GAY SOUL

WILL ROSCOE

RICHARD A. ISAY

MALCOLM BOYD

RAM DASS

GAY SOUL

EDWARD STEINBRECHER

INTERVIEWS AND PHOTOGRAPHS BY MARK THOMPSON

ANDREW HARVEY

CLYDE HALL

JAMES BROUGHTON

PAUL MONETTE

HARRY HAY

ANDREW RAMER

JAMES SASLOW

JOSEPH KRAMER

FINDING THE HEART
OF GAY SPIRIT AND NATURE

GUY BALDWIN

WITH SIXTEEN WRITERS, HEALERS,
TEACHERS, AND VISIONARIES

ROBERT HOPCKE

HarperSanFrancisco
A Division of HarperCollins*Publishers*

MITCH WALKER

For
Malcolm Boyd, soul mate
and
Ken Clements, soul guide

A TREE CLAUSE BOOK

HarperSanFrancisco and the author, in association with The Basic Foundation, a not-for-profit organization whose primary mission is reforestation, will facilitate the planting of two trees for every one tree used in the manufacture of this book.

Grateful acknowledgment is made for permission to quote from James Broughton's poem "Ode to Gaiety." From *Special Deliveries*. Copyright © 1990 by James Broughton. Used with permission of Broken Moon Press.

FIRST HARPERCOLLINS PAPERBACK EDITION PUBLISHED IN 1995

Library of Congress Cataloging-in-Publication Data
Thompson, Mark
    Gay soul : finding the heart of gay spirit and nature with sixteen writers, healers, teachers, and visionaries / Mark Thompson.
        p.   cm.
    Includes bibliographical references.
    ISBN 0-06-251040-1 (cloth : alk. paper)
    ISBN 0-06-251041-x (pbk : alk. paper)
        1. Gay men—United States—Religious life.   2. Spiritual life—United States.
3. Gay men—United States—Psychology.   I. Title.
HQ76.2.U5T56   1994
305.38'9664—dc20   94-26574
                                                                       CIP

95 96 97 98 99 ❖ RRD(H) 10 9 8 7 6 5 4 3

CONTENTS

The stalwart assistance of Melissa Limmer, who transcribed the interviews included in this book, is gratefully acknowledged. The author would also like to thank William Stewart, Joel Singer, Thomas Maguire, Doug Sadownick, Winston Wilde, and Jed Mattes for their support, as well as commend the fine guiding hand of Kevin Bentley. The generous commitment of time and insight into this project by Jim Wilson, Neil Tucker, Michael Callen, Essex Hemphill, and Assoto Saint is similarly appreciated.

INTRODUCTION

To talk about soul is not necessarily to know it. The more we try to define soul, to elevate it or fasten it down, the more it eludes our grasp. It is the source of all that we are, yet words alone fail in discerning its nature. A soul must be engaged—played with and worked on—not just analyzed, in order to know what it is. Soul speaks to us through dreams, reveals itself by the music, art, and poetry we create and behold. In a work dedicated to exploring the psyche's complexities, I am unable to say what exactly constitutes a soul—yet I know I have one.

My soul is the repository of all that I feel: my appetites and ambitions, sadness and joy. It is the place where inspiration germinates and from which vitality grows. It is also a place of perplexity and unfathomable fear. Above all, I sense that my soul is the inner arena in which life's combustible opposites collide, creating dissonance and upheaval as well as new harmony and stasis. Somewhere in this great container of ceaseless death and rebirth lies, too, the mystery of my being gay.

However one might attempt to characterize soul, being in relationship with this elusive center of self is what's important. To be aware of one's soul is to be soulful. By whatever means we choose to address it, the soul asks only to be honored, cared for, and relished. When not consciously reflected upon, the soul is left to its own domain—the unconscious—and there its workings confound us. If we do not seek to engage soul, we remain illiterate of ourselves. Then, rather than becoming the cause of celebration, the soul's constant act of dissolution and re-creation becomes the cause of our personal demons and doubts, our public hates and thoughtless actions. One could say that much of the world today is living in a dark night of the soul.

I hope, with this book, to shed a little light. The speakers gathered here not only have the ability to illuminate questions about soul—or, as the case may be, the lack of it—in contemporary life but they have the relatively unique vantage of experiencing soul through a queer prism. In each case, in varying ways, these sixteen men have encountered their souls and the souls of others through the facet of being "other" in a society of calculated sameness. In order to survive, let alone thrive, they have had to grapple with, descend to, and inhabit the realm of the soul during a time and place when such voyaging is not widely encouraged.

While it could be said that the soul is beyond categorization—that it is neither masculine nor feminine, heterosexual nor homosexual—I argue that the seeds of behavior and belief leading to modern gay identity are found in the soul. Like many of the speakers in this book, I believe that being gay—or at least that quality of being that is currently so labeled—is its own immutable truth. That despite a hundred years of theorizing about homosexuality, the very core of who I am as a "gay person" remains an inexplicable mystery waiting to be plumbed if only one were to know the right questions. The queries presented here are an attempt to fathom that mystery; they cut against the grain of accepted discourse about being gay, which says that it is primarily a historical invention.

During the past decade, gay and lesbian studies have been polarized around the issue of nature versus nurture. The *essentialist* point of view holds that the type of people currently labeled as gay have always existed in one form or another in human culture—that there is an indwelling, archetypal basis for their being. *Constructivist* theory holds that sexual identity, like our notions of gender, has been formulated by dominant political and social forces. Since the latter view continues to hold precedence in the growing ranks of gay academia, it is easy to see how the swift rise of self-identified gay communities around the world has been attributed to the efforts of a new minority group claiming its autonomy from the tyranny of oppressive norms. The reason for this half century of political struggle has been to overcome prejudicial social constructions of gender, sexuality, and "sodomy."

As with any group wanting to make its cause known and to be assimilated by the mainstream, notions about authentic difference have been downplayed. Reasons that might exist for a queer uprising beyond the need for tolerance and reform have yet to be explored in any depth. As justified as the gay movement has been in its pursuit of equality, to strive for a culture of conformity is to deaden the soul.

To achieve their aims, gay people have infused themselves with spirit— the resilient spirit of the disenfranchised, the empowering spirit of pride and hope. But too much spirit without enough soul is like an automobile running with a tank near empty. The liberation movement that has been carrying gay people collectively forward through the last half of the twentieth century is about ready to run out of gas. What is needed to refuel our progress is not more spirit but a deeper understanding and embracing of soul.

The appearance of queer people on the world stage has rewritten the script by which many conduct their lives; certainly the quest for gay liberation has been a force for widespread cultural change. Less recognized, even among gay people themselves, is their role as carriers of soul in a world that prefers to dwell on surfaces. All people, but especially gay men at this moment in their collective development, need to awaken to the freedom of the inner world as much as the outer. For I believe that gay men and lesbians possess the ability to lead society's next phase of cultural revolution—liberation of the soul—if only they realize that potential.

It is to that end that I've collected the voices of prominent and thoughtful gay men who have taken time to consider the deeper possibilities of their lives. More conversations were recorded than could be put between these covers, and in no way do I intend this assembly to represent any sort of definitive list of those who are meditating on these matters. If anything, this is a highly subjective sampling of the many gay men in this country and elsewhere who are profoundly committed to the inner journey and where it takes them. The speakers gathered here are men who, through friendship or the power of their written words, have intersected my life with sufficient provocation to make me want to pursue them further. Some I met for the first time during our interview; others I have interviewed before, a decade ago or longer, but I wanted to revisit them in order to see how their thinking has evolved.

It should be further noted that I have focused exclusively on gay men for two reasons: It would be presumptuous of me to expound on the spiritual issues of lesbians, who have been speaking for themselves on these matters for some time. Furthermore, I believe that the inner world of gay men contains its own reality and truths that need to be brought forth and separately examined at this crucial juncture in our collective development. I also want to acknowledge that while this book covers a wide range of beliefs—from Buddhism to Christianity, erotic ritual to Jungian theory—it is by no means a complete cross-sampling of queer-practiced spirituality. There are other cultural traditions at work in the gay male community besides the ones represented here.

As for the final concert of interviews assembled, the discussions include insights about the potentialities of otherness, the spiritual aspects of being gay, and feelings about life and death in the age of AIDS. The conversations are expansive in their scope, yet they are intimate and detailed; far-ranging ideas about gay nature have their roots in personal experience. As we listen, a commonality of shared secrets and struggles, of myths and archetypes, emerges. In almost all cases, being gay has been the conduit through which a closer union with soul—the divine within—has been forged.

By weaving together an eclectic but informed group of speakers, a collective history is also told: the stories of men living and working on the edge of the "global village" as teachers, healers, and visionaries. Another purpose of *Gay Soul* is to record and preserve the innermost thoughts and emotions of a remarkable community of men who are simultaneously engaged in acts of discovery and self-invention and with the responsibilities of catastrophic loss.

I am a journalist, so this book is primarily a work of investigative journalism. I came to the story of "Who are we?" not looking for definitive answers but with the belief that the inquiry is the important thing. Providing a lively forum in which substantive issues about our lives can be raised is the point of this effort. As for the answers that are included here, several important universal truths about being a gay man living today stand out, much like connecting currents.

First is the question of injury. In ways both subtle and extreme, most gay men are soul-wounded early in life through rejection by their parents and peers. Some of the reasons for this distancing are explored in depth in a number of the conversations here, but in whatever form the rejection occurs it leaves countless gay men emotionally injured, bereft of self-esteem and the capacity to love. Of utmost concern to gay men is to establish a healthy awareness about the nature of their soul-wounding, to heal its ill effects, and to perceive its spiritual value.

A second universal truth, and one of the most intriguing and valuable ideas put forth in *Gay Soul,* is the concept that gay men constitute a third gender—and, by extension, lesbians a fourth. While the word *homosexual* was not coined till slightly over a hundred years ago, 1868 to be exact, some would argue that the kinds of people who are now so labeled have always lived. Further, they say that, though our dualistic Western system of thought has only been able to conceive of two genders, homosexuals are as different from heterosexuals as men are from women. Individuals now categorized as gay and lesbian represent significantly different ways of being, and as some in this book believe, that implies that they have a purposeful social function, a function that is not contained by today's emphasis on sexuality alone. In other words, gender is about what we do—our contribution and value to society as a whole—rather than merely on what we *are.*

A third crucial view expressed in this book is that the way to the soul is through the body. Rather than being an abstract entity—something "out there"—the soul actually permeates every cell of our being. Explorations in ecstatic sexuality, breath work, and the essentially cheerful practice of "being here now" are means to accessing all that lives within us. Many gay men, including some speakers here, are on the frontier of understanding how flesh and spirit can be—must be—integrated in a soulful life.

Finally, and perhaps most important, is the concept of coming out inside. To be a traveler on the inner path is an activity that all gay men should pursue. Whether through psychotherapy, dream work, or other imaginal techniques, encountering and exploring the contents of one's soul is tantamount. Investigation of psyche offers lasting empowerment and true insight into the archetypes, shadows, and myths that govern our lives. Here, at the root of the soul, is where answers about the meaning of being gay are to be found.

As the psychologist James Hillman reminds us: "Soul is imagination, a cavernous treasury, a confusion and richness"—a world of passion, fantasy, and reflection. It is my intent, through this collection of soulful voices and visions, to uncover the still hidden richness of being a gay man in America today.

Los Angeles, Vernal Equinox, 1994

JAMES BROUGHTON

GAIETY OF SOUL

James Broughton's greatest teaching tells us that living poetically is an act of courage. There is much other wisdom to be found in his prolific work—some twenty books and as many independent films over the past forty-eight years—but following this irreverent, essentially cheerful, cue has been my best lesson.

I unquestionably needed poetic license, not to mention courage, the night we met in the autumn of 1972. I was a reticent college sophomore; he a much-celebrated poet and filmmaker debuting new work on campus. That night, James was extravagant and vital, the audience full of laughter. I scarcely noticed anything but the poet himself. Each spoken word, every image on the screen, shot lightning bolts to the back row of the theater—to my seat in particular, it seemed.

There were many things I didn't know about myself, perhaps had no way of knowing until then, that James saw perfectly clearly. Most important, he helped me understand that being gay didn't have to mean the things I had thought; it certainly was not the compromised, calcified existence I saw being lived by many of the gay men where I grew up, an artsy town on the central California coast. I was struggling to leave not just that locale but the place of mind where fear rules.

James's very presence signaled delight in being: no shame and scant indulgence of sorrow—just life lived in the here and now. "This is it," the poet said, so why not claim life as one's own invention? Instead of an undoing, use gaiety as the means for one's total becoming. Above all else, love unabashedly and well.

These and other messages ignited my mind as the evening progressed. Then, at the end, came an introduction and a chance to say a few words to the man himself. No time to hide in the back row now. With a bold squeeze of the hands, and a perceptive gaze into my eyes, the poet leaned forward. At that moment, my life changed. Something long asleep inside was forever awakened, summoned forth by his gentle kiss.

In the two decades that followed, I have often marveled at James's knack for affecting others as he did me. I've seen it happen time and again, that spark of unconditional love and permission passed from one man to another—a wake-up call to gay souls, wherever they are encountered. In this capacity, if for no other, James qualifies as a gay sage, a queer wise elder, of which there are precious few.

Then there is his body of work, as deep and lucid as a blue sky. He made his first film in 1946, a scraped-together production made with the help of friends and a borrowed Bolex. The Potted Psalm *premiered at the San Francisco Museum of Art and helped to establish Broughton's reputation as a West Coast pioneer of experimental cinema. He wasted no time in planning his next effort, an allegorical work titled* Mother's Day, *in which a cast of childish-acting adults struggles to come to terms with a remote and formidable mother-goddess figure. Complexity and playfulness infuse the work like polar currents. The way to unravel the psyche's serious business, the filmmaker implies, is with belly laughs and nonsensical glee.*

The attitude that life is an adventure, and not a predicament, is one that Broughton has always maintained. "I sailed in easy and laughing," he writes in his recent memoir, Coming Unbuttoned, *about his birth in Modesto, California, in 1913. "And because I smiled at everyone they called me Sunny Jim." A few pages later, Broughton relates the experience that would forever seal his optimistic relationship with the world: "One night when I was three years old I was awakened by a glittering stranger who told me I was a poet and always would be and never to fear being alone or being laughed at. That was my first meeting with my angel, who is the most interesting poet I have ever met."*

It was a communication that would serve James well in the years to come: through his father's early death and his mother's remarriage to a dour businessman, during education in a military academy and Stanford University, while he spent time on the open road and high seas as a merchant marine, and through a stab at a writing career in New York City. Still, even divine inspiration may at times lag a little, and by his thirtieth birthday the young poet's "greatest consolation was the thought of suicide." It was not until James returned to the West Coast after World War II that his most creative life began.

Broughton quickly found his niche in San Francisco's thriving postwar avant garde scene. He and a circle of fellow artists lived cheaply but well, channeling all available resources into the making of movies, plays, and books. His filmmaking continued, reaching a plateau in 1953 with The Pleasure Garden, *a satiric fairy tale celebrating the triumph of love and liberty over the joyless forces of restriction. Jean Cocteau awarded the film a special prize for poetic fantasy at the Cannes Film Festival.*

Though Broughton would not pick up a movie camera for another fifteen years (when he made the lyrically erotic The Bed), he continued to publish volumes of verse observing the sublime and the spontaneous turns of life's unfolding. His own life took a sudden new direction in 1962; even though Broughton had long collaborated—in love and art—with like-hearted men, he decided to explore marriage and subsequent parenthood. A decade of creative achievement and acclaim, family life, and professorships at Bay Area universities followed.

But in 1974 Broughton's renegade angel made a crucial reappearance, unexpectedly in the form of a young graduate student from Canada named Joel Singer. James was sixty-one and Joel twenty-six at the time of their first meeting. The strength of their connection to each other overrode anxieties about age difference and social censure; they were surely soul mates. "Joel brought me true 'psychic wholeness' by giving me the missing reality of myself," Broughton writes. "At last I could become fully my own kind of man, giving in as well as cutting loose. Reinvigorated I was ready to begin life anew." In the years since, the couple has flourished; they have traveled the world and made lasting friendships and a creative life together wherever they go. The last of their eight collaborative films, Scattered Remains, is a portrait of the poet by his lover.

James's indefectible sense of amusement about life—that "everything is going nowhere, beautifully"—reflects his passion for harmoniously integrating opposites. The dualities of light and dark, male and female, solemnity and gaiety—all have been mediated in his life with Zen-like inscrutableness. It's a crazy balancing act, for sure. Yet, as I've learned from him, inspired living requires chutzpah; it can't be won unless you're willing to risk all to find it. "Attain the inevitable; everything is an experiment in possibility," James is fond of saying. And for a generation of seeking gay men, he has modeled these words well.

When we meet for this interview it is on another kind of edge—the windy headlands of the Olympic Peninsula. James and Joel make their home there now, in the artists' colony of Port Townsend, Washington. Snow-capped peaks make a dramatic backdrop as we walk along the shores of the Strait of Juan de Fuca. Befitting his moniker of "Big Joy," and with a poet's care of language, James speaks of gaiety and its contribution to the art of soul-making.

How do you experience your soul, and what is gay about it?

Wherever I hurt, wherever I tingle, whenever I weep, whenever I guffaw, my soul is humming. It flexes with my desires and responses, my longing and my ailing. It operates in my heart, my deep guts, and my genitals. My soul entangles me in fantasies and surprising emotions. It is the playground of my instincts. Denials cripple it, denunciations squinch it. Cautions, taboos, leashes, sensible advice enrage the soul. It does not want to play safe, be insured, or think twice. It is involved with involvement. It relishes nature, not organization. It wants to plunge, risk all, and live it out. The greatest enemy of the soul is a literal mind.

Don't make Adam's mistake. Choose joy, not reason. Acknowledge the spontaneous responsiveness of your soul and you are on your way to experiencing gaiety.

At what age did you first experience gaiety of soul?

Though my solemn family tried to make me take life seriously, I came into the world an irrepressibly cheerful poet. My inborn nature was reaffirmed by my angel, who introduced himself to me when I was three years old. He blessed my merriment and told me never to fear being laughed at. He also urged me to believe in the unbelievable, worship wonder, and celebrate life. The world, he said, was a nonstop tournament between stupidity and imagination. He has been my helpmate throughout my eighty years, cautioning me always to heed my own soul, not someone else's mind. This has meant combating dogmas, alienation, and ridicule. But it has also toughened my gaiety.

If you have neither sympathetic pals nor guardian angels, find congenial gurus wherever you can. My earliest ones were Oz, Mother Goose, and Buster Keaton. Later I added Shakespeare, Zen, and Stravinsky.

Is there any separation between the soul and the body?

"Those who see any difference between the soul and the body have neither," said Oscar Wilde. The soul expresses itself throughout the body, in its members, organs, nerves, and cells, in all actions of desire, daring, and droop, wherever you ache and wherever you soar. Every nook and cranny of yourself can flutter and stretch, exude and hum, in experiencing the pleasures and pains of being alive. The body is a holy place of romp and renewal. It is not the shameful sewer that orthodox religions insist upon. Novalis said, "There is only one temple in the world, and that is the human body." From your tiptoe to your topknot you are throbbingly alive in the dance of the divine mystery.

The genitals, the anus, and the perineum are the holy trinity at the root of your torso's experience. The penis is the exposed tip of the heart and the wand of the soul. The perineum animates all the chakras. The anus is the transforming and recycling volcano that fertilizes new growth.

The proper activity in a temple is worship. Open your temple to love. Visit other temples. In my temple the names of gaiety's trinity are Always, Mary, and Bright.

Surely the soul has its shadows? What about your own soul's demons and despairs?

There are agonies in any temple, as there are wounds in any playground. There are as many ghosts in a parlor as there are in a graveyard. Most people live in a dank cell of their soul, in a fog of negation and despair. Rescue from this prison can come only from recognition that your soul is the instrument of the light of enlightenment. The only respite for the struggles with one's demons is to try to love them and discover what they have to reveal to you. You cannot love without a light heart. You cannot participate in the dance of life without a light foot.

Is sustaining that lightness part of your spiritual practice?

My spiritual practice begins each day with a meditation on the glory of God, the wonders of creation, and the delicious absurdities of the world. I like to laugh with God at his universe, connect with everything that's going on, big and small. This is to acknowledge the Almighty's instinctive gaiety.

My friend Alan Watts always claimed that his first meditation in the morning was to go out on his porch, hold his ribs, and laugh with God until his whole body just shook. That got him in a great mood for the day and its responsibilities. That's the way I've done it, too. I feel sorry for people who wake up upset. It's all a matter of calibrating one's cheerfulness. But you have to work at it. It takes practice to cultivate the sense of life as being a divine amusement, something that amuses the gods.

The kind of gaiety you describe is not easily found in modern life. People suffer from so much doubt and worry.

We have killed off the gods with rational thought and sent our demons into our shadows, so we suffer from a great lack of meaning in our lives. I have found it valuable to personify the powers that operate within us the way the Greeks did. Personify your symptoms and neuroses as gods. This helps to make them real and possible to understand. Otherwise you only have symptoms and miseries. We are each of us a whole universe right here and now; we are each a Godbody. You can never have a full measure of psychic wholeness by denying, scoffing, and doubting.

When you were sent to a military academy at age nine, what effect did that drastic measure have on you?

My initial terror was quickly replaced by my pleasure in the camaraderie of male society. Any military organization desperately needs gaiety. Remember Robin Williams in *Good Morning Vietnam?* He also enlivened school boys in *Dead Poets Society.* My angel came to the academy with me and counseled me to trust my need for love and not be afraid to express it. Thus I began to appreciate men early in life. It seemed to make all of us happier. Furthermore, I began to appreciate jolly brotherhoods such as St. Francis and his laughing crew, the Knights of the Round Table, Robin Hood and his Merry Men, Peter Pan and his Lost Boys, Jesus and his divine disciples.

How did sexual precociousness help bring you closer to the mysteries of life?

It introduced me to the mysteries of the body and to my first raptures of the soul. Sex is an avenue to bliss in the soul, and that bliss I have followed all my life. It led me into the arms of love, which belonged to a blond athlete several years older than I who taught me the arts of love and the pleasures of sturdy tenderness. Thus I experienced sex as a total wonder before I was fifteen.

Did marrying and raising a family during the sixties conflict with your gaiety of spirit?

On the contrary. A human life is a wheel of fortune, as the Tibetans picture it in their mandalas. A fulfilled life, which very few people experience, requires opening oneself to every possibility. Because in midlife I married and became a father, I have been accused of bisexuality. But why should this be a term of disparagement? It means you choose the best of both worlds. Bisexuality is natural; nature is pansexual. The soul is bisexual in everyone, or men and women would not understand each other at all. How else would Flaubert have created Emma Bovary, or Tolstoy, Anna Karenina? The soul is androgynous in everyone.

Isn't androgyny an unnatural state, neither one thing nor another?

Androgyny is the true image of the soul. It is not an amorphous freakhood located between male and female on the scale of human gender. It is a concept of wholeness, a guide to experiencing the full range of yang and yin. It is the secret portrayed in Shiva, Kali, and Hermaphroditus. It is the mystery of the total self. I touch upon this process every time I shed the skin of an outgrown attitude.

It is difficult to make this clear because our language and our culture is structured around the demanding concept of choosing either one thing or the other. We are always being told we must choose between a this or a that. One choice is as rejecting as the other. That is not the way the soul experiences things. That is the tyranny of the mind. We don't have words to describe the inclusive notion of both/and.

The most androgynous men, whatever their sexual preference, embody the sturdiest gay spirit. They are freer of the rat races and the desire to be like everybody else. What could give all men liberation and depth would be a realization that their souls include all the reaches of human possibility.

Are you proposing a new order of masculinity?

Don't you think it could use a new order? First of all, how about dumping the brutal and greedy drive toward career, riches, or empire? A man should be more than an aggressive mind with an embarrassed cock attached. A man who fails to develop compassion and tolerance is not completely human.

A man who expresses his sensitivity and imagination is closer to being a whole man than a one-sided, self-censoring man. These are the men who enliven and enrich the arts, for instance, for they value wit and beauty and outrage.

The majority of men resist acknowledging their own tenderness and empathy, preferring to project it onto another person who will carry it for them. This is called "falling in love." When the real person doesn't fit the projected image—end of love affair, end of marriage. A gay spirit doesn't censor his sensitivity, he enhances it.

Gaiety has no gender barriers. Isn't joyfulness available to all sexes? I do not condone heterophobia any more than I do other prejudices. I am uncomfortable with the dichotomy of Them against Us. I believe in the potential redemption of all men's souls. Wouldn't everyone benefit from more enlightened consciousness?

As the rap song says, denial ain't just a river in Egypt. Men have denied their softness and suppleness, their tenderness and sensitivity. They have taught their sons to be tough, contemptuous, and inflexible. This is a perversion of masculinity. Can we transcend the cynical thinking that denies value to the soul and to the quest for significant meaning?

I would plead for loving friendship. Keats called friendship "the holy emotion." Can we deepen our sense of friendship to be unafraid of trust and devotion? "The clasp of fond friendship is life's greatest collision," I once wrote.

Look for all that is beautiful in men, despite appearances to the contrary. Look for the radiance behind the mask of every face. Though you may not want to believe it, every other human being is as divine as you are. Rub against fellow creatures of all stripes, shapes, smells, tints. How else will we end the civil wars of the world and inherit a friendly future?

How does one maintain gaiety in a cheerless world?

"The world is on fire, and every solution short of liberation is like trying to whitewash a burning house." The Buddha said this centuries ago, but it is still true. The cure for the woes of the planet remains perennial: cure men's souls.

Do what you can. Begin by curbing your sneers and complaints. Heighten your spirits. Celebrate your existence, don't deplore it. Live in your body, not your mind. Eat more chocolate than beans. Fuck often. Follow your bliss over hill and dale.

Gay soul dances on the grave of the dead serious. Think of yourself as a dolphin child in a sea of light. A dolphin is swift and free and full of humor. A sense of humor is a divine grace. Be generous with joy and juicy with ripening. Keep your soul uncontaminated. Watch out for conformity. Middle-class morality is ever ready to kidnap you. Support erotic workshops, Radical Faerie circles, rainbow gatherings.

Gaiety makes us gods, said Frederick the Great. And love is what enriches gaiety. Nothing works well without love, and anything done without love is irrelevant or drab. Nietzsche called the practice of lovingness "the gay science." Rumi said love was the first thing God created. Lovingness is the essence of gaiety.

This earth is essential to our souls. Since we have treated it with ruthless contempt, doesn't that indicate how we regard the whole family of man? Loving the earth is the only way to redeem it. Love is the only solution to every problem. Pity that there isn't more of it available.

Be not shy of the love you can share with other men. Fear of love is fear of the sublime. Put lovemaking before moneymaking and troublemaking. To be a lover is to practice the major art of life. You must love even if it hurts. It will hurt more if you don't love.

When love makes the heart sing, nothing exists but courage and trust and the delights of fruitful action. Then you have gaiety of soul.

My "Ode to Gaiety" includes these lines:

Without gaiety freedom is a chastity belt
Without gaiety life is a wooden kimono . . .
Wrap killjoys in wet blankets
and feed them to the sourpusses . . .
Long live hilarity euphoria and flumadiddle
Long live gaiety for all the laity.

PAUL MONETTE

ON BECOMING

*On the day of our interview, a chilly Los Angeles afternoon in early
November, Paul Monette is the most famous gay man in America. His book*
Becoming a Man: Half a Life Story *has been on bestseller lists for months and
is nominated for the 1992 National Book Award for nonfiction, an honor it will
receive a few weeks later, when he makes a standing room–only acceptance address at the Library of Congress. The acclaim, the magazine profiles, the thoughtful reviews, all serve to underscore the reputation of a man long in the making.*

*Contentious yet gracefully spoken, frivolously witty but possessing a
sharp intellect that can cleave lesser minds with a mere sentence or two, Monette
brooks no fools, takes no enemies. For his victory is a deeply ironic one. Even as
he enjoys the rewards of the creative apex of a lifetime's achievement, the author
must face his own life's dwindling possibilities, having received his AIDS diagno-
sis two years ago. And yet this poet, novelist, memoirist, screenwriter, and activist
is still able to humorously proclaim that he has published more books than he
now has T-cells. Monette's struggles during the plague years, on both the political
and personal fronts, have been documented in the books* Borrowed Time, *a har-
rowing memoir of a lover's death,* Love Alone, *a collection of elegies for that
lover, and* Afterlife *and* Halfway Home, *novels of scathing indictment and rage.*

*On the day of our visit, the furies seem to be calm. Paul sits thoughtful
and collected, even in the midst of a household in some upheaval, even with the
AIDS drug Amphotericin B being slowly administered through a needle stuck in
his arm. In the distance, a gardener noisily blows leaves from patio stones; closer
by, a day nurse fussily attends and a lonesome dog whines for affection—all
while an answering machine records one urgent-sounding phone call after another. Despite the claim that he's "dying by inches," Monette speaks with
warmth, compassion, and an obvious delight in the becoming of life.*

o

*You've just come from a meeting with a priest. I'm surprised be-
cause you've taken no small pains in the past to condemn members
of the clergy along with all others whom you see as collaborators in
sustaining homophobia and disinformation about AIDS.*

I had this profound realization that worked its way into *Becoming a
Man* about the difference between living a life of collaboration and a life of resis-

tance. I've been furious and blunt, as you say, in my impatience and rage with churches and religions. But I have refined that rage, at least in my own head, so that my anger against the injustice and hypocrisy of religion goes where it ought to go, for instance, to the Vatican and the pope. Those people for whom God is only politics and not anything of the spirit—those people are evil. They are evil in all forms of fundamentalism, be it their own fundamentalism or Muslim fundamentalism or the peculiarly disgusting Protestant fundamentalism in this country.

And yet, in the midst of this nightmare and calamity of AIDS, I have seen such eloquent work done by people who are part of the clergy or part of a religious commitment or calling. Here I am close to the end of my life, and I somehow think that I am an atheist who is, for better or worse, still an Episcopalian.

Can you explain the influence religion had on you in your early years and where you are today at age forty-seven in matters of faith and spiritual belief?

Quite early on, by my teenage years, I came to feel that the pageant story of Christianity as it was taught to me when I was a kid was a myth. But it didn't feel uncomfortable to continue to go to church. I mean, I grew up in a small town, and you went to church on Sunday and dealt with ministers who were very good and kind people. So I didn't really feel myself estranged from God; it mostly was a sense of estrangement from Christianity, from the whole matter of faith.

By the time I finished college I was very lapsed. I didn't want to go to church. I was very impatient with the whole notion of an afterlife, of miracles—that seemed like an offensive idea to me. Still, I have to admit that I have had experiences of a mystery larger than myself. I remember when Stephen and I where in Turkey, and we were going to see the great city of Ephesus. There were about twenty of us on the bus, and the guide pointed out this column standing in a field, the last pillar of the Temple of Diana, one of the wonders of the ancient world. Then she directed us to look at a house in a little village, saying, "That's the house where Saint John finished the gospel." It's very difficult to articulate the shiver I had about all that. But there was something terribly exciting about this moment from the ancient world, from the pagan world—because I do in some ways think of myself as a pagan.

I have come to believe in the goddess of love and beauty, in the god of the sun; Aphrodite and Apollo are my gods, not Jesus. And yet, I was thrilled to see something that was part of the history of writing. I think John's gospel was written about eighty years after Jesus, so it's a poet's gospel, it's a poet's words. I'm not a big fan of the Bible for the most part—it's full of the worst sort of tyranny against women and gay people. And yet, it has some moments of extreme beauty that are as profound as anything I've ever read. Still, even this close to my death, I don't know how to characterize God.

> *How has your ongoing struggle with AIDS affected your spirituality? Do you believe in or draw strength from a higher power? If so, can you describe what that power might be?*

I have a friend who's in Alcoholics Anonymous who says that sometimes he wishes his higher power would beat up God. It almost disturbs me the way that my illness has not brought me closer to a rapprochement with the idea of the largest mystery. But I'm very comforted or held in place by Paul Tillich's description of God as the "Ground of Being." Certainly, I am struggling to stay the course of my life on some kind of ground of being.

> *But hasn't this calamity deepened your ground of being in profound ways? Are you now closer to the mystery within yourself?*

One of the ways in which AIDS has purified so many of us is in how much it tells us that this is not a dress rehearsal. You are being tested, even if there is no headmaster in the sky marking the grades or giving you board scores on those tests. We are being tested by something as deep in ourselves as we could ever be. If you needed any further proof that the material world is not enough to nourish you, that success and money and career are not enough, that the only real nourishment that you can count on is love and that love is possible for all of us, that we can generate it and find it, this is it. What's going to matter to people when they come to the end of their lives is how much they've loved.

> *You've had three very distinct love relationships closely following one another in your life: Roger Horwitz and Stephen Kolzak, who both died of complications due to AIDS, and currently, Winston Wilde. How does your sexuality interface with your spirituality? Is there a connection between the two? Does one inform the other?*

One of the great challenges to one's sexual nature in the midst of AIDS is that you're very much at odds with your own body, even more sometimes than it is at odds with you. Carnality is not as easy as it used to be. I find it more precious. But I've also come to understand in the last couple of years that being gay is about something more profound than my sexual nature, my carnal nature.

> *From the first page of* Becoming a Man *you make clear that being gay is somehow different from being straight. You eloquently speak about "the festering pretense that we are the same as they are." How are we not the same, and why? What is this profound difference that you just spoke of?*

It has taken twenty-five years since our declaration of freedom as a gay and lesbian people for us to begin to address this. There's a quality of exultation in our differentness—I think we just have it and it's part of our different nature. I remember reading about a similar kind of debate in the medieval church. They spent two hundred years deciding whether Jesus had the same nature as God or a like nature to God.

We have begun by reclaiming our history so that now we know something about the [Native American] *berdache,* for instance. We've begun to understand anthropologically the role of gay and lesbian people in tribal cultures, historically and around the world, and we've begun to challenge patriarchal systems such as the Roman Catholic church, which are terrified of them. It is still beyond mystery, however, though I don't think the Greeks would call it beyond mystery.

> *Do you believe there's some element of our psyche that is unique to us, a kind of homosexual genius, a kind of native, intuitive wisdom that is peculiar to the kinds of people that today we call gay? If so, what are the elements of that way of being?*

It's been my experience that gay and lesbian people who have fought through their self-hatred and their self-recriminations have a capacity for empathy that is glorious and a capacity to find a laughter in things that is like praising God. There is a kind of flagrant joy about us that goes very deep and is not available to most people. I also think that something about our capacity to live and let live is uniquely foreign—that we have learned in the crucible of the discrimination against us how broad our definitions must be for us to be fully human.

But that crucible in which we've been tempered was manufactured by society's strictures against us. Are these capacities innate gifts or traits forged by external circumstances?

Well, it may be that only an externally recognizable set of circumstances can give us, as in a mirror, what the deeper thing is. I don't know whether I can characterize it in words. This deeper core that we're calling "gay soul" is something we have to learn from one another as we grow more human with one another. It's a bit like trying to characterize the grace of God, you know, with a bunch of medieval theologians. You can spend all your time on that, but it's almost what it illuminates, or what it permits to flower or blossom, that tells us what it is.

Here's another way of coming at the question: What would happen if one morning every man, woman, and child woke up and realized that it's okay to be gay. No problem. No pressure. If that were the case, would the kind of gay joie de vivre, these capacities you speak of, still exist?

Yes. Without question. Not only would they still exist, they would be so unhampered by ignorance and homophobia that they would threaten the very core of the patriarchies—love of war, love of putting people down, and love of slavery.

If the strictures and the horrible censures on our lives were removed and we were allowed to fly as high and wide as we could, what would be the result?

I think that it would sweep us all forward to a place where the dear love of comrades is the law of the land. With us, there is an urge of selflessness, of altruism. It comes from that strange mystery of learning to understand yourself by understanding others, learning to love yourself by loving others. There are many vectors for this "getting out of ourselves" quality, which is as basic as our drag at Halloween. The paradox is that in getting out of ourselves, somehow we know ourselves more and grow more.

Becoming a Man is really a treatise about the legacy of self-hate that is seemingly endowed upon every gay person almost from the

moment of birth. You have achieved a pyric victory of sorts, rein-
venting yourself in the consumptive flames of agonizing self-doubt.
The book ends with you coming out to the capacity to love another
man and be loved.

Love is a terrific shortcut to some very profound places, but you and I both know that it isn't simple and that the years of programming, of self-hatred and self-recrimination, make intimacy very difficult. And intimacy is as difficult in a loving ten-year relationship as it is for someone who is struggling over a first date because intimacy is as deep as Walden Pond. I mean, once you begin to troll the shallows of this mystery of intimacy, it seems so easy, so ordinary, so pedestrian in a way, and yet you come up against barriers in yourself that draw you back from that awesome sense that two people can sometimes discover something that one can't alone.

What constituted "becoming a man"? How did you find your mas-
culinity? What was the central test involved?

Rilke says that what the world speaks to us finally is: You must change your life. My acceptance of that challenge is that I had to change my life from de-spair, distancing myself from people, and feeling out of place in the world. That decision preceded coming out, and it was totally the right decision. I see so many people trapped in rage about the past, and I so want people to somehow applaud themselves for simply having survived it, so that they can go on. Change is diffi-cult, but it doesn't begin until you accept the challenge of it.

I ceased to be merely the outline of a human being—you know those Magritte figures cut out like the shape of a man and you see the open sky through him. I filled in that space of myself. I can still be as despairing as I was when I was twenty but not with such a sense of hopelessness and not with such a sense of alienation. My will is a human will, though. It's sexless, it's co-sexual, it rings me in a circle of my masculine passions and my feminine passions.

If we do have this crucial moment of self-definition, this realization
that we can't go on with only an outline of self, we have to begin to
start coloring in the blanks. But with what?

It seems to me that when we start to color ourselves in femininity is re-ally the crayon. You can use it, use the sensitivity and the sense of magic and the sense of tribalism that is part of our unafraid female nature as gay men. It becomes your paintbrush for painting the masculinity with which you are comfortable, which is yourself, which expresses your style, which doesn't leave anything behind. Androgyny seems like such a concrete physical emotion, but it isn't really. It's really beyond physical, and it is, in a way, freed of the physical.

If we're talking about the geography of the soul here, doesn't this put us into a kind of brave new world, a relatively unexplored terrain?

Our queerness in the last generation is a sailing across a water of an earth that we know is not flat. We are not going over the edge. There is a new land, and that new land is our legacy to the gay and lesbian people who will follow, who can because it's a stronger ship and a better compass. We don't know what the new land can bring. It's a route to the East; it's a route to the deepest core of feeling.

Have you imagined yourself as one of the shipbuilders, or one of the sailors, or have you actually been to that new land and come back to tell of it?

I'm the humble captain of a ship like that. Or we're a conspiracy of captains. I'm very glad to have been a kind of role model even for myself in the last half decade because I know how barren the world was of that when I was growing up.

If there's anything that the flag flies on this ship into the new world, it is W. H. Auden's idea that we must love one another or die. We are people who have triumphed over affliction and suffering that would humble anybody else, that connect us to the Holocaust, that connect us to—I mean, I turn on the television sometimes and see these Somalian children dying, and I think, I feel closer to them than I do to my own neighbors. As gay and lesbian people, we have made a stand against darkness and put the wind in the sails of the ship.

Now that presumably you have become a man, what's next? What lies beyond that becoming? What, for instance, is the difference between masculinity in a gay man and a nongay man?

It is certainly true that if I can accept the high compliment of life that I have reached manhood, then it comes hand in hand with the paradox that I am also a woman. Manhood is not a separating, except from the bonds of the past and the bonds of other people's opinions. It is certainly not my way of separating myself from Woman, whose strength and passion and lyricism and exaltedness I seek to share.

I don't know if there is any extra wisdom that comes free with manhood, but the road is open. It means you know you're on the path, and that path is in the Ground of Being. Manhood is not terribly freeing—it doesn't mean you can fly—but you can begin to attach your own being or the struggle for your own being to something that rings out to the stars.

You are an ardent student of ancient Greek culture. What have your inquiries in that area led you to believe or affirm in terms of being a gay man today, even though homosexuality meant such a different thing in that civilization than it does in ours? Have you recognized any parallel realities that have really spoken to you across so much time and space?

I have come to see through the Greeks, and especially through Greek literature, this unbelievable illumination of what it means to be human. I am thrilled by their intimacy with their gods, so intimate that they can pour drops of wine on the ground to honor them, to give some back. Their gods were attached to forces of nature—the wind, the ocean, the tempest, the sun—and that seems so wonderful because the gods are available to something so far beyond the intellect. They are just living in the world. The old woman says at the end of [Truman Capote's] *A Christmas Memory,* "You know, maybe heaven will turn out to be just like this—walking among the cherry trees." And in that sense we experience heaven. I think the Greeks did. They tangibly thought of those gods as living at the top of Olympus because they thought of their world as heavenly. It seems to me that ancient Greece for a modern person is a glimpse of an ideal, which is expressed in the Greeks' comfortableness with a word like *kallos,* which means both physically beautiful and spiritually beautiful. There wasn't a difference. When Phidias would make a sculpture of a charioteer that physical perfection and physical exaltedness never ceased to be human.

And this is something that really speaks to you as a gay man?

Yes, yes! Gay is a modern appellation. There wasn't really anything we would call a gay person until past the mid to late nineteenth century. But despite all that, there is a connectedness between me and Pericles, or between me and

Achilles, that may just be romantic gush but I still feel at the deepest level. When Achilles rages in his tent because of the loss of his lover, that is as real to me as my raging in this house when Roger died. We have to build an ideal, a pagan world of reverence and connectedness out of the shards that are left in the steamrolling of history by religion.

Speaking of reverence, who are your gods? Who's gathered around this household?

Walt Whitman has a place by the fire, and there's probably a lot of ashes from his pipe all over him. He's very demanding, but the eloquence makes it worth it. There's a very austere room in this house where Anne Frank and Primo Levi lie down and rest. Surely Apollo, because he's not just a god of the sun but of youth, and a youth that strides boldly into life, a youth not afraid of losing youth. I also applaud the Greeks forever for having a goddess of love and beauty. That seems so unavailable to religion to understand that beauty is holy, that love is holy, and that art is one of its avenues.

What is the most effective way for gay people to free themselves from the shackles of guilt and shame that are used by the majority culture—the "heterosexual dictatorship," as Christopher Isher-wood put it—to keep them in their place? What is straight society so afraid of? What do they see in us that they must suppress, whether through actual physical violence or the covert disarming of our self-reliance and self-worth?

Coming out can be the most significant act a gay or lesbian person can do in their whole lifetime, but to come out is not to fully understand who we are. You have to take the energy of coming out and then you have to study. I mean, all of us who come out, at sixteen, twenty, fifty, whatever, have gone through a life-time of no images, no role models. You can't turn on the television or go to a movie or listen to rock music, or anything, and find an echo of our gay and les-bian experience or specialness. So I think that that's the private work we have to do, to leach out whatever's left of the stupidity and wrongheadedness of our own homophobia.

The one thing they can't take away from us is knowledge about our-selves. We have produced as a people an astonishing literature in twenty-five years. You'll have to know it. Ignorance is not bliss, and ignorance will not hold back the darkness. I believe that there is a great deal more homo-ignorance than homophobia in the world. I do think that hate is genetic and must be fought by the genetic altruism that one also has. I think it's a struggle every person has throughout his or her life.

But the illumination of our coming out to one another and to our families, co-workers, and friends is something we have to feed because we can in fact change minds, and we can reduce the paranoia that they have. Straight men especially have a strange paranoia about feelings, and they fear what they perceive in themselves and in gay men as weakness: femininity, softness, crying too easily. And you know, that's their limitation that's coming out. What they twitch from in us is what we have to nourish and make even stronger.

What do you do with your rage? Does it corrupt or empower your soul?

I have really come to understand that anger is not debilitating if it is against injustice. I need to attach my rage to injustice and then it is a very clean and an invigorating emotion. You know, I'm able to be this angry, this twisted up with anger at my government and the churches and the sullen ignorance of the world, and still be happy because the rage becomes a kind of sword of righteousness.

You would see rage in this case as being a spiritual good?

It can be a kind of singing. But it can also turn back on you and shrivel you up and leave you dead. If you have a lot of will, though, to force it into action and empowerment, it's their hate that shrivels up.

Some say that anger turned inward is a crucial factor in disease, physical as well as mental. How have you managed to turn anger around in your own life to use it as an ingredient in your soul-making rather than to let it fester?

It was a conscious decision, and luckily I had my writing as a vehicle. It was stronger than I many, many times in the last six years. The writing knew where it was going more than I knew where it was going. It was an automatic process; I just had to keep true to myself and true to it and let it lead me through words to feelings.

I have a certain respect for people who are finally overwhelmed by their rage and smothered by it—unexpressed rage as a description of depression. I also understand that it is rage of the day to day, rage at the frustration of standing in line and the pricks of the needles and the maddeningness, the maddening slowness, of the healing process. But all those day-to-day rages are not really what we're talking about. We're talking about a very large rage that is like tempests and storms. It rattles your bones and leaves you drenched, and the world is clearer afterward. And if you carry that with you, it's like that wonderful remark Jean Cocteau made when he was asked what he would save in a burning house, and he said, "The fire." By not being afraid to take the fire as an act of sacrifice, you also get to take the fire of inspiration and the clean newness of the world you walk into. It seems to me that rage is one of those two-sided powers: it can overpower you, and you can channel it until you are going across the sky like Apollo in his chariot.

> *As a person with AIDS, you have certainly given some thought to your death. How have you prepared for that? And what are your views of an afterlife, if any?*

All my life I have thought of physical death as the end. But I also understand that my memory for my loved ones extends me—gives me a kind of human immortality through them. You can't be a writer without having some hope that you do that through your books. Even though your books may be like the lost plays of Sophocles and no one will know them, somehow they are thrown into the ocean of hope. Sometimes death feels as close as the walls of this room—that's a quotation from Graham Greene—and at times I will look at my little shelf of books and think, you're more real than I am. I don't feel it ruefully; I think it gives me a sense of peace.

I am so attached to the human, to the eccentric uniqueness of the people I love, that no heaven as it has ever been described to me is good enough. This world has been very good to me. It's like something out of Milton: You can make a heaven of hell and a hell of heaven. I have looked into the face of hell in my years on this planet, and I don't have much answer to it. But I know that the best of what I have been and the best of what I have found in other people is what I have instead of an afterlife.

> *What is the most important thing you could say to a young gay man today, a queer teenager in the making?*

Come out, come out, come out. Though I know that's not so easy for people who live in tyrannical situations. Otherwise I would say, hold on: The fury of confusion and self-doubt will turn out to be a lifelong process of recovery and challenge, and it's worth it. It will get so it doesn't hurt anymore; it will get so that you are stronger and stronger the more you devote to understanding. But the major last thing I would say to that kid is, "You are not alone."

What has been the most pivotal thing you've learned about life from your ever-evolving experience of becoming a queer-identified man? What has helped to make your life story complete after all these years?

Other people. The really special people who have given me some wisdom and a helping hand and made things easier for me and put themselves out for me. There's no way I can repay a hundred different people for what they have taught me—sometimes completely unconsciously—but they form a kind of bridge of linked arms, and I'm on the other side. It's made of those I'm genuinely in love with, like Winston or Stephen or Roger, and also just strangers. They have made me stronger in my belief in myself and made me more joyous in my sense of self.

I don't realize how open I am compared to most people, and I'll say anything if it's going to make me figure something out better. There's a wonderful saying that in New York there are two things: there's talking, and there's waiting to talk. I think I'm a better listener than I've ever been, and sometimes in listening I feel that I express myself better than when I'm talking. But I profoundly agree with Socrates, too, that you don't have a clue what something is until you've talked it through. He didn't really much believe in books; he thought books were a kind of dead, impatient thing, that it was in the vitality of human intercourse that one finds the life force. I agree. Life is such a good conversation.

RICHARD A. ISAY

RISING TO LOVE

Clamorous rebellion and uprising have marked the dramatic course of the gay movement during the past twenty-five years. But on December 15, 1973, a more quiet revolution occurred, an action that would forever change the lives of millions of men and women previously labeled as sick. After lengthy testimony and, ultimately, a vote, the American Psychiatric Association removed homosexuality from its list of mental disorders. The terrible onus of pathology was lifted from being gay.

As far-reaching as the resolution was, it could not undo decades of harm perpetrated on countless individuals. Electroshock treatments, lobotomies, all kinds of grueling aversion therapies, and even incarceration were among the weapons used in the war of "normalcy" waged against homosexuals. Casualties have been high as a generation of gay men and women continues to struggle with lingering doubts about themselves, which were implanted by a social establishment armed with religious dogma in one hand and, until 1973, scientific injunction in the other.

One man caught in that conflict was Richard A. Isay, a psychiatrist and psychoanalyst whose long and arduous road to a whole and integrated self mirrors the struggle of many. After ten years of psychoanalysis bent on dispelling his homosexual longings, during which he married and had two children, Isay came out of the closet. His personal victory was part of the changing tide of accepted wisdom, and he has continued to contribute to the growth of equality and understanding for gay people.

In 1989 he published Being Homosexual: Gay Men and Their Development, a landmark study exploring the crippling effects that parental rejection, societal hate, and internalized homophobia have on the psychological growth of gay men. Going to the root of homosexual behavior, Isay concludes that gay eros is genetic in origin and projects its need at a tender age within the individual. For young gay boys, the target of this longing is usually their fathers (or available father substitute), a situation rife with conflict and tension. By the time they are four or five years old, says Isay, many gay boys experience a rupture in their relationship with the father, an emotional breaking off that seriously affects their capacity for loving themselves and others as they grow up.

As with most theories about homosexuality, Isay's view is hotly debated—particularly among gay men themselves. His Freudian-based analysis is one possible scenario out of many that might exist for the development of a gay soul. However, I do know that what Isay suggests happened in my own life. Somehow, quite early in life, I became estranged from my father; we were distant and apart, strangers in the same house. One of the predominate story lines of my adult life has been the recovery of his love—an epic search that meant forging my own self-acceptance.

Isay asserts that a gay boy, in projecting same-sex eros onto his father, may unconsciously adopt the mother's traits and mannerisms as a means of attracting his attention. In effect we become our mother's "best boy," all the better to decode the mystery of her allure, intensely bonding by way of our desire for the same man. In order to romance the father we learn and employ the language of "femininity." And in a culture so polarized around gender, such nonconforming behavior almost invariably leads to the father's discomfort and to the gay son's sense of alienation from the masculine world.

"It is most often the same-sex erotic fantasies centering on the father that initially makes these children feel different from their peers," Isay writes in Being Homosexual, referring to the early childhood of gay boys, a crucial period of development analogous to the Oedipal stage in heterosexual boys. "The child's perception of and response to these erotic feelings by themselves may account for such 'atypical' behavior as greater secretiveness than other boys, self-isolation, and excessive emotionality. Other traits that they soon label as being 'feminine' may also be caused by identification with the mother or mother surrogate. Such characteristics usually develop as a way of attracting the father's love and attention, in a manner similar to the way the heterosexual boy may pattern himself after the father to gain his mother's attention."

The drama Isay describes is all too recognizable to gay men, especially men of my generation—the gay Boomers, as it were. We're the ones who came out relatively young, often in our early twenties, largely the products of dysfunctional families and a striving, fragmented culture that further distanced us from our dads. The scenario of a father's love, rejection, and loss runs through our lives like an unnerving bass line.

In a culture so unforgiving of gender digression—and of one man's capacity to love another—it is easy to see why so many gay men feel wounded. It is to the repair of such injury that Isay, a clinical professor of psychiatry at Cornell Medical College, applies himself.

"If you're gay, and you've broken social stricture, there's not much else that guides us, except our own internal sense of what is right," he tells me once we've settled into his comfortable upper–East Side office in New York. "I believe that homosexuality is normal for gay men, and so I have tried to change previous theory so that psychoanalysts have a fresh vantage from which to work."

Certainly his task is far from done. Even though twenty years have passed since the psychiatric mainstream reversed its course, psychoanalysis and developmental theory have lagged far behind; the notion of homosexuality being an aberration lingers in the collective mind like a noxious cloud. Outer change, like inner growth, as any therapist will attest, is an incremental process. Over time, patience and the commitment to healing become their own rewards. But the goal, as exemplified by Richard Isay himself, is a recovered life fully capable of love.

o

In terms of inner work, what is the most important area that gay men have to address about themselves?

Self-esteem injury and the repair of that injury are issues that every gay man has to deal with at some time in his life. Of course, I think the best way that's done is through a loving relationship in which one can feel and return love. But the work that's necessary to get there is sometimes long and difficult.

Many people are attracted to becoming healers because of their own woundedness. What led you to do this work?

I wanted to be an analyst from the time I was a sophomore in college in 1955. I got very interested in nineteenth-century philosophy, particularly Nietzsche and Schopenhauer, who were convinced there existed an unconscious mind. Then I started reading Jung and Freud. It didn't take me long to recognize that my interest in psychology had to do with my feelings that there was something terribly wrong with me because of my attraction to other men. I grabbed on to what I could read about psychopathology of sexual perversions and labeled myself as sick. Not for one minute, and not for many years after, did I think that it was possible for my passion to be an expression of love.

I was also attracted to my college roommate. This was the first time I had ever fallen in love with anybody, and I attributed it to his being a very nice person, not to the passion inside of me that needed expression. It was a way to avoid labeling my own sexual orientation. I thought of myself as being neurotic and perverse—but not "homosexual." I knew that sometime in the future I would go into analysis, or some kind of treatment, and my sickness would go away.

How many years did it take you to feel okay about being gay?

I was depressed after graduation and after separating from my roommate, and then I became preoccupied with studying, so in the early years of medical school I didn't think much about sex. When I did, I always had in the back of my mind that if I was going to be an analyst, I would have to be straight and should get married, so I tried to put sexual thoughts and feelings out of mind. I didn't have any sexual contact with a man from the time I left college until I had finished almost ten years of analysis, much of it six times a week. I was a tough case!

I believe there are remnants, echoes, of the self-loathing you speak of in the souls of all gay men of every generation. It's something that has scarred us all at one time.

The hatred of society affects us. But more than that, society causes our parents and siblings to relate to us in particular ways. The relationship between the father and the male homosexual child is so important. If the father withdraws because he sees something he labels as not masculine, or he withdraws because he senses our wish to get close to him, then damage is inflicted on the child. I'll never forget when my father would take me out to the foundry where he worked, to be around the fires and the workmen. I was about ten. The work was rough, and so were the men. I suppose he thought I was effeminate because I wasn't at all athletic. I recall one occasion when he asked me to feel the muscles of a workman, saying he was a "real man." Of course, I knew he was really saying, "And you're not!" Even though I didn't know why, I felt humiliated and embarrassed.

You believe that gay male longing first manifests itself when we are quite young.

Between the ages of three and four. I am firmly convinced that all sexual orientation—heterosexual, homosexual, bisexual—is constitutional and inherited, genetically transmitted. My hunch would be that one effect of this genetic transmission is to push the homosexual male child toward the father and the heterosexual male child toward the mother. I'm only talking about men because

I know more about them, but the evidence points to the genetic transmission of sexual orientation in women as well.

> *There are some people who would argue with your observation. Many hold that sexuality is socially constructed. For instance, the very notion of being a homosexual is a late-nineteenth-century construct.*

Some academics, if I understand them correctly, say that if we had no word for "homosexual," then homosexuality did not exist. *Homosexual* is a late-nineteenth-century term, but in light of what we know about the biology of sexual orientation, same-gender sexual attraction has probably always existed. On the other hand, I do agree that being "gay" as we know it today is a product of our society. It is unlikely, for example, that homosexuals gathered in communities, as we do in large urban areas, until this century.

> *Based on your observations over years of clinical work with hundreds of gay men, how common is the experience of early erotic longing for the father?*

A gay man does not usually come into my office, sit down in the chair, and begin to talk about his attraction to his father. This is something that I pick up clues about over a period of time and infer from recollections and dreams. These memories are not necessarily direct, but they can be reconstructed. Or there can be indirect memories revealed in a gay man's relationships with other men that may repeat the relationship with the father in different ways.

If we have a proclivity to desire other men, the first man we love will be the man who is closest to us in our early lives: the father or father substitute. And if he's not around, we will find somebody like him to attach the desire onto. If homosexual desire is inherent, which empirical evidence increasingly suggests, the question is why it takes one form in some men and another form in other men.

> *That would depend upon who the individual is, as well as his family or social setting.*

That homosexuals are primarily attracted to others of the same gender is biological. But the form of this desire is determined by the nature of our interactions with both of our parents, our peers and siblings, and by social and cultural expectations, social norms and demands.

Clearly, if a boy starts out with an accepting and nourishing mother and a father who is nurturing of his desires to get close to him, then he is much more likely to be able to love himself and other people as he grows through childhood into adolescence and adulthood. If we have abusive, rejecting, or indifferent parents, then we're not likely to be able to withstand the abuse that we may experience from our peers, and we are certainly less likely to be able to withstand the hatred that we all experience in society.

We live in a society where fathers are often distant from their sons—whether those sons are gay or straight.

That's right. But they're more distant from a child that they sense is different. Our society is not tolerant of differences, particularly differences that rightly or wrongly may be labeled as "feminine." The idea of not appearing male yet being male is particularly odious to straight people. And not feeling masculine is odious to many gay men as well in our society.

How do fathers know that their young sons are different? What are the clues, or is it an unconscious sort of reckoning?

Most homosexual youngsters do not appear to be particularly feminine. It's difficult to get data on that; my hunch would be most are not feminine, in manner or appearance. But they are different in terms of some of their attributes, like sensitivity or perhaps not being as competitive as straight boys. Some view these attributes as not being masculine; many fathers do. However, I think fathers are more likely to be put off not as much by these differences as by the different need on the part of their homosexual child for closeness. Our longing for our fathers causes them to pull back, to be angry and anxious, to push us away.

When a certain stage of consciousness is reached, there must be an enormous outpouring of grief among gay men for what was lost.

Usually the recognition of the grief is gradual. Any time one takes a forward step, there's always a loss incurred. Whenever we become more independent, more ourselves, there's always a letting go of aspects of the past to which we are attached. And often we are attached to things that are not in our best interest, for example, a relationship with a rejecting, hurtful father.

We may hold onto an unhappy, unsatisfying relationship from the past with the hope that it will change. Or feeling that what little we got, even if it was bad, is better than nothing. We may try to recapture that relationship with our current lovers or partners. Letting go can be very painful because we are giving up the hope of ever being able to get from that person what we did not get but still long for—usually love. Hopefully, in the process of giving up the past, we can learn to get love from people in our current lives.

> *Everything you're saying rings true to my experience and to the experience of so many other gay men I've known. How does this rejection from the masculine affect our relationship with the feminine? You imply that gay boys tend to borrow their mother's physical and emotional vocabulary in order to romance the father. At such an early age, it's the only context available to them.*

Heterosexual, straight boys will become like their fathers, or some aspects of their fathers, in order to, as you say, romance the mother. I think that we as homosexual children often become like our mothers. I don't mean that we necessarily dress like her, but we may take on certain of her attributes, feeling states, interests, sensitivities. There may be some homosexual youngsters, particularly those whom one might view as being more gender atypical, whose feminine behaviors may be linked genetically with sexual orientation, but I do not believe this is true for most.

> *What is the best way to care for and nurture this indwelling repository of feeling and life experience that, for lack of another word, we call the soul?*

I keep coming back to the ways we have of viewing the hatred and rage that each of us, as a homosexual in our society, feels. And especially the way we are treated not so much by society but in our earliest relationships. I keep coming back to the capacity to love and be loved, how very important that is, and how society has crippled us in this regard. It has taken away our capacity to love other people and filled us with shame and disgust about something that binds us to others in close, intimate, passionate, loving ways.

I'm always trying to find the love inside of gay men that is often covered by anger, resentment, and hatred. When we talk about helping other human beings to love and be loved, we're talking about finding something spiritual inside of everybody.

The wounded aspect of being gay is not only a source of pain but is also the wellspring of so much of our creativity and power.

What you're calling the wound, I call self-esteem injury. Power comes from dealing with that pain in a psychological or spiritual way. Wherever there's self-esteem injury, there is rage at those who have hurt us, or at society in general. And society, in our particular case, continues to injure us. We've got to find ways to channel that anger. Clearing away the roadblocks to loving first ourselves and then others takes both a psychological and spiritual healing.

One thing I got from my own long analysis was the capacity to think about myself in psychological ways. And that has been very helpful. When I finished my analysis, I rather abruptly recognized that I had for so many years tried to please my analyst and that getting married had been part of that need. At least I was equipped then with the capacity to reflect on myself in order to find ways to deal with my difficult situation. That has been extremely important.

We have to know what is inside of ourselves and why it is there. We should understand and nurture the feelings that our anger unleashes so that we can use them in constructive and not self-destructive ways. If we don't know about our disappointments, frustrations, and injuries, the tendency is to direct our anger in self-destructive ways. I can live with all kinds of terrible feelings. The feelings that injure me are the ones I don't know about.

What have been the tangible results of dealing with that injury in your own life?

People who have come out feel themselves full of something that they have never experienced before: a sense of power. That power is caused, in part, by freeing the energy that we have previously been using to deny and disguise ourselves. I've sensed it in myself over the last twenty years. One of the things I was able to do, for example, was to get the American Psychoanalytic Association to adopt a nondiscrimination statement in 1991. It took four years of effort. It is an enormously conservative group that kept homosexuals who were comfortable with their sexuality out of training. If I hadn't been out and open about my sexual orientation, I wouldn't have been able to do that.

Is internalized homophobia how we're damaged most as gay men?

Internalized homophobia is undoubtedly part of the self-esteem injury. But let's broaden the concept to include not just what happened to us as adolescents, but what happens to us as youngsters in the family—the way our parents, siblings, and peers responded to us as children who were different. They responded out of fear and ignorance.

> *Why has our society organized this way? There have been many other cultures in the world that have found some way to value variant people within their cultures. What's wrong in America that we're not given some kind of meaningful place? Basically, we're a people with no stated social role or function, and therefore we are much more easy to dismiss.*

We have puritanical roots. That was not a help to begin with, historically. Americans also have a particular intolerance of difference. De Tocqueville would say this comes from our democratic tradition—the "tyranny of the majority" he warned us about. Gay men and lesbians may be acceptable to many in principle. But if we are visible, that's a very different story—one of intolerance, discrimination, hatred. As I indicated before, heterosexual men cannot stand to see anything they label as feminine in another man. That's why a gay man who appears feminine is more likely to be the object of verbal and physical abuse than one who looks straight.

> *Do you think that gay men have a particular vision? What about this much-debated thing called "gay sensibility"?*

I don't know if we have a unique vision, but I do think we're an awful lot more interesting than heterosexual men. We've been through more. We've met a greater variety of people. We've had to deal with more outside of ourselves and inside ourselves as well. It causes us often to be more thoughtful than straight men. Gay men who don't know themselves are not particularly interesting. Some are trying to live gay versions of conventional heterosexual lives and have blocked off a lot of what's different and interesting inside of themselves.

> *If you had one lesson to offer a young gay man coming out right now, what would you say?*

He should appreciate himself and his passion. He should, in other words, have sex—safely, of course—and enjoy it. Eventually, if he can value himself as a gay man, he's going to become attached to somebody. Being in a close, loving relationship is so important, particularly for gay people.

What about sex and relationship? Many gay men have problems putting the two together. They are troubled by intimacy.

There is a tendency on the part of many to split sex and love. It is very difficult in our society for gay men to bring their sexual passion into a loving, affectionate gay relationship. This split has to do with the way society treats our sexuality, the way we have learned to view our sexual passion as sick or bad, and with the kinds of self-esteem issues we've been talking about.

Incidentally, that doesn't mean that I feel long-term loving relationships necessarily have to be sexually monogamous in order to be good. Emotional monogamy is absolutely vital for any relationship. But for various reasons some within relationships feel the need for outside sexual exploration. Gay relationships are extraordinarily complicated, and whatever it takes for us to get them to work, we should do.

In your work, do you notice gay men having particular problems with sustaining emotional commitments because of soul injury?

Oh, sure. There's the rage, shame, and resentment that all of us carry with us—a need to express our anger at what society does to us. And then there's a need to re-create our early relationships. If we've been rejected by a father, for example, we will be inclined to enter into a relationship with a partner in which we reject him as revenge for what was done to us, or place ourselves in a position where we are again rejected. A lot of gay men feel it's easier to have sex in five minutes and go home. And while that's understandable, most of us need a relationship because of the injuries that we have sustained from family, peers, and society. We need to love and be loved to be healed.

How do you keep the embers of passion stirred in your own relationship after fifteen years?

First of all, I think my lover is one of the most interesting and beautiful men I have ever known. That helps. I get an enormous amount from him. Also, I've done a lot of internal work on the ways in which I might separate sex from love, sex from my relationship.

How do you personally cope with the anger and rage that every gay man in America experiences in this age of AIDS? We all feel society's indifference, the tragedy of our friends dying one after another. Do you just analyze or think these powerful emotions away?

I deal with my feelings daily as I work with sick or infected patients. Like others, I have had friends die. One can't deal with anger, frustration, and despair by analyzing them away. One can only deal with powerful feelings by experiencing them and making use of them. My writing helps.

I've always thought of the coming out process as never ending. Aren't you still coming out, in a way?

Soon after I self-identified in the midseventies, when I was still closeted, I began to look for sex and on one occasion was nearly arrested. After my initial shock, I recognized that being closeted was harmful and self-destructive. I knew I would gradually have to come out regardless of the consequences. Those consequences have at times been quite heavy, but nothing has been as important as the freedom being out has given me.

Being gay is an adventure because there are no guidelines for living our lives. We make them up as we go along. Sometimes I wonder what will happen when society is more accepting. Will we then become bound by convention? Life wouldn't be as challenging. I like being a renegade.

ANDREW HARVEY

REBIRTH THROUGH THE WOUND

Andrew Harvey is the author of many books of poetry and prose, including three novels—One Last Mirror, Burning Houses, *and* The Web—*in which his vividly drawn characters explore the intersections of the worldly and the sacred. An earlier nonfiction work,* A Journey in Ladakh, *tells of Harvey's arduous spiritual pilgrimage to remote Buddhist monasteries located in the highest region of India. Disparate as the author's writings may be, there is a rich vein common to all the work: from travelogue to verse, the real life humming on the other side of stale history is explored. Harvey is constantly pulling apart the fabric of cherished illusions. He challenges us to see through the woof and warp of mundane existence as if our lives depended on it. In fact, he believes they do.*

There's no doubt that Harvey is a man with a passion—an urgent calling made all the more clear in his recent autobiographical account, Hidden Journey. *The book tells of his spiritual awakening through the healing presence of the Divine Mother. Exquisitely written, grippingly told, the book is also cause for exasperation—especially to Western readers not used to circumventing the roadblocks of the rational mind. We will perhaps need to surrender our disbelief to accept Harvey's proposition that the Divine Mother could be the force to save the world.*

Harvey experienced the Divine Mother with the help of a woman called Mother Meera, whom he met in Pondicherry, a coastal town in southern India, on Christmas Day, 1978. He was twenty-five, a brilliant academic, the youngest fellow ever elected to Oxford, and he had just abandoned his career in England to return to his native India. "I was a paid-up intellectual and member of the British elite," he told me, "and had become immured in the frozen world which moved, if you could call it moved, in that college." As a result, the young scholar's life "quickly exploded into all sorts of forms of suffering. I became disillusioned about my world, my way of doing things. I understood that there was nothing whatever in this society to cling to—nothing. Unfortunately, that didn't lead me immediately to search for God, it just led me into an abyss of desolation."

Harvey's search, its stops and starts, its jagged turns and moments of profound revelation, makes Hidden Journey *compelling literature. The exasperation may come when the reader encounters Harvey's staunchly held notions about the nature of life. The sum of our world's parts do not necessarily add up to a greater truth, he says. To find one's real self, one must unquestioningly and* rigorously submit the ego to annihilation by the light of the divine, a mystical meltdown in which all shreds of former identity are completely, irrevocably burnt away.

Any person on a spiritual search is likely to meet all sorts of preposterous prophets; questionable messengers of the divine are almost certain to be encountered on the inner quest. Realness, however, is the best way to characterize Harvey, a man undeniably informed by deeply held convictions about who he is and what he has to say.

We meet on a flawless June afternoon atop San Francisco's Buena Vista hill. Harvey lives in Paris, but he is in California on a lecture tour and to take in the sights with his handsome life partner, Eryk. I begin by reciting a few lines from a favorite poet of his, the thirteenth-century Sufi mystic, Rumi: "Conventional knowledge is death to our souls. . . . Live where you fear to live, destroy your reputation, be notorious." Harvey acknowledges the quotation with a knowing guffaw, a gleefulness that infuses the rest of the day.

o

You really took Rumi's words to heart when you left Oxford. Why did you return to India and what place did the traditions of the East have in your understanding of life at that time?

India was essential to my life because the first nine years of my life were spent there. So I returned and had a series of unexpected and shattering mystical breakups that led me to experience the divine dimension. I prefer the word "breakup" to "breakdown" because I think you do break completely, but you break into another dimension in which you are at the same time infinitely more fragile, more awake, and more loving.

It was through this experience that I've come to understand what Rumi means: the absolute inadequacy of normal consciousness, the necessity to fling away all our conditioning of every kind if we are ever going to know the truth, the divine truth, about our real self.

How did this inner awakening affect your outer life?

When I came to think of writing *Hidden Journey* I had this choice: Would I commit public hara-kiri by being totally honest, or would I fudge and write about my "experiences" with a "wonderful Indian teacher"? To do the book nakedly would mean cutting myself off from the whole so-called literary world and my attachment to celebrity. But not to do it would betray the truth. Choosing not to betray the truth in its "madness" was a hair-raising thing, but it taught me everything that I think I know: that reputation is nothing and that the only valuable thing is to remain true to the soul.

Remain true to the soul, and life magically transforms itself around you. You go "mad" into the divine—like Rumi and all other mystics—and know the whole of reality as a dance of divine light. The world reveals itself as a field of what Rumi called *kibriya*—divine glory.

Is experiencing this kind of breakup, this madness you speak of,
actually a process of finding one's sanity in a crazy world?

It's not that you become sane; it's that you find the courage to stay "mad," to stay with an endless capacity for transformation—for going on and on dissolving your own assumptions and certainties. In fact, you come to trust enough to remain perpetually bewildered so as always, always to be vulnerable to miracle.

There's been a long tradition of intellectually constipated Western-
ers trekking to the East to find enlightenment—to "go native" as
the cynics would say.

India was not something exotic that I suddenly picked up in the sixties. India was my childhood, my source of legend, of whatever scraps of divine knowledge I had as a child. I'm not an exile in flight from England; I am not running away from anything. I am just staring at catastrophe. Since seventeen, I have been awake to the fact that I am living in a collapsing civilization, one that has lost all touch with the sacred and its power of love.

Seventeen was the age when I awoke to the realization that I was
gay. Was this also the case for you?

I was awakening to my homosexuality and my desire to be a poet. I also sensed the doom that civilization was locked in, and all of those three things inflamed and illumined each other. I withdrew from the world into a room at the top of my parents' house and just stayed there all summer reading Shakespeare and Emily Dickinson. It was in those months that it registered for the first time just how frightening it was to be alive in a civilization that is dedicated to destruction and exploitation, in which hardly any of the wisdom and culture of the past survives, and in which nobody I knew seemed to know who they were, what they were doing here, or why they were living.

In Hidden Journey *you movingly write, "From the deepest wound of my life grew its miraculous possibility." Most gay men, having been deeply soul-wounded themselves, would be able to relate to those words. Still, I want to know how we can best address the wound, to perceive and allow for its mystery. How do we transform the pain of being wounded from unconscious self-betrayal to self-discovery?*

Had I not been so wounded, I wouldn't have burned my life away in the ways that I have. I think I wouldn't have constantly hungered and searched, certainly not with the intensity that I have. After long years of mourning this wound, which is essentially my abandonment as a child by both my father and my mother, I have come to understand that it was in many ways the karmic preparation for the work that I have to do. The wound carved out a void I had to fill with divine love because all human love would fail me, necessarily. It compelled me to look for final healing. Emily Dickinson wrote, "The wounded deer leaps highest." The wound was savage enough to make me leap into the arms of the Divine Mother.

Was there a connection between the wounding you incurred from your parents and being gay? What kind of little boy were you? Were you a "sissy"?

I was an eerie little boy, fantastically precocious and full of imitations. I've seen films of myself in which I look quite camp—like a tiny drag queen. It must have been rather difficult for my father, who was a policeman, and I never felt loved by him. Now I see that longing for my father's love was something that defined my homosexuality just as my obsession with my mother must have. I've come to understand that it was really the impossible desire to have my father love me that propelled me to choose again and again men who couldn't or who, being like him, could only repeat the rejection. It's terrifying when you finally understand just how much of your emotional life is ruled by forces that are buried so deep in pain that you can't get to them.

Let's talk about the uncovering of the past.

I think that you first uncover it by suffering and causing a great deal of pain. Unconsciously, you repeat, in situation after situation, the devastation of childhood. Again and again, you find yourself running against the same spear, and the spear keeps going right through the same wound, widening it and making it more and more painful. Eventually, if you are lucky, you come to understand that there is something very damaged about the way you envision yourself and with the way you love, and you begin the long process of healing. Therapy can be valuable in revealing to you over a period of time exactly how your actions are permeated by self-hatred or the fear of abandonment. But the actual way I took was a mystical unraveling. What happens as you go through a mystic process is that your ego and its biography become crystalline clear. You undergo a therapy so final and so excruciating that there is nowhere for any corner of self-ignorance to cower. You have to face everything, things which would make people in normal consciousness faint from terror. What is revealed is just how hollow and conditioned almost every move you make is, and that's a very painful recognition.

What do you mean by mystical process?

I mean by the word *mystical* entering into conscious direct relationship with the divine. It must be conscious and it must be direct to be mystical. Mystical is not theological; it's not having a series of ideas about God, however lucid or wonderful. It's not emotional; it's not having a series of feelings, however deep and adoring, about God. And it's not intellectual, in any sense, even in the most refined sense.

What it means is having direct contact in the soul, the core of being, with the Source. That can take place in many different ways, but its primary ways are through an opening of what people call the third eye. Through devotion, mystical prayer, and the saying of mantras, all the senses of the subtle body—the spiritual senses, if you like—wake up and begin to see and interpret the world in a completely fresh way.

The world remains the same but appears now drenched in light and transparent and is experienced far more like a magical film than as something inherently real. The ego stops interpreting and deforming, and you begin to see the primal, divine world in its pain and beauty and to respond to it with the love of the soul, which is one with the love that creates all things.

Is this what some spiritual traditions call the "awareness of maya," having the sense that all things are illusion?

Yes. But I don't like the word illusion too much because I don't think of this creation as an "illusion." For me, it is a theophany. Theophany comes from a beautiful word, *theophania,* which means "showing forth of God." A mystic is someone who sees God in all things and all things in God. Everything we see or live is for me a shining forth of God, a radiance of the beloved, a radiance that can be terrible as well as beautiful, and sometimes both at once.

Why is this radiance also terrible?

There is a terrible aspect of God that cannot be avoided. There are hurricanes and plagues, there are collapses of civilization and stars exploding in the darknesses of space. There is agony on every level of creation. There is no joy without pain, no life without death. A mystic comes to learn to dance not only for creation but also for destruction—knowing that life and death are inseparable and part of the same process that transcends both.

That's a very vulnerable place to be, particularly in the brutal world of human cause and effect.

Of course, but then hearts were made to break. By accepting heartbreak and allowing the heart to break again and again without fear or consolation, a space is opened in the heart in which the whole universe can be placed. Such vulnerability is sacred, I believe, and the source of the highest and most luminous forms of strength.

I see that in the lives of many gay men, particularly in those who are gender nonconforming. There's nothing stronger or more right-on than a queen.

Nothing! Because they've had to face all the derision and all the projections of the world.

The real mystic search is about the very difficult uncovering of one's fears and self-hatreds, guilts and shame, and the irradiation of those things by the divine light. This means the divine light itself enters and takes over the whole being and subjects parts of that being to a real burning away. Saint John of the Cross has a wonderful image for this process, which is of a log burning in the fire. When you burn a log that has just been cut it hisses and crackles in the fire. The flame has to clean it, purify it before entering.

. That purification—which means looking into the mirror of the flame and seeing your whole life, every scrap of your vanity, pointlessness, and self-absorption—is really a death. It's far beyond the kind of death that conventional therapy wants to produce—it is a death while alive. The ego is dissolved in a larger fiery center.

Examining the wound is a preliminary and a very important stage for entering the divine fire, just as the log itself is penetrated by the flame, crackles in that union, and then sinks into a softer, sweeter union before it becomes ash. Everyone who is destined to have a spiritual transformation comes to the journey with a wound as large as God. They have to, to go through it. Very few people are going to undertake the massive stripping it entails unless there is something tremendously painful urging them on. There are very few people who become advanced mystics because they simply feel happy on Sunday afternoons.

Every human being walking on the planet is wounded in some way, but it seems to me that if you're a gay man, your wound is particularly big.

And I think this is one of the reasons why so many gay men are at the forefront of the spiritual movements of our time. Ram Dass, for example, has used his gayness in the most resourceful, hilarious, brilliant, acute, poignant ways—to illustrate his own search and also to scent and perfume his own persona. Ram Dass is somebody who is fearless in many different dimensions, and his fearlessness communicates itself to people. But there are many other gay men that I know who are leading the fight for transformation because they've suffered in their own lives from the limitations of this culture. They've gone on a very passionate journey to overcome those limitations in themselves and to live from a different center. So I think gayness, which is a large wound, is also a large opportunity.

I certainly see being gay as a kind of experiential soul food, something that can help to awaken and hasten us on our life journey. But obviously this is a largely unrealized potential good, not something that is universally recognized by every gay man. I mean, it's a door to walk through, but not every gay man does. You write in Hidden Journey: *"I realize that the voice, that inner voice, was telling me to bless and to accept my sexual nature, which had filled my youth with loneliness, pain, and guilt. I had to love my sexuality fearlessly before I could transform it. Suppression or denial would not work." But self-love is hard to achieve, Andrew, particularly when the very core of who you are has been systematically abused. How did you do it—find the joy of being gay?*

My quest for self-love is inseparable from my mystical journey. I had to face that I was, as everyone else is, inherently worthy of love. And that was a vast and healing revelation for me, a revelation that goes on and on unfolding.

What I have learned is very simple: Every human being is a Divine Child. My secret yoga, my spiritual path, is that of the child. I have no desire to be a master or a guru or a teacher; my only desire is to be the Divine Child of the Divine Mother. All I want to do with the rest of my life is serve the beauty of her vision with whatever gifts I have and to play and work and sing and dance and love as her child.

The Divine Child is an extremely important archetype.

It's the essential archetype of the mystical life.

I also see it as a very central archetype in the psychology of gay men.

For me, it is the key. So let's explore what might be called the mystical meaning of gayness. In a sacred world, which we do not live in, every human being, whatever their inclination—sexual or otherwise—would be given at birth a series of options through which they could develop their mystical capacity. Gay men and women would clearly be seen for what they are from birth—as beings essential to the health of society, as people who are freed from the responsibilities of procreation to cultivate the artistic, the spiritual, the values of living itself, as people who point to an inner fusion of male and female, a holy androgyny, that all beings could aspire to. God is both male and female and beyond both. In a sacred world, the gay being would be seen as the living presence of that nondual, male-female character of the divine and revered as such.

Now, let us take this one step further. Reality is created by yin and yang, but the yin and yang are held within the Tao. And the Tao, the mysterious transcendent that governs all things and in which all things move, is the all-embracing Divine Mother. The homosexual male, because of a peculiar vulnerability to the feminine, is deeply in touch with the sacred transcendent feminine and so is open to being initiated into the Tao.

Is a realized mystic a kind of archetypal Androgyne?

Yes. A mature mystic fuses within his or her being the male and the female aspects of the psyche and in so doing consciously realizes the goal of human life, which is to be at once as immanent and transcendent as the divine itself. When the male and female aspects of the inner being fuse they give birth to the child, the Divine Child, the complete being at one with all the yin and yang forces, free from conventions, barriers, burdens, and definitions. I think the homosexual, by virtue of his or her makeup, may have a greater chance of realizing this androgyny and its end in divine childhood.

I'm very interested in exploring how this connects with homophobia.

Homophobia is entirely about extinguishing the feminine and extinguishing the child. Because what are the two great enemies of the masculine myth—the woman and the child! The woman—whose powers of feminine strength, love, and intuition eclipse and accuse those of the clumsy operators that men have traditionally opted to become. And the child—who is free from the savage laws with which men scourge themselves and everyone!

Nor can homophobia be isolated from the very battle for life on a dangerously misused and overpopulated planet.

Of course not, because if homophobia is rooted in the derision and fear of the feminine, so is the destruction of the earth. The destruction of the earth has resulted from our ignorance of where and who we are, which is totally interdependent with everything else. The patriarchal folly that we call Western civilization is rooted in a willful separation from the earth, from nature, and from one another. Gays have a unique function in registering the cruelty and the craziness of patriarchy and in working to transcend it

Let's face it, any conscious and spiritual homosexual today is trying to invent a new world in the bloody and frightening chaos of a collapsing civilization and in the bloody and frightening chaos of a plague that affects us. These two kinds of chaos can either destroy us or provide the pain and energy for our transformation and press us to define ourselves more clearly and fiercely. There is a Tibetan proverb: "In a bad time, let obstacles become the spurs to enlightenment." We have to learn how to become phoenixes and rise again and again out of the ashes of humiliation, desolation, and grief.

What about the role of AIDS in our lives?

AIDS is a kind of training ground for the apocalypse. I feel that those people who are dying of AIDS are going through in their bodies what is actually happening to the earth. The earth has AIDS because of the way we've treated it. The gay plague, if you like, mirrors that huge natural disaster. In another sense, I think the bewilderment, the total stripping of illusions, the humiliation, and the horror of AIDS mirrors what is happening to the entire planet.

AIDS is a challenge to all of us to become as awake and enlightened as possible, to live as intensely and presently in love as possible. I see on the one hand the despair and desolation in the gay community that arises from the fact that people in a corrupt civilization are given no spiritual help; nobody is helped to really understand the nature of death. On the other hand, I see in certain individuals who are pursuing paths of self-healing amazing transformations taking place. People who five years ago were self-absorbed and hedonistic are now giving their whole lives over to serving their fellow beings. That is a tremendous and prophetic sign to the world at large.

If we, as homosexuals, are going to claim our position as mystical and spiritual leaders, as I believe we should, there must be an unsparing embrace of this plague and its possibilities. We are very far from that radical embrace: there are so many denials and fears as well as widespread ignorance of what a spiritual transformation is and how much it has to cost. People have to believe that enlightenment is possible and worth any amount of suffering—and that is a huge leap for Westerners trained to hate pain and the loss of control.

> *I am reminded of something one of the characters in* Hidden Journey *says: "The heart must break to become large. When the heart is broken open, then God can put the whole universe in it." Those words really spoke to me.*

AIDS can, if we let it, shatter our heart absolutely open. I think we have to stop thinking there's going to be a miracle cure. We've got to accept that this plague is going to carry away many of the people that we love most. This is terrible, but then so is the nature of this world. I think it's time for us to face what samsara is. Samsara, say Buddhists, is the endless, unending round of birth and death, and everything in samsara is designed to break and be inadequate: we are not meant to be comforted by or safe in anything. The only safety is in the realization of our divine nature, a condition of complete simplicity that costs not less than everything.

We have a responsibility to be wise and lucid in hell, to be signs in hell of divine knowledge. That is what all my gay brothers who are on this mystical path are trying to become. There are many of us, and we are awakening to the same truth and the same task and to the immensity of the honesty and sacrifice needed to fully realize them.

> *Let's go back to the word* soul—*how do you define it? And what's the difference between soul and spirit?*

I would say that soul is the diamond and spirit is the shining of the diamond. Soul is the divine essence in us that is changeless and unaffected by anything that happens and is always at peace, always in a state of calm, bliss, and love.

Spirit is the agency, if you like, of the soul—like the Holy Ghost is the agency of the Father and the Son. It's the creative fire, the creative effulgence of the soul that acts in life to permeate different activities—from scrubbing the toilet to writing poetry. But no human words can ever be adequate to the subtlety of the interaction between the spirit and the soul. It might be said that the soul is like a sun and the spirit are its rays. The rays and the sun are one, but the rays have a different function; they are the glowing agents of the soul, working in reality to transform reality.

What is your best prescription for the care and nurturing of the soul? Do you follow a daily spiritual practice? Do you mind talking about it?

I think that it's essential to nurture the soul, and the best way to do that is to continue to remind yourself of its existence. Sitting in simple meditation and following your breath is a very good way. Or repeating the name of any divine person who really moves you, repeating it in your heart and imagining the divine light drenching your body and mind as you are doing so. Those two forms of meditation are extremely simple and can be done anywhere, under almost any circumstances.

Very slowly you will come to realize that your whole life can flower into a kind of meditation, and you become not disassociated from your life but freely detached from it, able to watch it and so able to manage and love it with generous dignity. As Blake wrote: "He who binds to himself a joy / Does the winged life destroy; / But he who kisses the joy as it flies / Lives in eternity's sunrise."

After you've gone through this fiery process of transformation, where the ego and all previously held perceptions of yourself are reduced to ash, what do you know?

You're beyond the point of knowing. You are in love with a mystery. You trust it and go on and on moving deeper and deeper into its heart of light.

When you've finally taken really deeply in your heart the bodhisattva vow, which is to serve humanity with what limited gifts you have, then you're given the divine energy to realize your vow. As you open to love's service, you're given the energy of divine love to enact it—otherwise you couldn't. Love engenders action: What's remarkable about the lives of nearly all the greatest mystics is that after their illuminations they work, work tirelessly. They build monasteries or write books or go on and on explaining, communicating—Buddha didn't just sit about after his illumination; he tramped throughout India for fifty years giving what he had been given away!

This cannot be stressed enough: the mystical transformation doesn't lead to passivity nor to a higher sublime form of narcissism; it leads to the most passionate, unstinting form of action in the world, which is the action of love and service. That is what all homosexuals, especially in this time of AIDS, have to learn. We should make ourselves signs of active love so that people just by being with us can realize the end of fear. But we have to end fear in ourselves before we can communicate the end of fear to others.

This is key—the end of fear.

AIDS brings up every conceivable fear. Fear of being derided, fear of being abandoned, fear of a horrible death, fear of physical ugliness. In a homosexual culture as addicted to beauty as ours, what disease could be more afflicting? But there, in that complete stripping, is one opportunity.

Being queer and choosing to come out is another kind of stripping away, isn't it?

Very much. One of the reasons why gay men can be so open to mystical experience is that their choice to come out is a choice for what Keats called "the holiness of the Heart's affections." And that is a brave thing to do in a world like ours. Through that leap of courage the first step toward divine love has already been taken. By choosing human love and paying the social price, you begin to find the strength to choose the highest love of all.

I'm still surprised, even dismayed, by the great numbers of gay men who reject this potential in themselves.

I completely understand it. Religions have done nothing but tell gay men that they were either sinners of the worst kind or people who needed reformation. The only religions that don't spout rubbish about gay men are Hinduism and Buddhism. And even they are often morally reactionary.

I'm not asking gay men to join religions! What I care about is the mystical tradition, the core of every religion, often the persecuted core. If only gay men understood that mystics have shared throughout history so much of the same derision and persecution as they have, for some of the same reasons, because what they incarnated was the banished feminine, the derided powers of intuition, the powers of sacred love and sacred joy. If gay men could be guided to understand their own sensitivity and yearning for love as coming from within their innermost core, which is a divine source, then I think you could really see a spiritual revolution among them. But I entirely understand their cynicism. Why should they believe in God as God's been interpreted for them by the religions, which have done nothing but to make them feel humiliated?

That's why gay mystics are so important: they show gay men that there is a way to enter into direct communication with the divine source and its unconditional transforming love that bypasses all dogma and punitive moralism.

Who are some of these gay mystics?

In Plato we have a very complete vision of the ladder to transcendence in the *Phaedrus* and in the *Symposium*. I'm amazed how few gay men have really seriously studied those. And in Walt Whitman we have the most extraordinary guide to mystical tenderness and fraternity between men and to its vast consequence: the discovery of a new form of love that would bring peace to the world.

How does one survive the fire of transformation?

You mustn't want to survive the fire, you should want to burn away in it. We don't survive AIDS, we use AIDS to go beyond the idea of survival at all, to experience our immortality. That's the only way to use it. It's like in judo—the secret of judo is to take the strength of your opponent and use it against him or her. If we do not become the reality behind reality, we will just go on being victims of fantasy and change and death.

In Hidden Journey *you tell us how your life has been transformed by your contact with the force of the Divine Mother. Can you define the Divine Mother?*

The Divine Mother, for me, is the mother-aspect of the nature of God. I see "Her" as the power of love that infuses the entire creation, the force that is continually creating the creation and also the transcendence that holds the creation forever in arms of light. Everything is born from "Her," and "She" loves all things with a tender passionate love. The Divine Father, or father-aspect of the nature of God, can be stern and judging; the essence of divine "motherhood" is unconditional love. It is the boundless and unconditional love whose force heals, redeems, and transforms all those who truly turn to it.

She's creating the universe, but isn't she also taking it apart at the same time?

Yes, she is the force of creation and destruction as well as the eternal light in and beyond both. As to the relation of the Divine Mother and homosexuality, it is natural, blessed, and sacred and with its own function in the world—otherwise it wouldn't be there! I don't think homosexuality is more sacred than heterosexuality—all forms of loving sexuality are sacred.

Don't you think that gay men need as much equilibrium or honest relationship with the Divine Father?

Yes, but with the real father, not the psychotic vision of him. In my own healing journey, it was very important that I come across the divine and sacred male. Only I couldn't find him in my own culture until Tibetan teacher Thuksey Rinpoche showed me just what a complete being a realized man could be. By having my heart, mind, and soul broken open by him, I was initiated into the sacred man in myself. This enabled me to claim my maleness, something that I found very hard to do in the West because up to then I associated what maleness I had with the maleness that I found bleak and cruel in the men around me. Experience of the Divine Mother led me slowly out of the shadow of the "false" father into the light of the real one. This is a pilgrimage all modern men need to make.

Gay men seem to have a natural propensity for intuiting and dancing with the feminine. But in modern culture, our problem often lies with locating the masculine.

We've had a false masculine presented to us, an ideal of control and domination that is really a frozen hysteria, a condensation of panic and fear. It has nothing to do with the real masculine. In fact, gay men are closer to the real masculine than the so-called masculine ones are. Gay men in the way in which they interpret and live masculinity might be models for straight men, models for a deepening of the heart, a more tender and playful humor, a greater acceptance and tolerance of diversity.

The Divine Mother is not about a new dogma of femininity. She is not saying, "Get rid of everything else and only choose the feminine." She's saying, "Bring everything into balance, marry the opposites within you." That means bring the derided and negated feminine into the picture so completely that a real balance is established between yin and yang. And out of that real and mysterious balance a new order, a new love, is born in each of us in the ground of our being, beyond all categories of "gay" or "straight." This love is the fountain of enlightenment.

When you say that someone is divine, what are you really talking about?

All of us are inherently divine, and knowing and being what we really are is the point of human life. Some people will completely realize this in this life, and they could be called enlightened beings. They have the power, within certain limitations, of an enlightened consciousness and work with that power in the world and do immense amounts of good. There are also a very few beings whom I would call avatars or bodhisattvas—*avatar* means "descent from the divine"—divine beings who descend into this dimension to do a specific transformatory work. This sounds fantastic and outrageous, but my book *Hidden Journey* is an attempt to show people that this force and this light are really working here. Thousands of people have known them all over the world and know them intimately and normally. It's essential for the gay community to know that incarnations of the Divine Mother are here. And also to know that incarnations of the "real" Divine Father are here. The Dalai Lama is one, for example. He reveals so beautifully what true maleness is like in all its lucid strength and grace.

A great deal depends upon how the most responsible members of the gay community work with the power and light of the divine to transform themselves and become leaders in the only revolution that can now save us—the revolution of love, of love-in-action.

But doesn't self-forgiveness have to come first? How do we release the suffering of the past, let go of our guilt and shame?

By allowing the sun of love to awaken in us and shine through us, we come to feel and taste our inner glory. Slowly the illusions of shame, guilt, and impotence melt away, and we assume humbly the beauty and tasks of our true royalty.

If you had one thing to say to a young gay man just coming out, what would it be?

Please discover who you essentially are as quickly and directly as possible, and don't get trapped in any of the illusions either your gay culture or the culture around you will try to project on you. Realize that you are the child of God, and embody it. Live and act passionately from your divine center of love.

ANDREW RAMER

TRIBAL WISDOM

In the litany of sorry, broken relationships between gay men and their fathers, Andrew Ramer has a different story to tell.

"My father did the best he knew how as a straight man to introduce me to gay culture," Ramer recalls, even though he is quick to admit that those attempts were frequently "terrifying." Andrew's parents would often argue over their young son's nonconforming behavior, his father advocating tolerance. "You can't change people," he'd proclaim. "Let's see what we can do to make him happy as he is." So when Andrew became old enough his father took him to gay parties. Although Ramer senior was not himself a homosexual, his job as an interior designer put him in contact with plenty of men who were. It was the midsixties, and Andrew still remembers those outings well.

"All the men were screaming queens," he says, with a slow shake of his head. "They all had on little cashmere V-neck sweaters, were incredibly skinny, had bad skin, and wore penny loafers and very tight pants. I thought I'd turn out exactly like them." As the evenings progressed, the men "got drunker and drunker and sat around the piano singing Broadway songs, which I knew but wouldn't admit that I did." Despite the teenager's discomfort, it remained clear to him that his father wanted to support him "in the best way that he could."

Born in 1951 to a left-wing, atheist, political, Jewish family in Queens, New York, Ramer had plenty of other lessons about being different while growing up. "I was raised in an environment where I was taught that in a tribe, which was Jews, we have a responsibility not only to educate the world about who we are innately but also to support one another, take care of ourselves, and make lists of all the famous Jews that have ever done anything of significance in world history."

It was natural, then, for Ramer to come to his gayness through his Jewish sensibility. Dispensing gay tribal wisdom with heart and soul is the work he brings to the world today. A longtime teacher and writer, Ramer excels in his role as storyteller—a mythologizer for his queer tribe. In widely distributed essays such as "Two Flutes Playing" and "Priests of Father Earth and Mother Sky," Ramer weaves lines of anthropological research, spiritual philosophy, and personal insight into a unique vision of who gay men really are—and always have been.

The alcoholic queens he visited in his youth may seem like arcane figures, tragic stereotypes from the past, but to Ramer they represent a bitter legacy that continues to this day. For all of the social progress that gay men have *achieved since the era of* The Boys in the Band, *in his view they still have little perspective about their true place in human culture as harbingers and mediators of new consciousness.*

A wholly likable, engagingly articulate man, Ramer now lives in suburban Northern California, not too far from the Institute of Transpersonal Psychology in Palo Alto where his life partner is completing doctoral studies. He has long been familiar with the West Coast, having moved to conservative Orange County with his mother after his parents divorced when he was fifteen.

"I had never seen so many blond people in my life the day we got off the airplane," he says. "Almost every day after that I experienced some form of anti-Semitic harassment. One boy at school even told me he couldn't be my friend anymore because he heard that I was Jewish. He asked me where my tail was. That was a real shock to me. I couldn't believe what I was hearing."

Such bald prejudice helped prepare Ramer for the homophobia to come. It also no doubt strengthened his resolve to fight damning myths with fables of his own invention.

°

Your father was apparently an extremely sensitive man. If only all fathers could be as perceptive about their gay sons.

I had a solid foundation of acceptance. I still remember him saying the one thing that has been utterly critical to the work I've done as a man who loves men. One day we went to an exhibit of cave paintings, which we both loved. At one point he turned and asked me who I thought had created them. I said I didn't know. "It had to be the fags," he explained. "All the other men are out hunting and killing. There's a bunch of fags sitting in the back of the cave, complaining about how ugly it is, wondering what they can do to make it look better. So they decide to paint some bison on the walls." I never forgot that conversation. Years later, I realized that my father was consciously trying to say to me, "I want you to understand that you have roots, that you have a history." I grew up being told all these stories about being Jewish. That's part of my tribal consciousness. But except for a few things my father said, like that day at the museum, I realize that no one tells our gay stories except for ourselves.

Is this how you regard yourself, as a gay storyteller?

Thousands of years ago people were sitting around a fire, telling stories. And here we are today, sitting around a tape recorder with two little red lights glowing like embers. It's all that's left of the fire, but that's enough. There's somebody who asks, What happened? And there's somebody who tells why what happened happened. And the rest of the tribe is sitting with us.

What is the most crucial thing we can be telling each other as gay men?

The most important thing we can tell each other as gay men is that we are here for a reason and all of us know what the reason is. We know when we sit with ourselves and notice who we are, what we do, and what we bring to the world. There's a line from a Native American medicine chant that I really love: "You bring to all of life your special touch." We gay men know what our special touch is.

Perhaps a few of us know, but don't you think that most gay men are unable to express what their "special touch" might be? After all, we live in a homophobic society where there is little or no supportive imagery about our lives. What's so special about being gay?

The first thing I noticed when I came out is that I could feel who was gay. There is a certain energy that we carry. I don't know where it comes from exactly, but I think it's something in the body that's different. I used to practice by going to Grand Central Station at rush hour and just standing there with my eyes closed. I could feel just by somebody walking by who was gay and who wasn't.

Can you describe that feeling, perhaps associate it with a tone or color?

Straight men's energy is sharper and more direct; it's more horizontal, spikier. Whereas the energy that gay men carry is rounder, softer. It's kind of like the difference between a porcupine and a peacock. If I was going to pick a color, I would say that straight men are yellow and gay men are green. There are also more overtones and undertones in the energy of gay men. We have access to internal feminine parts of ourselves and that comes out. Another way of putting it is to say that gay men are plaid and straight men are stripes. We have another weave going in another direction. However one might describe being gay, it's very different from being straight.

> *In "Priests of Father Earth and Mother Sky" you describe a great circle in which the women-who-love-women sit in the North, the men-who-love-men sit in the South, the child-bearing women sit in the East, and the nongay men sit in the West. Isn't that another way of describing a four-gender society?*

The more I become who I am, the less like a man or a woman I feel. The more we gay men become ourselves, the more we do become different. I think the future of the world, the hope of the world, depends upon us, that men who love men are the only people who can save the planet. That's our job, our purpose. We carry this other kind of energy that no one else carries, and it's entirely in our hands to save the world. On an archetypal level, every tribe has its own characteristics that are woven out of the total fabric of what it means to be a human being. However, since we are talking about gay men specifically here, it is my belief that we are the ones that stand at the outermost edge of transformation.

My role is to keep supporting other gay men in recognizing that the visions we carry, the creativity we hold, are pushing us to do this work. I have no idea how we're going to do it, but no one else has the daring, the madness, the folly, the seriousness, the pain, and the delight to do it but us! However wobbly our tribe is—we come from every single other community, age, race, and religion—we're somehow still a tribe. We are the United Nations of the future. The way that we have been learning to come together since AIDS is a model for how life on the planet can be. That's our job.

I believe that certain people are biologically separate from the child-rearing pool, that nature in some way has invited gay men to exist separate from that process in order to do soul work, to be both a mirror in which everyone else can look at themselves and an inside-outside voice to express things that are going on in the whole tribe. By virtue of our creativity, our passion, our humor, our exuberance for life, by virtue of the fact that we come from every other group, we have the ability to model what it's like to be a human being on the planet for all of humanity. It's time that we do this, publicly, together, separately, and in our families. The world is looking to us even though it doesn't know it. The world is depending upon us because no one else can do it. It's us!

It's one thing to say that we can save the world, but can you explain the tools and abilities we'll bring to that task?

There are four basic abilities that gay men have. First, because we live on the edge of gender and on the margin of society, we are consciousness scouts. Any tribe has scouts that run ahead to see what's beyond the next mountain and then come back. But what's happened in the world we live in today is that we keep going out to scout and no one wants to hear from us.

Society is not particularly interested in most of what we discover, except marginally. If gay men are making theater, eventually straight people will come. If we invent a new way of dressing, eventually everyone will dress that way. So in little ways, we're still doing our innate job for the whole society. But because society doesn't really honor who we are, many of us become bitchy and angry, or we just sort of wander off.

Like those roomfuls of sad gay men your dad took you to see?

They were that way because they had been disenfranchised by society. Almost all of those men were hairdressers or interior decorators; they were in the business of making beautifulness.

And that's the second thing we have the capacity to do. If there's theater, we're doing it. If there's art, we're doing it. If there's music, we're doing it. If there's writing, we're doing it. If all of us decided to stay home for a week, the entire cultural life of the planet would grind to a complete halt. In one of my stories I talk about different names for gay tribes: the Makes Beautiful Lodges people, which is my synonym for interior decorators, the Fixes the Hair people. We do those things; we've always done them and always will—it's one of the attributes of our energy.

Our third major attribute is taking care of people. Some of that is very specific; there's a way of nurturing people by just fixing their hair. But the biggest piece of what I'm talking about is something I call Midwives for the Dying. In my mythological vision of how the world is/was/always will be, women are the midwives of birth and men are the midwives of death. But I think men got a little bit confused about that and started killing people. Standing at the closing door made men feel like it gave them the power to push people through it very quickly, before their time.

So it's been left to gay men to be the guardians of death, who now stand at that door. Because we live between genders, we also live between matter and spirit, between this world and the next. In a very ancient way, we have the capacity to sit with someone when they're dying and shepherd them across. AIDS is especially awakening this memory in us; now we're really good at helping the dying.

The only thing that's missing is the mythological container in which we can understand these capacities. My job as a storyteller is to say that our being nurturers, our being midwives for the dying, is something that's innate within us. And not just physical death but the dying that occurs throughout all of one's life: I've heard so many conversations where people are dying to parts of their life and the person that they turn to is a gay man, whether they know it or not.

Assisting in the spiritual or psychological deaths that allow us to go forward in life is traditionally the job of the shaman.

I believe that all shamans were once gay. And it was only later when we started to get disenfranchised that other men had to learn, with great difficulty, what we know innately.

What is the fourth gay attribute you mentioned?

I'm going to call it "hunter energy." The only way that it's survived is in the way that we stalk each other, in the way that we cruise, the sex hunt. In cultures where we could have been drawn and quartered or burned at the stake—and were—it didn't stop men from having sex with each other. Nothing has stopped us. Not damnation, not imprisonment, not all kinds of psychological labels, because this energy in us is so strong. It allows us to survive, to feed our souls and feed the culture. Because this energy has been reduced to the smallest thing we only see it in terms of our sex hunt. But when we really live in a whole container of who we are as a tribe we're going to be able to use that energy to change life on the planet.

I distinguish hunter energy from that of the warrior, which to me is destructive. The capacity to bring home food to the tribe is one of our jobs, and what I mean by the tribe is the whole world. We have the capacity to go out, find stuff, bring it back, and use it. People like Dag Hammarskjöld and Bayard Rustin epitomize what is possible.

The attributes you've described sound great, so wonderful. What intelligent society wouldn't want people who have the ability to do these things? Yet we live in a culture that has rejected queer energy for centuries. Do you have a clue as to what that rejection is about? What are the roots of this dislike?

The reasons are multiple. The emergence of male-dominated religious-economic systems necessitated the suppression of certain kinds of power, certain kinds of vibrations. But I believe in reincarnation, and I think our immortal souls made decisions about where humanity was going to evolve that transcend our particular definitions of gender. In other words, the most militant feminists today were probably oppressive robber barons a century ago, and some of those robber barons had been enlightened women a century before that. Things are constantly going around. In looking at the evolution of what we call the patriarchy, we can't be pointing fingers because it's everybody's evolution.

The religious-economic complex is male-dominated. And the round, fluid energy that men who love men carry threatens that system every step of the way, as women in their own power threaten that system. Some of the roots of homophobia come from the suppression of goddess cults, the suppression of free sexuality and of the temples where having sex was considered sacred. All that's left of prayer now is the words that come out of somebody's mouth, but once when you prayed you could use your whole body. From early historical times to the beginning of the Christian era, if you wanted to pray, you could go to the temple and have sex with a man or a woman.

That's not the kind of energy that supports the development of technology, of city-states that become nations that become empires. So some of the roots of homophobia come from the suppression of that energy. The energy is scary, it's different. Our culture keeps insisting we have two containers only: Male and Female, Column A and Column B, no other choices. However, babies keep popping up that are neither A nor B. It's very upsetting. We keep trying to get rid of them. Like any taboo, like any great fire that you want to contain, if there's that much fear, then there's something really magical.

Another reason for homophobia is that the culture we have evolved suppresses everybody. Homophobia is an expression of people's own wounds. Human beings are not welcomed at birth into a world that says every person is their own essence and totally free to express themselves. The people who hate us are projecting onto us their own limitations. And because we're Consciousness Scouts, because we are Hunters, because we are innately living out a vibration that pushes the container and stretches the boundaries, we're really threatening to them.

How prevalent is homophobia in gay men themselves?

It's universal. We will die with it inside us, in the same way that because we're raised in a racist culture we will all die racists. The question, then, isn't whether we're racist or not but what we do about it.

What form does that homophobia take within you?

The easiest example is when I'm angry at my lover, feeling that our relationship is not going to work. One of my very first thoughts is that I'm not really gay. That's the problem. If my brother's having a fight with his girlfriend, he doesn't stop the conversation to totally deny the nature of his sexual preference. He doesn't stand there and say, "I'm probably gay and that's why we're disagreeing." But I do that again and again.

And what do you do about it?

I notice it, I laugh, I cry. I sometimes wonder if it's true. I try to come back to what's really going on—the capacity to deny my own self in crisis. What I see moving in the world is how often I distrust other gay men for a variety of reasons and with all kinds of judgments: he's too bitchy, too closeted; he's too out, or not out enough! I can walk into a room and make judgments about other gay men in a second.

But I can also feel the same things as a Jew. I was raised in an anti-Jewish culture, and it's a part of me: Jews are too loud, too pushy, too materialistic, all of these things that I was told. I can walk into a room and instantly have all of those feelings, too.

There's the larger question here about finding our joy. But before that can happen, don't you think we have to find the means to deal with our injury, our soul-wounding? Most of us have been deeply hurt by rejection and humiliation, often quite early in our lives by our fathers. What is the best way to heal?

Our suffering, our wounds, can't be separated from our joy. Although we may say we don't have masculine initiation, rejection is an initiation of a kind.

It's a cutting away. People in the men's movement get me really angry when they romanticize initiation rites, for instance. They talk about Native Australian boys being put out to live in the wild and subjected to all kinds of trials, but they neglect to mention that one-third of the boys died from the stuff that happened. Given the choice between dying and having my father not love me enough, frankly, I would prefer the latter. It's a kind of initiation because every initiation is a separation.

Even if we were loved by our fathers and not rejected when we were five or six, there would still be a point where we'd be different from them. What happened to most of us is the initiation. It's tempered us, it's made us stronger. Those of us gay men who have survived have lived through the kinds of ordeals that other men hunger for.

When I went to see the Names Project AIDS Memorial Quilt, I thought, This is probably the saddest creation ever made by human beings in the history of our planet. I don't know how we go on, but part of our strength is that somehow we do. It's not just enough to talk about our wounds, however. I've sat around for years with gay men talking about their wounds: the lovers that rejected them, the jobs that rejected them, the fathers that rejected them. What we haven't talked about is our capacity for joy.

> *There's been much revisionist thought about gay male life in the seventies, all the drugs and other hedonistic indulgences of the time. We were surely experiencing our joy, but perhaps it was being released without the proper container. Can we learn to channel our joy in a more purposeful manner?*

Joy is a prime frequency of the universe. And our journey as embodied spirits is to become the transmitters/receivers for this energy. Through releasing our pain and cleansing ourselves of old wounds, we make our bodies capable of resonating with this joy. That's the focus of all soul work in every society on the planet, to make the body a vehicle for receiving and expressing joy. Jesus said that the Kingdom of God is within you. That's another way of saying, Joy is already here if you allow yourself to experience it. All it takes is remembering that it is here. Take a deep breath and remember.

Joy includes honoring the body, both the body of yourself, your peers, and the body of your tribe. A lot of what gay men have done in the past wasn't respectful of their bodies. I've watched gay men push themselves endlessly without taking care of themselves. We confused manic behavior with joy. A lot of what we did was necessary rebellion against our stuffy, uptight, heterosexual culture, but I don't think it was well grounded. What we're learning now is that joy starts from loving the body.

You and I seem to share certain assumptions about the essential nature of being gay. What do you say to those who believe otherwise—that being gay is a socially constructed identity?

I would say that we're living on a two-way street and traffic is going in both directions. Coming out as a social construction is one direction. But there's another direction on the street, which is what I call coming in. There's coming out, there's coming in—and what we're talking about in this conversation is about coming in. Coming into who we are, energetically, spiritually. Both directions are necessary, and both of them are true. There's nothing in the street itself that says north or south. Except for the markings down the middle, it's one street. It's all the same asphalt.

You may not be able to afford, physically, financially, emotionally, religiously, to come out, but everybody can come in. One of the things that I dislike about only looking at coming out is that for so many people coming out is a sexual act. Coming in can include sex, but coming in is about essence—not about experience.

Speaking of essence, what is your definition of soul? And how does that differ from your concept of spirit?

A soul is an energetic piece of the absolute container for everything that exists. It's what we used to call God. Whether I now call it the Tao or the Great Spirit, I believe that the soul is real and timeless and not limited by space. One of the desires of the particular kind of soul that we are is that it embodies itself in this physical world. There's a weaving together of something that is limitless and timeless into something that is born and dies.

Spirit is the interface between the soul and the body. It's the transformer, the stepping-down device that allows the soul to penetrate and enliven the physical body. I used to think about this theoretically, but last spring I experienced what I believe was my soul. I was in a workshop doing extensive breath work when I found myself in an altered state of consciousness. I was lying on the floor in a luminous field of golden light. I was utterly clear that it was my soul and that it was interpenetrating my body. I had always imagined that my soul was very tiny and that it lived in my heart. Much to my surprise, it was much bigger than my body, and my body was floating in it, like a fish floating in the sea.

In healthy, organic cultures, somehow the soul is able to weave itself into the body completely, harmoniously. But in this culture, where we distrust our bodies and deny that people have some kind of energy that is both indwelling and yet greater than the body, the soul has a lot of trouble getting in.

Given all that you've said, do you believe that gay men are carriers of soul for a society that denies the validity of both?

As I said, we have this particular vibrational energy. The vibration preexists us, the same way that joy preexists us, and all of these frequencies exist in the same place. This room is filled with every single television frequency yet they don't get in each other's way, they coexist. The gay vibration is one of many different kinds of energy fields that exists on the planet. All of us have access to it, and within that gay energy is all of gay history, all of the experience of all the gay people that have ever lived. A lot of the personal work that I do is about going into that field, the gay channel as it were, to listen and watch.

How do you do that?

I guess one could call it a meditation practice. But all gay people do this, in their way. For example, you grow up all by yourself in a tiny isolated town, and several years later, when you get to San Francisco or New York, you discover that you have all these things in common with all of these other men whom you never met before. It's a meditation that we do unconsciously.

Many gay men are in pain because they're picking up this energy all the time, but they're living in a little town in Texas, and they don't know what the hell they're picking up that's different from what the other guys are picking up. People jokingly say we only use 10 percent of our brain, but I think that we only use 10 percent of our brain consciously. The other 90 percent is picking up information all the time, only we're told not to pay any attention to it. To call it a meditative practice implies that you have to learn something obscure or very difficult, but actually it's very easy.

Offer a short exercise about how to do this.

Sit very quietly and know that in the same way that television broadcast signals are filling your room there is gay consciousness, the gay vibration, that is also surrounding the planet. It has information about who we are, why we exist, and what we offer to the world and to ourselves—that which nurtures, grounds, and sustains us. All you have to do is tune into it. You may want to put your hands on your chest to feel the beating of your heart and have that be the trigger, or switch, that lets this energy in. Notice what you feel. What is the vibration?

And then, whatever images and feelings come, trust what they are. Whether it's a picture, a word, or a sentence. In one of my favorite dreams, I was listening to a lost Sappho poem. I don't know whether it was an actual poem, but it seemed real in the dream. Maybe it wasn't, but I was in the energy—there's so much information there.

We weren't told the stories of our people, but I think that they do exist. So my work has been to record stories that have been vibrating in the gay collective unconscious, picking up the stories and making them conscious. Our history is with us and we have a right to know it. Stories feed the soul the way that food feeds the body. And we have to feed our souls.

Is there a particular gay story you'd like to tell?

I'd like to tell the story about the gay son of Adam and Eve. It says in Genesis that they had Cain and Abel, and then Seth and lots of other children. And their children spread out all over the world, and one of them noticed that he was not quite the same, that he was different in some way.

In the story, he is looking around for someone like himself, but there's no one there. So he walks and wanders, and in time a nephew is born to a sister and brother of his, who is also different. And eventually these two men find each other. The moment that they look in each other's eyes, they recognize something about each other that has no name yet is perfectly understandable to both of them. It's about the soulful coming together of their bodies; it's about their bodies expressing something together that cannot be expressed any other way. And so they go off, and they tell that story for the first time by living it. And we've been telling it ever since.

HARRY HAY

REINVENTING OURSELVES

In the spring of 1925, fifteen priests from the Hopi nation made a ceremonial trek on foot from their two-thousand-year-old pueblo in Arizona, traveling across the dry mountains and plains of the Southwest to the shores of the Pacific Ocean. The journey had been ventured every quarter century for as long as anyone could remember. But highways, fences, and other encroachments of the industrial age were making the Hopi's ritual passage increasingly difficult.

Harry Hay was thirteen years old the day the Hopi leaders arrived at a deserted strip of coastline near Laguna, California, perhaps for the last time, to gather salt and offer their prayers. Linking hands with fifty other local boys to form a giant half-circle on the beach, Harry helped keep a respectful distance between the Native Americans and a curious crowd of noisy bystanders. As he stood in silent vigil with the other members of his boy's club, the sensitive youth felt powerful emotions stirred by the Hopi's rite. The realization dawned on him that other windows through which to see the world existed beside his own.

Harry's encounter with the Hopis led him to Los Angeles' main library, where his natural inquisitiveness was fed by hours of reading about Native Americans. As he studied, Harry would occasionally come across an illustration or a reference to an odd-looking figure called a berdache, the term early European explorers gave to cross-dressed men found in North American Indian tribes.

"The Spanish and French missionaries who wrote these historical accounts called them 'degenerates'," recalls Hay. "Because they looked at women as degraded creatures, they thought that if a man gave up his manhood to wear a women's dress, he was a degraded person, too." Still, somewhere between the tangled lines of Eurocentric history a glimmer of truth about who the berdache really were deeply resonated.

For all of their strangeness, Harry could relate to the berdache as being someone like himself: "Not a man, not a woman, neither—something other . . . someone other." Harry, who had long been labeled a "sissy," felt this quality of neitherness fit like a comfortable suit of new clothes.

Living a contrary life has become an art as much as a practice for Hay during the seven decades since his discovery of the berdache. He has been an actor, teacher, laborer, and political organizer and has espoused many causes: Marxism, Indian rights, and gay liberation, to name a few. But throughout his varied life one role has remained central: that of a challenging yet nurturing k'oshare—or Sacred Clown—who can't leave stagnating conformity alone.

Hay is most widely known as the visionary "founding father" of the modern gay movement. His open stand against homophobia—in society and within gay people themselves—led to the formation of the Mattachine Society in 1950, the nation's first ongoing gay political organization. Hay's ideological struggles with the burgeoning movement, his separation from it, and his eventual move to the New Mexico desert with his companion of now thirty-one years, John Burnside, have been well documented.

Perhaps less known is the fact that Hay's queer activism has continued over the years, however far removed he's been—either physically or philosophically—from the center of a movement intent on assimilating into the mainstream. His commitment to creating a new system of values, a real ethnicity for gay- and lesbian-identified people, has been lifelong. From organizing the first gay demonstration on the streets of Los Angeles in May of 1966 to taking a brave public position on gay rights and other just social causes in isolated New Mexico throughout the seventies, to addressing the world beyond—from New York to Moscow—during the eighties and nineties, Hay has remained steadfast and fearless. Neither his passion nor his principled beliefs about spiritual neitherness and its social purpose have diminished over time. If anything, the mantle of neitherness that Hay invested himself in so many decades ago has aged superbly.

At eighty-two, Hay remains one of the most daring and original theorists of the gay movement. His ideas about gay people being "a separate people whose time has come" have been hotly debated, especially among gays themselves, many of whom are uneasy by any notions of difference. If anything, the gay movement's thrust during the past forty-five years has been about achieving sameness—without which, presumedly, we can find no place at the American table. But Hay continues to question whether we want to be seated at that table at all, particularly if we are, at best, a misunderstood and barely tolerated guest. Rather than show up at the door as a stranger with hat in hand—or as a stranger kicking in the door—Hay suggests that we let our strangeness be our guide. No one, least of all gay people themselves, yet knows what it really means to be queer in America. Or, for that matter, what visionary political and social gifts we have to contribute.

Answering that puzzle is something Hay has spent his whole life trying to do. From those early days devouring books in a downtown library to now, he has been absorbed by the role that "the other" in Native American cultures once played. *Existing beyond the duality of male/female, the berdache once occupied a position in their societies that was neither—they were a third gender. It was a role steeped with meaning, a sense of place, quite unlike our own society where anyone who differs from standard gender categories is assigned little or no social value. Hay claims that being gay may place one beyond the social margins but not away from the social responsibilities that third-gender-type people have traditionally upheld; he thereby emphasizes what we can do rather than merely who we are.*

People currently labeled "gay" are already experiencing life outside of rigid gender norms, so they are better equipped to transcend opposites of all kinds, Hay says. This enables them to unite disparate ideas and constructs into new forms of expression, pushing the whole culture creatively onward.

But relatively few have been willing to make the required leap across cultures—and of faith—in order to make Hay's understanding their own. The Radical Faerie movement, which Hay and Burnside helped to found in Los Angeles in 1979, has colorfully represented this strand of thought within the greater gay community. But some Faerie-identified men, let alone gays who are leading comparatively mainstream lives, are at a loss to explain what exactly Hay means. That being gay has a social purpose beyond unfettered consumption is an idea that remains largely ignored.

True to his nature, Hay is undaunted. That much was revealed to me the first time we met, over fifteen years ago. Rushing through a crowded airport terminal, I nearly collided with Hay, who was patiently waiting to greet me. Our eyes met, and I was confronted with a face lined by remarkable contours. I saw courage and strength, stubborness and humor—the markings of a great survivor, and more than a hint of inspired contrariness. And beyond that, especially when I looked more deeply into his eyes, I saw loving kinship.

For myself, and for a generation of like-seeking men, Harry Hay's unwavering vision has exemplified the freedom of spirit found in leading a truly queer life. There are no easy answers, he'll tell you, but anything is possible if we believe it so.

o

You've witnessed so much of your original vision come true. What happens to a dreamer when his dream becomes reality?

What happens to a dreamer is that his dream never comes to an end—it just keeps getting bigger and bigger. A portion of my dream has become a reality, but the part that isn't yet realized is twice as big as it used to be. There are all kinds of new explorations.

For example, I've been very interested in the results of a recent study at the University of California, Los Angeles, that show there are more connections between the right and left hemispheres of gay men's brains than in other people's. This supports my view that gay men are those who are constantly trying to put their dreams into words, music, and motion—into new ways of talking to one another. We find the means to bring into articulation our innermost visions. That's why it's tremendously important right now for gay men to be in sensual and sexual contact as much as possible—it enables that articulation.

I don't see any lack of that in the gay male community. Are you wanting to see a new kind of touching between gay men?

In the sexuality found in bathhouses and backroom bars, gay men keep making objects out of each other. The ensuing ejaculatory affairs undoubtedly result in an eagerly sought release, but they end up being spiritually negative if not, indeed, spiritually taxing in many cases, not to mention a drain on the immune system. I'm more inclined to feel that some of the things that go on in tantric practices are as important, if not more rewarding, in the long run.

In tantra, instead of exploding you implode, but the energy is still something you want to give out to others and let flow back into you again. It's about creating an interflowing relationship between loving brothers, the kind of marvelous collective expression you had with other kids when you were nine or ten years old, before you discovered that all these things were dirty and nasty. We have to get back to those kinds of healing relationships and carry them forward as adults.

What has been your greatest satisfaction with the Radical Faerie movement, and also your greatest disappointment?

I don't like to think of it as a movement, because the word *movement* institutionalizes it. Development is much better. Radical Faerie development is moving toward the idea that we carry a special contribution, and we want to be able to share it. The development of the Radical Faerie identity is probably the most advanced form of the gay movement up to the present time: we need to continually *re*-imprint within ourselves our recognition of ourselves as a separate people—a third-gender people with the potential for many movements and movement developments in future times.

The disappointment is that neither John nor I were prepared to appreciate just how enormous the psychological damage wrought by meddling heteros or hetero-oriented shrinks getting deviant teenagers clients comfortable with their "unfortunate dysfunction" would be. This has molded many young gay men into negative distortions of their gay identities, liberally layered over with a thick crust of self-loathing. It is true that when the faeries finally hear in themselves the call to self-discovery they manage to heal outer layers relatively quickly. But there is so much more healing that must take place before they're healed enough to fly on their own. So we can't grow as fast as I would have liked us to have grown.

What happened at the first Spiritual Conference for Radical Faeries in Arizona, September 1979, was what I hoped would happen in the Mattachine Society in 1950. We began to free ourselves of the old habits of behaving like heteros; we began inventing, discovering, even rediscovering, more honest and genuine expressions of ourselves. This revealed what I call the beautiful faerie prince hidden beneath the ugly green frog skin of hetero-imitative conformity. This is the dream I always had; this is how I thought my brothers and I would find ourselves relating to one another. But in the early fifties we were faced with the fact that we needed first to develop a positive gay identity, which we didn't have. In those years we didn't even have the words. As far as I'm concerned, a number of us in the gay movement, totally fed up and turned off by the assimilationist blight that was creeping all around us like a corruption, were ready finally to spread our faerie wings and move in new dimensions after 1979.

> *How important are words and theories to a movement? Theories about the origins and purpose of being gay abound, yet they seem pretty distant from the lives of gay people themselves, who continually challenge all kinds of tidy notions about who they are. How did you deal with this issue, for instance, during the early days of the Mattachine Society?*

We found that for "the love that dare not speak its name" we had to create a language, as a first step, which truly bespoke us. You can't have theory without language that conveys the lengths and breadths of our very different outlook on reality. And you can't have concepts in that language without pungent words to strike sparks behind your meanings, if you are serious about fundamental communication. The feminist movement discovered this—to their utter dismay and frustration—when they tried to talk about their issues in hetero-male terms and values.

To answer your question, let's look at the invention of the word *homophile*. During the early days of the Mattachine Society Steering Committee meetings, Chuck Rowland would bring in a sheet of Latin and Greek suffixes and I would bring in a sheet of prefixes and we'd pair up combinatins. We went through dozens and dozens of variations trying to find a word that would mean what we wanted it to mean or at least sound like something we could handle. We finally came up with the word *homophile* because it meant "lover of same or similar." The Mattachine Society featured the word in all their leaflets and publications, as soon did *ONE* magazine [launched in 1953 as the nation's first publicly sold, avowedly gay publication]. We had no way of knowing that similar European groups were using the term by the twenties because United States postal regulations kept foreign journals for homosexuals from entering this country until a Supreme Court ruling in 1958 allowed otherwise.

Every time a court case came up, we would insist that the lawyer use *homophile* instead of *homosexual*. Then some judge or newspaper man would ask us what it meant. That's how we were able to define ourselves as we wished to be seen and heard; otherwise people would have just gone on with their old assumptions. By 1957, judges were instructing juries on the correct definition of the word, so we knew *homophile* was catching on. Brothers were obviously beginning to feel good about themselves; a positive gay identity was beginning to take hold.

By 1969, the homophile movement had done its work. A new generation, born of the Stonewall explosion, would choose to think of itself as positively *gay*—except for one nagging doubt: gay pride! No matter how noble the sentiment, no matter how passionate the intent, slogans like "Two, four, six, eight, gay is just as good as straight!" end up implying that being gay is *almost* as good as straight. In this fatal hetero-imitative comparison game we are invited to reveal some of the deeply hidden or unexamined self-loathing roots ferociously implanted in us through society's coercion to socialize us by forcing us into accepting hetero identities and behaviors against our wills. The louder and more strident we proclaim ourselves on Gay Pride Day perhaps the more hysterical is the unexpurgated spiritual panic.

So finding words to describe us led busy brains like mine scurrying to uncover concepts discerning our parameters reaching not only back to the past but forward to the future. V. I. Lenin's definition of a nation had helped me to appreciate us as a social and cultural minority, acknowledged as "specialists of the spirit" by many societies past and present. The early Mattachine Society's adoption of the theory of us queers as a contributive minority culture in whatever societies we have appeared in, and continue to appear in, was—and remains—a crucial contribution to the modern gay movement.

> *Speaking of theories, you've long advanced the notion that gay men are constitutionally different from nongay men. Many have contested that belief. What do you say to those critics?*

Frankly, I don't say anything. As you know, I don't ever proselytize. I've always said just one thing: I tell people about my vision, which is that long ago our brotherhood was made up of people who had talents and gifts different from the settled majority, different from the social conformity in which they lived. In the oral culture of a tribal community, the collectively held consciousness—or co-consciousness—could be acquired and retained only by being verbally described. It could be reactivated year after year only by being enfolded within a ritual or ceremony rehearsed collectively by rote and passed on to the next generations only by remembering. The vast accumulation of ideas and practices, then, could only be held in the common mental treasury by assuring that most of the people lived and thought in total conformity with one another.

So the very few in each generation who were predisposed by nature to rebel against patterns of conformity would be observed early as those strange ones who walked to a different drummer. Oral cultures long ago learned to train these strange ones in special, often spiritually trying or even dangerous, ways.

It is my vision that our gay windows are indicative of our natural inclinations to perceive manifestations of the throngs of the seen and unseen, the perimeters, planes, dimensions, and denizens of the known horizons and the unknown. Do we occasionally also confront such manifestations? No, we did not—and do not now—confront spirit manifestations. That is the role of the shaman, who has the power to transform—a function that is subject-object in character.

Shamans are discovered in most co-conscious societies to be heterosexual, and so are seekers of power in many shapes and forms in their respective villages. We third-gender men, being nonjudgmental by nature, do not seek power because it is subject-object in character. We mediate subject-subject consciousness instead.

It is my assessment that in the close collective of sedentary tribal life we were early recognized as being neither hetero man nor woman, nor did we seem to incline to sexually relate to either hetero man nor woman. We wanted nothing from either of them. Instead, in what appeared to be nonjudgmental fashion, we seemed to be enabled to see and hear each of them as they might wish to be seen and heard. From the tribe's point of view, we might have been appraised, as did the Di-ne [Navaho] so perceive their Nádle-eh, as specialists who might actually be able to balance the interrelationships of the two sexes.

It is my vision that we Celts, as the Indo-Europeans are now called, also shared this level of co-consciousness with Native American tribes, West African tribes, and with a sheaf of Pacific Rim communities. In [Roman historian] Tacitus's time, it was noted that women shared equal rights with men in tribal and collective governance, that bards and glee-men always seemed to travel and live in same-sex related clans, and that mimes, mummers, and players did likewise. But as our old enemy the Christian Empire spread north and west of the Mediterranean, we third-gender folk were gradually stripped of our functions and of approved outlets for our special skills, even as the traditional peasant villages we had served were razed and the peasants themselves now turned out to fend for themselves. By the eighteenth century, between the Inquisition and the sixteenth and seventeenth century witch hunts on one hand and the destruction of the traditional peasant culture on the other, our third-gender talents and mediational traditions had been thoroughly diminished and demeaned. Theatrical memories of our many former services and our lovely sexuality were all that were left of the vast divergences between first- and third-gender social demeanors and life imprintings.

But to return to your question, it's a little bit like the sixteenth-century College of Cardinals coming together to debate the flat earth: the earth is round, whether you debate it or you don't debate it. That's another way of saying that the people who contest my vision could very well be the people who don't share it. The Faerie gatherings are a beautiful example of those who do share a certain vision about what it means to be gay. The moment brothers at gatherings hear the word *faerie* and recognize what it really means, they start talking about themselves as faeries without any trouble.

At one gathering, for instance, there was a young man who asked if he could be a faerie and also be president of IBM. I said I didn't think that was possible. When I saw him at the end of the gathering a week later, I asked, "How's the future president of IBM?" He said he now saw himself as a person who didn't enjoy competing. He'd been competitive in the past because the other boys were, but now he knew that competition was not natural to him.

I'm using this incident to illustrate the actual characteristics of ours that are quite different from those of the heteros. At Faerie gatherings we discover that we want to share rather than compete, that we like to listen to one another and exchange our touch in loving ways. We begin to recognize that we're moving in a different direction from that of the world we left behind. We speak of ourselves naturally as faeries because we need a word to talk about those ways in which we are different from what we were outside. Words are the tools, the transmitters, by which we communicate our ideas to one another. And when we finally find the *right words,* we will be able to communicate *our* visions to the society around us.

You use the word co-consciousness. *What does it mean?*

Co-consciousness signifies those semi-civilized tribes, past and present, whose vast and varied reservoirs of cultural increments were, more often than not, acquired higglety pigglety by accretion, rather than by any organization of ideas or by analysis. Being oral rather than written cultures, meanings and the use of words as meanings were generally acquired by rote or through ritual and so remembered. Third-gender men who had memory skills were in great demand since once a discovery or invention of a tribal grandfather was blurred or temporarily knocked out of sight, the chances of recovering it might be a devastating zero. Rituals were often devised precisely to enable a community to collectively remember vital patterns, to keep them constantly in mind lest tribal life itself be in jeopardy.

Co-conscious societies, then, had perhaps evolved to the stage of being able to think about things, but not to the level of *thinking about* thinking, making it possible to think abstractly, to analyze, and so reorganize conceptualizations. In some ways, the earlier level of development may have been, to date, the best of all possible worlds. Because within the collective all members were still responsible to and for each other, and the community life of spirit was still accountable to its collective belief system through the devoted service of its third-gender brotherhoods.

> *There is often a great misunderstanding about the notion of gay people being different. That different somehow means better—or worse.*

This is typical hetero-oriented subject-object thinking: things are always seen as comparative in a worldview whose standard is total conformity. What is the problem? Of course we're different! We hate competition. We rebel against conformity. We don't honor the leadership role. We prefer to function by consensus. And we've obviously been that way certainly since the time of little Faerie-brother Jesus. We're different in that we are other, and otherness is neither better nor worse. It's simply different from the way that heteros see.

> *When did you first begin to realize for yourself the meaning of being different from others?*

When I was eight or nine years old, the other boys on the playground suddenly knew I wasn't one of them. So I asked the girls about it. "Well," they said, "you're not one of us either—you're something else." I was in limbo, as it were. I didn't belong any place, and I was alone and terrified. But in the stories I was reading and dreaming about and then acting out, "John o' the Woods" had his friends the animals, the birds, and the butterflies to talk to. And Roland had Oliver, and Hero had Leander. And as soon as I met "that other"—who, in the dream I had most every night, waited for me to come and catch his hand so we could run to the top of the hill—I would know what a nice place, *with him,* it would be.

I intuitively understood how free we would be being neither boy nor girl. I could relate my feelings to the berdache, who were also perceived in their several cultures as being *neither* man nor woman. This neitherness fascinated me, as did the responsibility that the berdache had to others in their tribes. The notion of my secret dream being ready to assume responsibility appealed to me very early: you must be ready to assume responsibility because your given collective needs you and your vision, you and your secret shining ideas!

The first gender consists of those who carry the responsibilities of warriors/herdsmen/hunters/farmers/husbands/fathers—the inseminators and protectors of the bloodline. The second gender consists of those women who function as wives and mothers but who were equally responsible for homes, gardens, and fields. In Latin, the word for farmer was *agricola, agricolae* [feminine]. And it has never changed. These two categories are presumably what the human race is all about. But third-gender people were and are those who were assigned responsibilities for discovering, developing, and managing the frontiers between the seen and the unseen, between the known and the unknown. Seen from a gay perspective one might say that homosexuality may present itself to a person simply as an instinctual behavioral given. But when it is acknowledged and lovingly embraced, it supports and in itself demonstrates the primary trait of gay nature, manifesting in a strong personal power to withstand the dictates of traditional belief when such dictates stand in the way of a genuine advance.

Under its own autonomous development, gay nature develops a gay window through which to critically examine the workings of tradition, to create new ways for shaping the culture, and to adapt to changing conditions. Creativity is a hallmark of gay nature.

Since the primary need of the two procreative genders for carrying out their responsibilities is stability, they are by nature and by necessity bound to traditional ways. In contrast, those whose nature is adapted to discovery and invention need to be recognized as so very different as to constitute a third gender.

> *In the late nineteenth century, the idea that homosexuals constituted a kind of "third sex" was put forth. What's the distinction between the third sex and being a third gender?*

The nineteenth-century projection of a third sex was a groping for the metaphor we now recognize as a third gender. But in the nineteenth century, the emphasis was on sex and sexual behavior, not on cultural, community roles implicit in the word *gender*.

> *What's the difference between being a faerie-identified man and a man who regards himself as third gender?*

I believe the concepts of being a faerie and a third-gender man will eventually become synonymous. *Faerie*, however, doesn't necessarily imply responsibility as well as *third gender*, which assumes that you do have a particular responsibility. Faeries simply are. If they do take on this responsibility, fine, and if they don't, nobody gives a damn. The point is that a great many of us wish that we could assume a responsibility that ties us back into the continuation of the race as a whole. Gender, among other things, talks about the things we can do and gives us the channel by which we can make these contributions.

> *Being a faerie is to be fabulous, and we should all be as fabulous as we can. But are you now saying that being fabulous, in and of itself, isn't enough?*

We all know that we carry within us something we want to do, something we want to contribute to the greater whole. Third gender is the channel through which we can do it. It suggests that we do have something important to contribute.

> *If you're a third gender, does that mean you're beyond dualistic, either/or ways of thinking?*

Either/or belongs to the two-dimensional world. This is the world where the hetero male assumes that either you're with me or you're against me, either I'm the king of the mountain or you are. There is no other way. Third and fourth gender—which might apply to lesbian nature, but that is for our lesbian sisters to say—implies that there are not just two windows on the world—there are at least four, and therefore maybe more.

People have said to me, "Why don't we just put the four together and say that's human nature?" To which I answer, "What about the others we haven't discovered yet: five and six, seven and eight, and so on?" Humility is what is required here, not the arrogance of the hetero male who says there is either his way of seeing or none at all. That's a Eurocentric way of seeing. There are all kinds of windows on the world. We are so accustomed to thinking that our hetero, male, white world is the only world that is. The nonlinear mindsets coming to us from Africa, Indonesia, and Asia have many ways of perceiving. And until we are open to them all we're not going to be able to hear the actual marvelous world of stars and wind that is coming to us from all kinds of different places.

> *What's the difference between a faerie-identified gay man and a gay man who is not? Are faeries just gay men who have found a particular means to tend to their soul-wounding, or do they actually represent some kind of next stage in gay consciousness?*

Average gay men, insofar as I can see, accept without question a large measure of hetero imitation in their lives. As a result of that, they are sort of half in and half out. They still want to be in competition and in the running of the competition. They're still trying to be accepted by the white hetero world out of which they feel they have been thrust.

I don't think that gay men belong in that world. The mainstream has the job of physical procreation to maintain the mainstream we all came out of. But I believe that gays are a specific development of humanity who have a particular contribution to make to the culture. We're about multidimensionality, among other things. You might say we're the feathers on the wing.

> *The gay movement has reached a critical mass in terms of visibility and political clout. Does that mean that society will now begin to see us for who we really are rather than as a figment of their negative myth? Assuming we do have a unique contribution to offer, what would that be in today's world? Before gay liberation, it seemed that openly gay men were allowed only the most ephemeral tasks, like window decorating or being a hairdresser.*

The gay movement's critical-mass visibility is still largely ephemeral. What society sees, by and large, are the middle-class, hetero-imitative assimilationists. The gay movement has not developed even an illusion as yet of a vigorous, anchored-in-rock grassroots foundation. Our political clout is still to be demonstrated. With 81 percent of the American public still insisting that homosexuality is wrong, with half our friends and relatives being as middle class as we are, we still have to rousingly defeat the religious right.

The work of dressing the hair and body or dressing windows in order to sell products is a hetero occupation of competition. Every man is in competition with everybody else, and he wants to be in competition so that he can control you. In competition there is always somebody who wins, and each hetero man wants to be the winner. He views everybody else as objects to be put under his control.

Now, insofar as gay men are concerned, we really don't care about that type of a struggle. If anything, we would like to share in helping you win. We are able to dress a woman's hair or body because we have no interest in possessing her whatsoever. Therefore, I can listen to her tell me what she wants to be and how she would like to look and then help her do that for herself. Every hetero man wants her to be an object: to excite him, satisfy him, do something for him. He thinks of her as an object in his competition game. I see her as she wants to see herself, and so I can share with her all of the talents I have at my disposal. I'm sharing in her joy in herself because I have no interest in her as an object. This is the essential difference between the one who is in competition and the one who wants to share. This is how the third gender can help the whole culture move in a variety of new directions.

> *For years you subscribed to and practiced Marxist theory. Now with the collapse of the Soviet Union, what are your feelings about those earlier beliefs?*

The Marxists in this country, including myself, suffered a horrible shock when we discovered the reality of what had been going on in the Soviet Union, about which we had been lied to for sixty years. I had begun to take a second look in the sixties, realizing that things in the Soviet Union were not good because the people who called themselves Marxists were being scientific in philosophical form, which is a contradiction in terms. To be dogmatic is the death of Marxism and not the confirmation of it. Karl Marx had a marvelous concept of a self-maintaining political process in socialism, but what he didn't know was that the shining promise of socialism could not be fulfilled through subject-object consciousness.

In the next century, I believe our entire culture will begin to shift away from competing with one another to wanting to help one another. Instead of subject-object consciousness, the collective will move toward subject-subject consciousness, which I believe comes naturally to gays. That's what we have to contribute to the world of tomorrow.

> *Would I be correct in assuming that you see the rapid emergence of gay people in the latter half of the twentieth century as being less about a movement for civil rights and more about carrying forth this new way of relating? And, if so, why is this emergence happening now?*

It's happening because ever since I formed the Mattachine Society we have been reinventing ourselves. Having been obliterated by organized religion to an almost catatonic point, having nothing left of our glorious three-dimensional selves but our deviant sexuality, our skyrocketing comeback through the vigorous use of civil rights—despite the electrifying tool that it is—is a scathing embarrassment. It's happening because daily we are finding new words to legitimate it.

The point is we've been carrying subject-subject consciousness in the right hemisphere of our brains for an awfully long time. The brain's right hemisphere, as you know, has no words, no logic, no way of dealing with these processes. So long as subject-subject consciousness is kept in the right hemisphere it's only experienced in dreams and formless things. But as we carry it into the mind's left hemisphere, we begin to find words for it, mathematics for it, poetry for it, metaphors for it, ways of putting it out so that we can communicate it between each other. This is all happening in our lifetimes.

What is the difference between spirit and soul?

Spirit is the distillation arising from the rich and bubbly brew in the pot, out of which new possibilities keep emerging. The world of spirit is made up of an ever-expanding continuum that finds new ways to touch and enhance the human world. Soul seems to be something that has been abstracted from that by various religions for their own particular purposes. Soul, to me, is cold. It seems to belong to the ruling class, and they love to make people think that "soul" is a commodity. Of course, the source of this is papal. What do you think the papal indulgences of the early Renaissance were? Other than rich men buying "soul"? Now the ruling class is selling. But there are no myths about selling your spirit! With *spirit* is where I want to be.

You don't think you have a soul?

I don't give a damn. I'm not interested in soul. Soul is something that the church tells me they have; it's something that's either approved of or not approved of by the pope. I like spirit!

If there is no soul, where do those elements that you're calling the gay elements of human nature reside?

I see no need to look beyond the neuronal networks of the brain and other as-yet-to-be-discovered aspects of the living body to account for the totality of our gay natures. But I'd also like to answer your question by evoking the image of the Great Mother standing by the Cauldron of Life. The cauldron to me is that from whence gay spirit, the froth of the brew, the distillation of essence, emerges, out of which new possibilities are always developing. The old possibilities and all the contradictions they become dissolve back into the cauldron, ionize, reshape, bubble into newer compounds, and eventually become part of the new. That's what the cauldron is all about.

One of the things I found when I was researching material for the Mattachine classes I taught in the early fifties was that the witch's cauldron of black sabbath folklore was an actual practice. It was one of the ways by which the peasantry stayed alive during periods of famine or extreme repression. When food was scarce or forbidden to them by lords, the people were literally reduced to roots and what they could pick out of the forest. The things that went into the witch's brew were snakes and rodents, for example, not necessarily the nicest things as far as flavor but rich in protein. All kinds of interesting herbs were added to make a rich, thick stew that everybody was able to have once every two weeks.

That's very interesting, but how does it relate to what we were talking about?

Well, we are talking about the Great Earth Mother's cauldron, what it contained, and what its contents were for. The witch's brew was a way by which the peasantry stayed alive through terrible times. The essence, the aromatic distillation arising from that cauldron, was the medium, the whiff of invention, upon which the souls of poets and bards, the spirits of visionaries, feasted and from which the new ideas and directions dispersed. Gay spirit wove together the distillation of earth as well as of air, for the directions of their responsibilities were fourfold and not just of air. The faeries assume responsibilities for the discoveries and inventions they engender.

That's poetically said, but can't you be a little more concrete?

The first and second gender procreate children of the flesh. The principles in radical faeries' consciousnesses developed in heart-circle sharing over the years are spirit children waiting pertinent occasions to be brought to term. This is our third gender way of procreating in the service of the human family. Many such spirit children have been produced between John and me, as well as by many more temporary arrangements. We believe that one spirit child can lead a hundred of the physical children out of the woods. Therefore we give freely of our ideas, our poetry, our art–in other words, our spirit children. In this way we reach out to all kinds of people, we speak in many different dimensions. We bring the world to the village.

Hetero men need to possess facts and absolutes upon which they can hang conformity, their subject-object way of thinking. But in today's world, one must increasingly learn to live on the edge of doubt. And, above all, we gay people—the people of the paradox—know how to live in doubt.

WILL ROSCOE

THE GEOGRAPHY OF GENDER

Will Roscoe and I met in the summer of 1979 during the first Radical Faerie gathering. Gender-nonconforming and spiritually seeking gay men from all over the country were convening in a remote spot in the Arizona desert. Under a hot Southwest sky, bodies and souls were bared in a brave attempt to shed a lifetime of hetero-imitative habits. The day was naked, in every way.

Roscoe, then as now, was among those asking the most articulate questions about the dynamics of queer life. Foremost among the inquiries of the moment was whether there is some indwelling quality in being gay, a uniquely gay way of perceiving and relating to the world, a factor that transcends time and place. Or whether, as some would put it, "We're no different from straights except for what we do in bed." These differing perspectives would come to be known in the eighties as essentialism *and* social constructionism, *although the terms were unknown to us then. Even among the dunes of the American outback the gnarled debate about gay consciousness was beginning to rage.*

In the fifteen years since that conclave, opinions have become if anything more entrenched. Roscoe, however, seemed to take the synergistic energy of the gathering and use it to propel himself on a career that has investigated core questions about gay identity in unique and daring ways. Now an independent historian and anthropologist of growing reputation, Roscoe has based most of his insight on studies of the Native American berdache—third-gender-type individuals who performed priestly and other mediating social functions within the life of tribes throughout North America.

Roscoe's award-winning 1991 book, The Zuni Man-Woman, *tells the story of one such figure. The biography of We'wha, the cross-dressed "Zuni maiden" who traveled to Washington, D. C., in 1886 as a cultural ambassador of his people, has offered gay readers strong clues about the roles they might serve within their own society. The premise underlying Roscoe's work is audacious, with far-ranging political and cultural implications. He examines gay people in terms of gender and not sexuality, a stance that challenges the basic assumptions of the modern gay movement and its growing ranks of university-trained scholars.*

Like anyone cutting against the grain, Roscoe has paid a price for his beliefs. Even though he rapidly obtained a Ph.D. based on his independent research, and despite the acclaim and honors he has received—the prestigious Margaret Mead Award from the American Anthropology Association is among his citations—the outspoken scholar still cannot find a job within his chosen field. Instead, he travels widely, lecturing on campuses and to groups around the nation. Everywhere he speaks Roscoe's vision is greeted with a gleam of intuitive recognition.

Like the berdache, Roscoe follows a contrary path. He can trace feeling different from others back to his first days at school. "I didn't know what it was that the boys did during recess, but I wanted to jump rope," he recalls. "So I brought a jump rope to school, only to discover that it was a 'girl thing.' I didn't choose jumping rope because it was a gendered activity. I chose it because it was personally right for me." His persistence in staying true to himself continued throughout his upbringing in the small town of Missoula, Montana. There was no gay life to speak of, and books on any kind of gay subject were kept locked tight in library cases, but Will delved deep into finding out about himself. "I always thought that I was destined for something, anything that was larger than life, anything transcending the ordinary surroundings that I grew up in," he says.

His expanding interests included the Native people in Missoula, "Indians who were dealt with in an incredibly shoddy fashion," Roscoe remembers. His research resulted in an article, written while he was still in junior high school, titled "Bitter Exodus of the Salish." Published in Montana Historian, *the piece marked the beginning of Roscoe's career as an investigator of hidden history. Today, with a mature mind sharpened to the task, he continues to dig in meaningful—sometimes surprising—places.*

°

You were among the first of the post-Stonewall generation to announce your gay identity in college. Historically, that's a unique precedent. What was your coming out period like?

It was in the beginning of 1975, and I discovered there was a small network of gay people at the local university I attended. We formed this intense little queeny gay world. And we were just terrible. We terrorized that town. We had no fear of anything. At one point four of us, three women and I, were taking a sociology class in participant observation. Our project was that we would have people act in obviously gay ways while other people wrote down the reactions of whoever was around. Bowling alleys, restaurants, shopping markets, dancing together, dressing like queens, wearing suits and ties but holding hands—we tried all these combinations all over town.

There was one friend—"Prissy" was his name—who was a real role model for me because he knew how to do everything. He could sew, he could make dresses, he knew how to do drag, he knew how to make a delicious meal with four dollars, and he could fix his truck. And I thought, That's it! That's the way to be. No limits at all. I've never left that image; it's been the core of my message about gays. We ought to be able to do anything, and we do.

> *You were mirroring a phenomenon that was happening in many*
> *gay lives across America during that time—an explosion of self-in-*
> *vention. Did this somehow lead you into studying the Native Amer-*
> *ica berdache?*

My awareness about the berdache first came through Jonathan Ned Katz's book, *Gay American History,* which I shoplifted as a poor student and absorbed. I was already interested in gay history; I had spent the summer of 1976 in New York as a volunteer at the National Gay Task Force, where I researched the history of the gay movement. I was already beginning to sense why gay culture was essential to a gay movement. People didn't form movements because they wanted to pass some stupid law but because of a culture that bound them together, that was shared.

In 1978, I moved to San Francisco to serve as an intern at the Pacific Center in Berkeley as part of my degree program. After I graduated, I really plunged myself into San Francisco gay politics. But I was very young and still naive. Gay politics there were tough, and my idealism got a little bruised. So when I learned about the first gathering of Radical Faeries, I was determined to go. That's where I finally met Harry Hay.

> *Hay has played a profound role in your life, as he has in many oth-*
> *ers. During the early eighties you came to Los Angeles for several*
> *months in order to work with him. What did you learn?*

What I discovered was that Harry had really sought out our role in history in the way a good historical materialist would—not in terms of individuals who were there and happened to do things but in terms of functions and social groups, classes and roles, that existed and were a part of history. And not just any accidental part, since his historical materialist vision was at that time [the 1950s] a progressivist vision of society rising through certain places and ultimately leading to socialism. If there was a niche for us in history, it was as a part of this story of how our civilization reached its present place—it was something important, necessary, and essential. In his research, Harry was using the word *berdache* to head all of his notes: "Berdache—origin of the priest craft specialists in ancient Mesopotamia," "Berdache—medieval fool traditions," and so on.

> *Others have also applied the traditional tribal roles of the berdache and the shaman to the roles gay men play in society today. But are these comparisons really that applicable? Some say that this is an appropriation, a cultural rip-off.*

Berdaches and shamans are different, and it's very important at this point to draw out this distinction. Shamans classically belong to small tribal societies, although not exclusively. They are involved in ecstatic experiences and contact with the otherworld, and they work very much on their own. The shaman is extremely liminal and ambivalent morally and socially. The berdache is a social, collective figure—a specialist, a cultural worker, a priest, an artist. A berdache is a person who mediates the divisions and contradictions within the community, as opposed to the shaman, who works with the outside.

These are very important traditions. We know all about the shaman because he appeals to Western, individualistic, heroic patterns. We don't know about the berdache because they wore dresses; their history has been suppressed and their voices squelched. Even gay people today feel ambivalent about the berdache. But to me the berdache figure is the one for us to look toward as gay people. They did magics of healing, mediation, and unification. They could foretell the future and predict the weather. And you didn't ever want to get one mad at you because their curses had an uncanny way of coming true.

Now, the things that I've just told you hold true for the *hijras* in India, the *mahu* in Polynesia, and the *galli* in the ancient world. But no one is asking the questions of what were these powers and why? What is it about being queer that enables you to read someone's aura or foretell the future? Or heal? That's what I wanted to know.

> *Do people resonate with your point of view when you go out into the community to speak, or do they think you must be crazy?*

They love it, they're hungry for it. I've been in every part of this country, and I've talked to every kind of gay audience, and they absolutely can't get enough of it. Even the straight people are excited about the idea that there could be a third or a fourth gender. My goal is to take my magic wand and say to gay people, "You're all berdaches." I want to help gay people realize that.

Is the notion of a third and fourth gender a way out of the nurture versus nature, social constructionist versus essentialist impasse that most of gay study seems mired in?

Well, no, because that impasse is an issue of self-esteem. Until individuals can get past this lack of self-esteem, they're not going to be able to get past the kind of very narrow, assimilationist perspective that underlies social constructionism.

What do you mean by self-esteem in this case?

People with a strongly ideological social-constructionist stand are saying that we have nothing in common with the berdache—that they were socially constructed differently. They claim you cannot use the word *gay* when you talk about the berdache, that we were invented when the term *homosexual* was invented in 1869. One of the leading scholars in gay studies recently published a book titled *One Hundred Years of Homosexuality,* and he really means it. He thinks it's a great thing to be able to announce that we have only one hundred years of history.

We've struggled so far to find gay presence in history, and now we're losing it. Why? Because the problem is that there's a long, interesting history of social practices, of ever-changing forms of identity and social roles. But it's a continuity of radical queens and not of nice, polite, middle-class, bourgeois, academic homos.

Now, I'm picking my words extremely carefully when I say "social practices and social roles." I'm not talking about some kind of gene or something like that. I'm talking about things that people learn, a continuity of learning.

It's almost a truism now to say that some people are homosexuals, which describes a sexual act, but some people are gay, which is an identity based on something beyond whom we fuck. I could go into any gay community in North America and make that statement, and ninety-nine percent of the people would know exactly what I mean. But the majority of gay academics I know would hate that. They would have all these intellectual arguments against the essentializing that's involved. And that's why we're stuck.

You've got the grass roots who believe one thing, but the gay leadership and intelligentsia who won't see the queens and the radical body experiments or hear the strange things we say, like, "I know I'm different from straight people; I know that I can do things socially and spiritually that straight people can't do." They're smart enough people to know there's something there, but then they create these elaborate rationalizations like social constructionism in order to say that there's nothing there. They still very much want to reach the top of the hetero world for love and recognition. They need the acceptance of straight people more than that of their gay brothers and sisters.

That kind of behavior is typical of the survivors of abuse. We're all survivors of abuse because our parents raised us to be straight and we're really gay, and despite all their best intentions that's one of the worst forms of abuse there is. So we learn that it's safe to hurt the ones you love. You don't hurt the ones who are truly dangerous and evil because you're afraid of them. We reserve our greatest judgmentalism for others just like us.

How is the berdache relevant to our lives today? The image of a cross-dressing tribal priest or craft specialist seems so remote, almost unrecognizable to modern people.

We've got to realize that as long as we live within a heterosexist system that decrees that there are only two genders and therefore only one sexual orientation—the attraction between these two opposites—we're going to lose out. We're going to be counterfeit, substitute, anomalous, half-men or half-women, failed men or failed women, sick men or sick women. The best that heterosexism has to offer us is androgyny. But androgyny is still contained within the male and the female.

Most gays still won't open their eyes to this horrific structure Christopher Isherwood called the "heterosexual dictatorship." But as long as we're contained within that, we're just not going to come off looking very good. A third gender and fourth gender is entirely consistent with our understanding of the social construction of gender; that is, if it's socially constructed, then why can't there be more than two? A third and fourth gender helps us to imagine ourselves as complete, autonomous, integrated, coherent, logical beings, not necessarily having anything to do with male or female.

All this relates to the story I told about the jump rope. I did what was right for me. I didn't want to identify with male or female. I think my experience characterizes the gay attitude toward gender, which more than anything is actually indifference toward gender.

One of the most disastrous assumptions about gays is that we are a people without social purpose. A person without a meaningful social role can be more easily dismissed.

That's why the berdache is so important. The social responsibility, the accountability, the function—it's not just that these people were accepted out of some sort of notion of liberal enlightenment. That's completely foreign to Native American tribes. Berdaches were accepted because of the work they did, because of the work that they did for the community.

You have recently turned your attention to the galli, *a third-gender-type caste of priests in the ancient Mediterranean world. Why this group, and how and where are you reading between the lines of history to find out about them?*

Just like the berdache, they're only written about by outsiders. They're never given subjectivity or intentionality. They're all assumed to be determined by social forces or other factors. But there is a wide range of references to them, and there are various ways to get at them and understand their practices.

The religion of the goddess Cybele, known as Rhea to the Greeks and Magna Mater to the Romans, originated in central Anatolia [now Turkey]. Its characteristic iconography, which shows the goddess flanked by two lions, has been found in Neolithic sites going back seven to eight thousand years. The religion spread outward from Anatolia after the conquests of Alexander the Great. The galli appear to have come out of central Anatolia at this time, where they had been the priests in city temples. They appear to have become wandering missionaries who survived by begging for alms. They continued to perform some form of the Great Mother religion's rites, in particular ecstatic dancing, trance possession, and prophecy.

Then at around 200 B.C. the Romans for some reason decide that they need this goddess. The Romans were very practical, and they were always appropriating other people's gods and goddesses. So they send out a delegation to Anatolia, and they get this misshapen meteorite rock that represented the goddess from the central temple, and they install it in Rome. Whether or not galli priests accompany the rock at this time is not clear, but by the early empire, in the period just before the birth of Christ, they begin to be prominent within Rome.

Now, Imperial Rome is going out and conquering all kinds of lands and bringing back vast numbers of slaves from places like Syria and Phrygia, which is a part of Anatolia, and these people are bringing their beliefs with them. Add to this situation the desperation of slaves, and you have an environment ripe for revivalistic movements. Magna Mater, the Great Mother, which is an official cult of Rome, now begins to become popular among the slaves and the freedmen, the poor people who are not slaves but who are not citizens either. So the cult is working at all kinds of levels within the culture and becomes one of the last major pagan cults to compete with Christianity.

The galli were the Sisters of Perpetual Indulgence [a cross-dressing group of gay men in San Francisco] of their day. Like the Sisters, they lived collectively, acted outrageously, and their public performances effected a catharsis in others. Now, when you read what the early Christians say about the galli, you would be hard pressed to distinguish it from what the fundamentalists say this very day about gays. The holy war continues, absolutely. It's paganism versus the Oedipal organization, the God syndrome, monotheism, right to this very day. Nothing has changed as far as that goes.

So, once again, what do we have here? It's not a gene or something built into the brain; it's a set of social practices—social forms and techniques and roles. They occur and reoccur in many times and places because they work and because of the way we are psychologically. They've been rediscovered but also I think passed on from generation to generation more than we may have known. These social forms are there to be rediscovered and implemented again and again.

But as these apparently ancient social forms are being rediscovered, they're also being reoppressed. Is this a dynamic that will exist throughout all of time? Will the oppressors always end up winning because there are simply more of them than us?

No. They need us. They've made us. We know that. But what we don't know is that we make them. The slave makes the master. The slave gives the master its power.

The galli, as with the berdache, were very much in service to the Great Mother. What is the connection between them and gay men living today? Do you see gay men being mother-fixated?

We haven't talked about the fact that the galli practiced self-castration. Being castrated, they were vehicles of the life energy of the goddess. There may have been many ways of doing it; they may have just bound the genitals. The goal was not the motive of castration that Freud attributed to it. It was not done out of individualistic motives. It was a social custom, a rite of passage. The point is that, whether they did it metaphorically or literally, it enabled them to be the intermediary who could channel the goddess' energy.

They had their own patron god, Attis. He was not a male, patriarchal god nor a maternal, matriarchal goddess but their very own, independent third figure. Attis, a shepherd, embodied the sexual politics of the maternal world versus the paternal world. This was a society that was thoroughly male-dominated, but it constantly worshiped the goddess as the source of life. In other words, it was a society that was extremely ambivalent about male and female, with deep, repressed guilt about what they did to women, who they worshiped in an abstract sense but treated as slaves in practice.

Attis's myth is that he gets caught up between this. For the father, he needs to be an heir and carry his name. But Attis wants to go with the Great Mother and be a follower of her religion. So he goes mad. He is possessed by the Stygian Fates, who are nothing other than representatives of the repressed feminine. If you deny the feminine, she comes back and she's real nasty. It is in this state of mind in which he alters, or castrates, himself. He changes his body. He takes it away from the father, but he doesn't give it to the mother either. He becomes his own being. Attis is the first galli, the founder of all the other galli.

There are, of course, positive and negative aspects to any archetype. Isn't it a temptation to focus only on the positive qualities of serving the Great Mother—the beneficial role of being a healer, creator, and mediator? What about the darker aspects, Mother the vengeful destroyer, for instance?

I've tried to be balanced in my views. Not all berdaches may have been nice persons or talented in any particular way. As I go along, the galli material makes me look very much at both the positive and negative sides. Studying the galli is much more relevant to us today than the berdache because we live in a vi-olent society and we repress the feminine. Certainly we pay a terrible price for that. Like I said, she comes back, and when she does, she's a bitch.

Do you see contemporary gay men repressing the feminine?

I see gay men today who have a lot of hostility toward the mother and even more hostility, deeply buried, toward the father.

Let's talk more about that. In particular, tell me about your rela-tionship with your own mother.

It's been very hard to reach a point not where I am independent of her super-ego voice but to feel like I am free of her super-ego voice. I've internalized her mother, my grandmother, who died when I was still very young. She was ex-tremely hypercritical of everything and left my mother with almost no self-esteem whatsoever. My mother is like that but a little bit better; she's very critical and not good at expressing support in an unqualified kind of way. Afraid, sort of tough—but not really tough. Hers is an extremely moral voice, in a Catholic sense.

Were you close to your father?

No. Dad was an introvert, a mercurial figure, gentle, quiet, musical, and talented. He lived to do nothing so much as fly-fish and retire as a gentleman farmer. He always had pets—ducks, wounded hawks, dogs, all kinds of ani-mals—but he couldn't relate to people. He was married five times. The last time I saw him was in 1975. It was not unpleasant; there was not an apocalyptic inci-dent or anything like that. He had conservative views. It was just. . . . He was killed by a drunk driver in 1991, so I guess I never had the chance to resolve things with him.

Maybe there was some other reason for the distance between you. There's a theory I'll call, for lack of a better term, the reverse Oedipal complex. That is, young gay boys borrow from the lan-guage of the mother to attract the attention of the father. Their ho-mosexual libido is being projected onto the masculine, so of course it's going to the father as the original masculine source. The father picks this up on an unconscious level, and a rejection of some kind, or a distancing, usually occurs by the time the boy is four or five years old. What do you say to that?

It's still a heterosexist view of us, or a heterosexist model. I think that the gay boy's first romance is certainly with a numinous male figure. But let's try to take out the ethnocentrism of this model so that it might have some use for all the people who don't come out of a patriarchal, nuclear family, which is most people in the world. So let's just say a numinous male figure who could be the father, an older brother, an uncle, or the guy next door. That's our first one.

What do we do to attract him? That doesn't seem to me like the way that an infant's mind works. The infant just gives his heart and his love to this person, and then he finds that it may or may not be accepted initially. Now, I believe from what I recall and what was told to me by my mother that my father was exceptionally affectionate with me up to a certain age, that he doted on me. So, in my particular history, there was a love relationship that was then broken. Others never made that bond.

When was it broken?

By the time I was in first grade. Maybe he realized that I loved him as much as he loved me. But whether I was male or female, that would have freaked him out because he could not deal with emotions and people's love.

But certainly there was a projection of libido from you.

I won't speak for other gay men, but I just don't have any sense that I used my mother's language to attract him. As far as I was concerned, it was natural, it was me, it was what felt right in a moral sense. But where would I, before age three, ever have gotten the idea that I was not a beautiful, loving, attractive thing in my own right? As a third being who was between my mother and father, who was of the two of them and therefore neither of them? No! All that comes later. Identifying with the mother, hanging out in the kitchen, learning her language, all of that comes in later. I think the initial romance is free of all that crap for us.

As you travel around the country what is your reading of gay men today? What is the inner work we need to do collectively?

Nothing is going to happen until we deal with self-esteem. I wish I could say, "Now it's time to address our relationships with our fathers." But that actually would be a second step. The first step is self-esteem, of taking yourself seriously. The tragedy of so many gay men today is that they don't want to be special. All these shamans and berdaches running around, shamanizing and berdachizing, and wanting to be nothing so much as just an average person.

Let's start with our frivolity. Let's start paying attention to what we're doing with this humor, this teasing camp humor, that brings everyone down to the same level. It creates a social contract and a social space and points out where your ego is inflated, or where your self-image is out of whack with your looks. Start by seeing how this powerful sense of gay humor accomplishes all these things. It heals and creates a space to be within. It establishes equality among participants. I have so much respect for gay humor and camping because I look at the work that it does.

In a way, our humor is the sword we use to make a place in the world, isn't it?

Well, that's kind of phallic. I'd rather think of it as the honey that we spread.

This leads to the issue of living fully to our potential. Yet, many would ask, what exactly is that potential? What is the fulfillment we really seek beneath our demands for political equality and social justice? Certainly there must be something else beyond obtaining legal and social reform. Isn't that what you're talking about?

I think we're seeking the opportunity to grow. We're blindly creating the possibilities of growth, even though so many of us are being dragged kicking and screaming to growth and self-exploration. That's the purpose of all these gay subcultures and networks, the parades and drag balls, and all the other social forms that we are involved in creating and expanding upon. Maybe vaster numbers of people will take advantage of that space in a future generation and say, "Ah-hah! That's what this is for." This is a laboratory for growth—Castro Street, South of Market, Fire Island, whatever. It's a laboratory to grow in. It's not just a neighborhood to live in.

So you would say that to be truly gay one should live in service of spiritual awareness?

Our service now has to be to the truth of ourselves, to finding what feels right—if it's a jump rope or whatever it's going to be. Only by doing that can we come to our powers. Politically speaking, what we need from society is protection so that we can have our space, so that we can come to our powers and give them back to the larger community.

However, the work that goes on in this space is best kept out of their eyes because they can never understand it. It's absurd to seek social acceptance, for example, for S/M. What is the point? It's not a socially acceptable practice. It's an extra-social practice, and it's not for everybody to engage in. The more limited and more responsible the people are that do it, the better. We're not going to get anywhere wasting our time trying to explain it, to put it into a language they can understand.

> *So what you're asking for is not necessarily understanding but a*
> *certain kind of tolerance for gay space?*

Space requires more than tolerance because space in our society is property, and property has a value to it. No, it requires society to understand the contributions that we will make if we are allowed to grow and do our work.

> *But aren't we already making those contributions?*

Until we reach the day when someone like Rudolf Nureyev can say, "My gayness is intrinsically part of my greatness and the art that I give to the world," then we've not reached that point. And we are very, very far from that.

> *Do you believe there is a particular matrix of archetypes at play in*
> *the psyches of those men that today we call gay? What would be*
> *the characteristics or archetypal qualities of the third-gender figure*
> *you speak about, for instance?*

The berdaches that I know today all have an extra-large ego—lots of awareness of the self and a certain degree of narcissism that goes with it. They are what you call big queens. When they come into the room, you know it. They make the party a good party. They connect, they speak the truth, and they're blunt. They're fearless as far as they'll do anything without consideration of social convention or gender boundaries. They're also indifferent to gender, maybe hostile to it.

Berdaches are aggressive, sometimes extremely sexual, but not necessarily. They very much feel like two personalities crammed into one little body, although sometimes the body gets kind of big, too. They literally are big queens because there's an expansiveness, a stretching outward. They're key in organizations or social events, and of course, they are trendsetters. As Judy Grahn said, "They go first." I look for that intensity as the key quality of a person who is working through the berdache archetype. Berdaches are pushy queens. I wish I could reduce it to some other archetype, but unfortunately I can't. We've got to insert that archetype into the repertoire.

But not all gay men display those characteristics.

No, they don't. But they nonetheless ought to look to and examine and follow those people who do because straight archetypes will do them no good. Not everybody has to be, should be, or is required to be a flaming queen. But our growth lies through examining the flaming queens among us.

You've got to be comfortable with that queen. You've got to take her hand and walk down the street—and I mean that literally. If you've never gone in drag, if you've never hung out with some gay guys while they're in drag in public, I don't think that you've made the progress toward self-acceptance that you need to make. You've got to learn to feel comfortable with the most outrageous and sometimes degraded images of us. You can't just love the good parts of gay men; you've got to love the so-called bad parts if you're going to love yourself as a gay man, too.

Perhaps liberating the flaming queen that has been oppressed inside each one of us is another stage of coming out.

Well, of course. Every person who achieves spiritual insight in any culture moves from recognizing that what the average person takes to be literal is a metaphor. You'll see this, for example, in the career of Hastíín Klah, a Navajo berdache. He did not cross-dress, didn't need to. He got the message and understood it was a spiritual cross-dressing. He was indifferent to many taboos that the Navajos religiously followed and were concerned with because he understood that the taboos were metaphors for appropriate modes of behavior and conduct. He could go straight to the heart of the matter.

So in the same way, I don't need to wear a dress all the time, any more than I need to take acid all the time. I've done both, and I remember the experiences and integrated what I learned from them quite well. I don't need to repeat the experiences again and again.

The berdache and the archetypal androgyne are both imagined as figures containing male and female characteristics within one being. Yet they're quite different figures. Can you explain the distinction?

The androgyne, of course, is half male, half female, or the soup you get if you boil the two down and mix them up. It's a projection of healing for heterosexuals. You'll see gays relating to the androgyne because in a heterosexist culture it's the only available image. But I believe there's nothing there that's going to help us out—there's got to be something more. I'm not comfortable with using a language to describe individuation that is reliant on terms ultimately reducible only back to male and female. I want to go past that language. What we're really yearning toward is Harry's notion of "spiritual neitherness." Neither hetero male nor hetero female—that which is not contained by the two.

It seems that this category of "neitherness" has been so deeply repressed it's not even available to us.

That's right. What's the opposite of being a third gender? That's a very interesting question. There may be an opposite, or it may be that we are out of dialectics and into something completely else.

C. G. Jung, in his dutiful, straight-man kind of way, sensed that our culture was moving toward the image of the self as the necessary integration of its archetypal themes, and he sensed the dialectical nature of gender as it's been constructed, and the individualistic nature of our culture, whereby the individual becomes the site for unity versus other ways that a culture could have unity. And queers are the ones, we're the ones who are in the best position to achieve this wholeness. Because of what society has done to us, how they have set us aside and persecuted us, we're the ones who are enough outside of the dualistic consciousness to begin to take this up and do it.

You're saying that heterosexuals can learn from gays, just as we learn from them? Perhaps ways to heal their split souls?

What we have to offer them is what's beyond androgyne space. Once they've reached the point where they can bring their split-off half back together again, then they'll be ready to talk about moving beyond even that, beyond gender, beyond male and female, beyond the play of opposites.

You sometimes strike me as being a very angry man. Given the loss of loved ones to AIDS, the antigay discrimination that has kept you from finding a job in academia, and even the denial by peers of the things you are talking about here, this is understandable. But I need to ask, where do you put your anger?

I talk a lot, I bitch a lot, I push that energy into other channels and try not to get obsessive. The opposite of that is depression. And I get that way, too.

Given that depression is often the result of repressed feeling, what would you say to a young gay man who is experiencing the same kind of awakening but also the same frustrations as yourself?

I would have to say, honor yourself. Take everything about yourself seriously. Pay attention to your desire and where it's taking you. It's all significant. But don't take things so seriously that you stop having fun. By all means, don't deny yourself pleasure.

Has all of your research into the past somehow worked to help restore what has been taken from you?

Well, yes, and to lead me into my powers as a queen.

CLYDE HALL

GREAT SPIRIT

Clyde Hall was raised by his grandmother in a one-room cabin on the Fort Hall Indian Reservation in southeastern Idaho. On long winter nights, after the fire had burned down, she would tell "coyote stories," he recalls. During the hot, dusty summer days he would roam the countryside, sometimes with a posse of other boys. They often frequented swimming holes on the reservation—"well secluded with overhanging trees and green grass on the banks"—and it was at one such spot during a late August afternoon that the eleven-year-old Clyde discovered his attraction to other men.

His best friend and he were swimming alone that day, the kind of day, says Hall, "when the air is barely moving and heavy to breathe." They dove into the cool water, one after the other, and when they surfaced the friend put his arms tight around Clyde in a passionate embrace. "I knew then that this is what I had been waiting for," Hall remembers, "and I have never looked back since."

A Native American of Shoshone-Metis descent, Hall left home some years later to travel the world, a young man in search of himself and trying to get away from a place where "everybody knows everybody's business." Part of his journey was about integrating two vital parts of his identity into a greater whole: the Native part, proud and intact even after the horrendous history of genocidal, Anglo practices against his people; and the gay part, essential yet misunderstood, no less so than among his own tribe whose knowledge of the tubasa—or "two-spirited" one—had faded in recent times.

Restoring the long-lost traditions of the "two-spirited," those individuals more commonly known today as berdaches, has been an important aim in Hall's life. Over the past twenty years he has joined with other gay and lesbian Native Americans in giving new life to the once-honored roles that third- and fourth-gender individuals had within dozens of tribal cultures before conquest and colonization. In so doing, they have enriched mainstream gay culture's perception of what it means to be queer in America while at the same time revising Indian society's Christianized view of the gays in their midst.

According to the founders of Gay American Indians, an outreach group founded in San Francisco in 1975, if the wisdom of Native American tribes concerning gay people is reasserted, "all of us will benefit." Among the organization's ongoing social and political work has been the production of a landmark book, Living the Spirit *(edited by Will Roscoe), a collection of essays, myths, and poems further defining the rich heritage of gay Indians as healers, artists, and providers for their people.*

Hall practices the legacy of the two-spirited in his daily life. He moved back to the Fort Hall reservation a decade ago, where he serves as a magistrate and attorney. The talent to mediate differences is one quality attributed to those who bridge the worlds of male and female, the visible and the unseen; another is the ability to uphold sacred ways. Hall functions ably in this role as well, actively preserving and perpetuating the traditions and customs of his people.

The issue of self-esteem—or rather the lack of it—weighs deeply on Hall, since it's an issue shared by Native and gay people. As he travels between the separate worlds of Indian reservations and gay ghettos, he's witnessed time and again the harmful effects of deficient self-worth. And for those straddling the two worlds—for those who are gay and Native—there is a double dose of disenfranchisement with which to contend. It worries him that gays and Indians alike can't be more accepting among themselves, and he compares the infighting in Native communities to what often happens in the gay community. "It's like, let's tear each other apart rather than hold each other up," he grimly remarks. "Let's devastate what little we have."

But Hall holds his concern more as a challenge than as a condemnation. The way to honor oneself and others is to lead a spirit-filled life, he emphasizes. It's a message Hall carries wherever he goes, from mentoring the young people of his reservation to the many classrooms and other groups he visits around the country. In a time of increasing disharmony, Clyde Hall fulfills the spiritual role that the tubasa *of his tribe always used to.*

"Hang loose and rattle," he tells me as we sit down to talk. "It's an old Western saying, and that's what everybody's got to do right now: Hang loose and rattle."

o

Despite the hardships of life on a reservation, the upbringing you describe in Living the Spirit *sounds quite idyllic.*

I was born April 8, 1951, in Pocatello, Idaho. It's a tradition among the Indian people for the first-born of a generation to become what they call "old people's" children. And because I was the first-born in my family, I was raised by my grandmother, Hazel Truchot, on the reservation at Fort Hall. It was a good life. Truchot is a very old Metis name, which my grandmother had because she was Shoshone and French. The Metis are interesting people because they practice both cultures. And that's one thing that my grandmother really instilled in me—to take the best of both worlds.

In those days, Indian people were looked upon a lot like blacks were in the South. You couldn't sit in certain areas of theaters, you couldn't even go into some restaurants, because you were Indian. In fact, if you could pass for something other than Indian, you did. It's kind of ironic that the people who owned this land were treated like that, referred to as "reds" or "prairie niggers"—that's the mentality white people had toward Indians in those days.

When I was about ten years old we went to Blackfoot, Idaho, which is still no great shakes today as far as its treatment of Indians goes. There was a sign on the hotel that read, "No dogs or Indians allowed"—in that order. I asked my grandmother what the sign meant. She said, "Well, my son, some people are like that. But just remember, you come from a very old and proud family, and you're as good as anyone else. Don't let anyone ever tell you that you're not." What she instilled in me was good, basic truth: pride in oneself and in one's family, the idea that the world was open to you, and not using "I'm an Indian" as a cop-out. Too many people do that. They use being an Indian as an excuse for not getting an education, or a job, or whatever. That's a lot of bullshit as far as I'm concerned.

Do you think that what has happened to Native Americans during the past several hundred years is similar to what has happened to queer-identified people in recent decades? It seems that alcoholism, infectious diseases, and suicide rates within both the Indian and gay communities are way above the national average.

There's a parallel there. Something you didn't mention that's very important is that when you're oppressed you feel powerless to attack other people, so you start attacking people like yourself. It's really a tragedy because nothing is ever going to get done as long as we tear each other up. Give people a little bit of power, throw them a bone, and then they try to protect that power by tearing at anyone that'll come and get at it. You find that in Indian society, gay society, in all oppressed groups.

Despite all the good lessons about pride and self-worth, is this something that you've still had to struggle with in your life?

Doubly so. Because I'm a Shoshone-Metis Indian, and I also happen to be gay. Or as they say nowadays, I'm "two-spirited." I've made a pretty decent life for myself. I could have collapsed and said, "The hell with it," or become an alcoholic or something nasty like that.

How have you survived and thrived?

It's been through the greatness of Spirit. Years ago, when I prayed with Spirit, I said: "I put my life in your hands, a totally blind leap of faith and trust. You do with my life what you want. And Spirit, I want to share things with other people, not only Indian people but all people, red, white, black, and yellow." I've been going ever since. For the last twenty years I've traveled all over the world and met all kinds of different people. Spirit's taken care of me and seen to my needs.

When did you first know you were gay?

I've always been that way. I knew that I wasn't going to have a wife and children and all that kind of thing—it was something that Spirit didn't have in mind for me. I knew this even when I was very, very young. When I was about seven years old I had scarlet fever and nearly died from it. After that things were a lot different in the ways of Spirit. For instance, I started having an intuitive knowledge of what was going to happen through dreams. And I could see things—Spirit—that weren't there to ordinary people.

What do you think about the notion that gays are a socially constructed people, in other words, that there was no such thing as "homosexual" people until a hundred years ago?

Pshaw! Gay people have always been around. I mean, from the remotest indigenous tribal circles, we've always been here.

What would you say to someone who says you're making this up just because you want to feel special. What proof do you have?

Look at the history. We're the people who bring the beauty into the world and actually create the culture. How many movers and shakers were people who were either what we would consider exclusively homosexual or at least bisexual? What have they done for the world? Either pro or con? Because it can manifest either way. There has to be a special race of Spirit in order for these people to accomplish these things. It didn't just happen, you know. We're the people who make Spirit move, and the world is much richer for it. All gay people, in one form or another, have something to give to this world, something rich and very wonderful.

So you believe there's a spiritual potential to being gay?

Well, one thing I've always known is never doubt Spirit. Always trust in Spirit and in what Spirit's trying to tell you. I live a Spirit-led life, you might say, even to the point of what I'm going to wear in the morning when I get up. I've learned not to question or doubt. If you try to talk yourself out of living a life with Spirit, you get yourself into all kinds of trouble.

Is this an inner voice, or your intuition speaking, or what?

In Shoshone, we have the word *poha-kant*. It describes a type of person who lives a Spirit-led life, who is a conduit for Spirit. They're the kind of person who Spirit ebbs and flows through, more powerful at one time than another. That's why when New Age–type people say, "I'm a shaman," I look at them and think, Honey, do you know what you're talking about? Because to tell you the truth, most of the real shamans I run across or have done research on are gay people or at least bisexual. You have to have that.

Why do you say that?

Because you walk in both worlds. Because you are elements of both male and female—but you're neither. You don't fit in, you're a go-between. And consequently it's easier for you to transcend from the physical to the spiritual realm.

Have you found this to be the case in your own life?

Yes. And if you look at any so-called primitive or indigenous peoples— and this goes for ancient Europeans like the Druids and Celts as well—their shamans were usually two-spirited people. American Indian societies are no exception.

When did you became aware of the berdache tradition? Did you hear anything about that growing up, or did you have to find out about it later for yourself?

I really don't like the word *berdache*, which is French. Indian people don't put labels on themselves; they don't think of themselves as being one way or another. It's just the way you are, unconsciously—a state of life. Still, contemporary gay Indian people are re-creating the berdache tradition, which kind of makes me happy because it gives them self-pride and purpose. Now we're using the term *two-spirit* because there are two elements in Indian culture.

There's what you call your manly hearted or brave-hearted women, who are for the most part very masculine and do everything that men do. They ride motorcycles, fix trucks, and are basically good old boys. But they're not necessarily just butch because many of them have children. They are very nurturing people. They live the way they want to live and are a very tight group a lot of the time.

What about the gay men in your tribe?

The men do not really get along with one another. They'll stab one another in the back as soon as look at one another. Of course, some of them are very much in the closet. There's a lot of self-hatred among them, a lot of lashing out. Actually, the women are more together than the men are. A lot of the men are really tragic people because they don't realize the spirituality they have right there in their hands that they could use to better their lives and their community. Instead, it's all enveloped in self-loathing.

What is the remedy for that in your view?

It has a lot to do with pride in oneself and in having a connection with it. Most gay Indian people have that connection. They don't have to go up on the hill and be medicine people and seek vision because traditionally they're beyond that. They practice a good life and a clean-spirited life and get respect for that. But then you've got your Indian people who are in the bars all the time, looking for one-night stands and that kind of thing. They don't practice the spirituality at all. Maybe some of them don't even know it exists, which is a tragedy.

That kind of behavior must be very painful for you to observe.

It is. I quit drinking even wine for dinner about two and a half years ago. I did that because as a judge and magistrate these past fifteen years I've seen the damage that alcohol does to my people, to their families, and to the tribe as a whole. I've seen the devastation that alcohol has done to my people, and it's not a pretty picture.

Tell me about where you live.

My tribe has a vast area of land, some 500,000 acres in southeastern Idaho. On that reservation there are about four thousand enrolled members of the tribe, fifteen hundred Indians from other tribes, and about a thousand non-Indians. So it's a big area of land with a lot of open spaces. It's not uncommon for us to jump in the car and go a hundred miles to visit someone. The center of the reservation is a little town called Fort Hall. It was established in 1835 by Nathaniel Wyatt during the fur-trapping period.

In this group of about sixty-five hundred people, how many would you estimate to be gay men?

Well, let me tell you this first. Everybody knows everybody else's business. You live in a glass house. The tribe is like a large extended family. When I came back to the reservation I figured I'd been out around this world and knew the kind of lifestyle I wanted to live. I decided I wasn't going to hide being gay; I was just going to live my life and to hell with what people think.

Anyway, I remember once in late summer there was a group of us gay men and we were picking berries, which is kind of a thing that Indian women usually do. You dry them in the sun, grind them up, make patties out of them, and use them throughout the winter. We were coming around this curve and there were three good old girls there fishing, which is a masculine kind of thing to do. That was kind of crazy, because we were picking berries and they were fishing. We just waved at each other and had a good laugh.

Does any of your family have problems with you being a gay man?

They're very accepting about it. It's never been hidden, and of course I dress my nieces and nephews in the best Indian clothes. I spoil them. I always knew intuitively that I wasn't going to be like other people, that my life was going to be different. Of course, in an Indian values sense there's always a place for everyone. There's definitely a place for gay Indian people among or within the extended family, and there always will be.

The role you've played within the life of your tribe seems very reflective of the work that the berdache have always done.

Keepers of culture. The last twenty years of my life have been devoted to collecting Indian art. I have a great love of tradition. People come to me and ask, How do you do this? Or, How should this be made? Or, What kind of song should be sung here? I mean, that's what I'm doing here. I have not just stayed on the reservation, which is a very enclosed environment—you know, some people live and die there. But me, I've always gone out and dragged people back in, and vice versa. In other words, I practice what I preach. But I don't like to put a label on myself. The word *berdache* is convenient, but even among reservation society it is not really known. The traditional word in Shoshone is *pasa ta-int* or *taina wa-ippe*.

How are gender-variant men received on your reservation today?

Well, there is a type of Indian man on the reservations whom you wouldn't know whether he was a man or woman. Those are the people that would have been the old-time berdache. And people look at them as being that way today, if at times kind of humorously.

But isn't it a misconception that all berdache were effeminate and cross-dressed?

It is. Some became very valorous warriors, since to have a berdache along on a war party was considered good luck. This person was in great communication with Spirit.

You mentioned that it was the berdache who went out to cut the the center pole for the Sun Dance ritual. Why is that?

Because of who they were. They walked in both worlds, the physical and spiritual, and they were honored in that way. It took a person not of this world to do something like that. For instance, the best rocks to use for rattles are those that were dug up by the ants and never touched by human hands. The best kind of earth to use in setting up your altar is gopher dirt because it was dug up by something other than a human being. If you can get that otherworldly spiritual connection, it has a lot of power.

What is the most important thing that white people still don't know about Indian people? What are some of the big lies and cultural myths that still linger on?

That Indians don't laugh. We laugh about everything, that's the way we survive. It's kind of a dry, insane sense of humor. It's better than crying—we do that, too. But anytime you laugh about something it shatters it. Then it doesn't have any power over you. Where that thing about the stoic Indian comes from I don't know.

Another major thing that non-Indian people don't understand about us is our consciousness of time. In Western society, time is a linear thing—past, present, future. With Indian peoples, time is perceived more like a spiral—past, present, and future are going around together. There's just a whole different consciousness about time.

That would significantly alter how one views life.

We believe that everything in this world is a circle—plants, animals, people, everything is part of that cycle. Nothing is square except the rock, which has the power to destroy, which is part of thunder and lightning.

Do you see gay men today as having a kind of tribal culture? And if not, what are the values and traditions gay men should be upholding more?

This country is all oriented toward the acquiring of possessions, power, and money. Gay people and Indian people have fallen into that trap as much as anyone else. The development of spirit has been sadly lacking. The tragedy of AIDS has forced some men to realize that they're not going to be twenty-one forever. In fact, some aren't even going to reach the age of forty-one. You'd better make peace with that, become strong with that. We're living in a period of great change, and things are not going to get any better for some time to come.

Do you believe that gay people have some kind of mediating role to play in the world at large?

Yes, a helpful role. Gay men and women, two-spirited Native people, we have a very important part to play in the restoring of balance. I can't emphasize that enough. That's the problem with the world right now—it's gotten severely out of balance. That's why we're as crazy as we are now, and why things are happening the way they are. And until the people and the animals and the environment get themselves back into some balance in some way, things are going to continue the way they are, perhaps even get worse. It scares me.

Let's go back to this idea of gays being the keepers and the creators of culture. Where do you think those instincts come from?

It's something that Spirit gives you when you're born. These powers and talents are an integral part of a way of being. They have to manifest one way or another because that's what we were given to do in the world. For instance, my people are masters at bead work; we are known worldwide for the stuff we do. But it was the gay men who started a trend of literally painting with beads. They've totally broken away from what you would think of as traditional Indian beadwork and have evolved this new style.

I believe that being gay in this society has created an opening of my soul, a kind of sensitivity to the world. Has this been your experience?

Most definitely. You know, you're always the outsider looking in, and you see things differently. That's why you can call bullshit, bullshit. There were times when I was an alcoholic or I went through the tragedy of breaking up with lovers. I got out of that through use of Spirit; I survived because of Spirit. I'm anxious to get on with what the next twenty years will have in store for me. I trust entirely in Spirit that it's going to continue and it's going to be a good life for as long as I live on this earth. There's always going to be something exciting happening.

Like, there's this gay Jewish fellow from Brooklyn who came to study under me. His name is Larry Two Turtles. He said, "Damn, you live a hell of a life. In the past year, you and I have been in some really strange circumstances." The crazy thing about it is that he thought he was coming out to learn about Indian culture and spirituality, and what he's found is more about himself, his own people, and his own ways of believing. That's what happens to people who come around me wanting to be enlightened, so to speak; they end up getting the mirror held up to them and being forced to look at themselves. And that's the way it's supposed to be!

> *Let's talk about spiritual authenticity, particularly the difficulties in following a Spirit-led path in a dispirited society. What, in your view, is a spiritual life?*

It's a way of being and living in balance. Balance has a lot to do with it. Not letting anything get heavier than the rest. Anytime you get out of balance, it's going to lead your life willy-nilly some way. A lot of living your life in balance has to do with listening to Spirit, listening really hard. If it tells you something, or leads you a certain way, intuitively trust that that's the way things are going to be. And when it tells you you're out of balance on something, try to get back. Living with Spirit and trusting in it—that's the most important part.

> *Do you have a daily spiritual practice?*

Yes, I do. I always carry this medicine bundle around with me. It may not look like much, but it's something that has protected me and helped me along all these years. If you opened it up, all you'd find is bits of stone and hanks of hair and different things that have been given to me by Spirit. And I burn sweetgrass during meditation. That's a way of welcoming Spirit when you say your prayers and meditations. Sage and cedar are kind of a deterrent, that's for clearing. The sweetgrass is for welcoming.

> *When you refer to Spirit, what do you mean exactly? The imma-nent Spirit that infuses life on the planet, or is there one particular spirit?*

We call it *poha*. The Sioux call it *skan*. And it's defined as the power that moves. It's part of everything; it's part of us, the trees, this world, the universe. People personify it as God, or in my case, *dammenappe*. But that's only just one manifestation of it. It's a very powerful force that people, if they know how, can tap into for either good or bad, since it's completely neutral. Everything that we think of, the gods and the spirits, the wood nymphs and all these different things that we personify, are manifestations of that power in some form or another.

Of course, two-spirited people, or the berdache who practice these ways, don't have a corner on it. Anyone who comes to it either through prayer or meditation, or by any means necessary, can tap into it—for good or bad.

You say that anyone can, but aren't you also implying that queer folk are a little bit closer to it?

A great deal closer to it, if they only knew how to tap into it and not short-circuit themselves.

Surely it's not as easy as opening a door and saying, "There it is." Were you trained or taught how to do this?

I was taught by a number of teachers over a long period of time. But I think anybody who's pure in heart can do it. I once met a woman who had studied under Tibetan lamas for some time, and we got along fabulously. We came from two different methods of teaching, and yet we were on the same level and could talk about the same kind of thing. So there are all different ways of making a cake from scratch.

How do you define soul or having a soul? What is your soul, and how do you care for and nurture it? Or is the word a Western notion and not anything that belongs to Native tradition?

Different Indian people have different consciousnesses of it. In my neck of the woods, up in the Northwest among the equestrian, plains-oriented type of people, there wasn't any concept of heaven or hell until Christianity came along. There was no concept of sin. But there were ways and mores that held the tribe together.

When a person died, or went to the other-side camp, as it was called in traditional language, what you had was just a continuation of the good things in life. In other words, you just moved camp, went from one world to another, and continued on with the type of life that you had always lived, only more of it, better. You weren't elevated to be on the right hand of God or to be with the angels. The Indian people think of the two worlds being separated by a very thin veneer, like a curtain.

But what do you believe? Do you feel the spirit of your grandmother is near, for instance?

Yes, because as long as there are people and places and things in this world that keep you here, you're going to have an input into it. Of course, that passes with generations. If you love a place and you care about people, that's going to keep you here in this world.

Our society deals in what it considers to be reality, but in truth it's just one of the realities. In non-Indian society, people think everything's dead! They don't take into consideration the other realities. When people see things like spirits and ghosts—which I have—they don't have any place to put them in their reference. That's why it scares them. With Indian people it's all part of the whole.

Indian people believe that if a person commits suicide or dies in some violent way, then that person's spirit is going to travel around the earth until somebody shows him or her the way to the other-side camp. My grandmother always used to tell me not to go into whirlwinds, the little ground twisters. "That's a dead person, a troubled person," she'd say. "You go in there, and you're gonna find yourself in some strange place when you wake up."

What can non-Indian gay men learn from gay Indian traditions or beliefs that would be of most value to them?

The most important thing is survival. Survival as a community. Survival in a spiritual sense, individually and collectively. Indian people, of course, were devastated a hundred years ago by diseases and warfare. At one point we were called the vanishing American. But we're still here. And that's what gay men have to think about, what with AIDS, political unrest, and fighting for basic rights. Spirit willing, we as gay people will still be here a hundred years from now, and we will look back at what we've done to make it.

What has come out of being gay that's helped you in your own survival?

My little grandmother's homespun words say it all: "Be true to yourself." Pride in oneself, walking in balance. Being able to express that pride, and living it. When it comes down to brass tacks, that's what it is, right there.

James M. Saslow

CROSSING THE CATEGORIES

Sometime during the first months of 1532, Florentine artist Michelangelo Buonarroti met Tommaso de' Cavalieri, a handsome Roman nobleman, and fell deeply in love. The fifty-seven-year-old painter and sculptor was smitten by the younger man's beauty and intelligence, and he made his feelings known by sending Tommaso a series of four drawings on mythological themes. Among the work was a drawing depicting the rape of Ganymede, an incident in the ancient Greek myth about the shepherd boy who became cupbearer to the gods. As the story goes, Zeus, looking down on earth from his throne on Mount Olympus, spied the attractive, young Ganymede tending his flock, transformed himself into an eagle, and plucked the object of his desire from the fields and into the heavens above.

Michelangelo's drawing of Ganymede's abduction was no doubt meant to convey his innermost emotions about a young man who, too, had captured his soul. But the impassioned image of an enormous bird carrying a naked lad aloft is more than just a coded love note; it is one of the most transcendent representations of same-sex love ever created. The eagle, majestic in midflight, grasps the boy from behind and seems to be penetrating him. The boy, arms entwined on outstretched wings, appears serene, even blissful. No violent struggle implying rape is depicted here; the two figures are unmistakably clasped in radiant union. In Michelangelo's numinous image, youth and maturity, the earthbound and the airborne, the physical and the spiritual, are harmoniously bound by rapture.

Since Michelangelo's heartfelt rendering, Gaynmede's ascension has been a motif often used by artists. But with almost each succeeding interpretation, the potent homoeroticism of the scene has been downplayed or ignored. As the centuries passed, this inspiring archetype of gay love has been devalued to little more than an allegorical picture about a winged creature carrying off a misfortunate field hand. The sacred quality implied within the master artist's gift to Tommaso has been left in the mud of ignorance and fear.

In his ground-breaking 1986 book, Ganymede in the Renaissance: Homosexuality in Art and Society, historian James M. Saslow examines the use of the Ganymede myth as a metaphor for gay love, showing how images of Zeus's bonding with the beautiful Trojan boy frequently appeared in the iconography of the time. In some ways, the High Renaissance was a period not unlike our own: a confluence of divergent cultural forces and new technology pushed European society into startling leaps of expanded consciousness. Thinking about all areas of human life—including sexuality—was advanced. The cultural and intellectual freedom of the era was short-lived, however, as political conservatives and religious zealots reasserted their hold on society, ushering in the reactionary age known as the Counter-Reformation.

The tension between expression and suppression, the irrational and the ordered, is, of course, one of the grand balancing acts of history. But the tug-of-war between the Dionysian and Apollonian is not necessarily limited to epochs and nation-states; it is a ceaseless debate waged within the psyche of every individual. Saslow has heard the argument from both camps and has made his preference known: how much better to go flying on the wings of an eagle than to be left counting sheep.

The forty-six-year-old scholar was born in New Jersey to a middle-class Jewish family. "I was a bookworm, not the least bit interested in sports, and very creative," Saslow says about his childhood. "The word everybody always used to describe me was artistic. But there would be this slight pause before they said it, so I knew they weren't just talking about my ability to draw. There was something larger the word seemed to refer to, but people would never quite say what it was out loud."

One of Saslow's defining embarrassments as a child happened on the playground in second grade. "I was playing catch with the girls when the ball rolled away," he recalls. "And as I ran to retrieve it, I tripped over a football some boys were playing with nearby and fell. I broke my arm chasing after a little pink ball."

Experiences such as these resulted in Saslow being painfully labeled a "nerd/fag," he says. "They were closely connected concepts and presented the only category others had for me." The stigmatization he endured while growing up was later to inform the historian's keen interest in deflating categories of all kinds. Since coming out in his midtwenties while living in a counterculture commune in Boston, Saslow has worked tirelessly on behalf of gay liberation while at the same time questioning the assumptions many gay people hold about being part of a continuous historical presence. As his study of the West's cultural heritage has revealed, being a lover of the same has meant different things at different points in history.

Yet, for Saslow, I suspect that being gay in the late twentieth century is perhaps not all that distant from how the queer artists of the Renaissance might have felt about their own sexuality: a source of mystery and wonder, the fire for a *creative life. One day, a few years ago, Saslow says he "was talking to somebody about coming out. I meant to say, 'I came out in 1973.' But what I said by mistake was, 'I woke up in 1973.'" It was a telling slip of the tongue. "I was a zombie up until that point," he says quietly, shaking his head. "Not miserable, but not alive."*

An associate professor of art at Queens College, City University of New York, Saslow is also the author of The Poetry of Michelangelo: An Annotated Translation. *Among the shelves of books, piles of research notes, and student papers waiting to be graded in his cluttered office, one can see pieces of lace, costume jewelry, and richly decorated fabric incongruously brightening the room. As serious a scholar as James Saslow has become, it's clear that a part of him is still happily chasing the little pink ball.*

o

What do you hope to find in the study of art that will tell you something about yourself?

In one of his poems, Tennessee Williams says there is no cry more dangerous than the cry of "Brother!" He was talking about paintings in museums and how people looking at them come to an awareness that they are in a state of brotherhood with other people. I saw the visual arts as a place that was the whole repository of everything human beings had ever felt, done, seen, loved, or lusted after. I wanted to get into that sandbox and dig around and find the images that I could say "brother" to and thereby create a historical tradition for gay sensibilities. When I started I was fairly naive. I assumed everybody who was gay was more or less the same throughout history. I didn't know the complications that would come up in trying to make sense of all this material.

Would it complicate matters further if I asked in what ways did homoerotically inclined men in the Renaissance view themselves similarly to the ways gay men see themselves today?

I tend to look on the Renaissance period as embryonic of early modern times. There are already suggestive bits and pieces in the fifteenth and sixteenth centuries of thoughts and ideas that are somewhat the ancestors of the way we look at homosexuality now. Orthodox social constructionists would say that the way we look at homosexuality today didn't—couldn't—exist until at least the eighteenth and probably the mid–nineteenth century. But you can find individuals in the sixteenth century—Michelangelo, Sodoma, Leonardo, among others—who clearly were homosexually inclined. Some of them began to articulate that they knew they were different from other people, but they couldn't quite escape feeling guilty about their difference because it was a heavily Christian society. Yet there are examples, too, of people not being terribly upset about it. What I've been interested in looking at over time are the very earliest roots of what would later become a more richly expressed gay consciousness. And it's there!

> My recollection of viewing Leonardo's Annunciation in the Uffizi Gallery in Florence supports what you say. The image, especially the figure of the angel, touched my soul in a way I find difficult to articulate. Somehow, across the expanse of five centuries and dichotomous cultures, it was clear that another gay man had created this wondrous painting. Why do you suppose I felt this way?

Spirituality enclosed in a very beautiful male form—I don't think you have to be gay to be aware of those things or to create images of those things, but it helps.

> Compared to work by Leonardo or Michelangelo, the art made by their contemporary, Raphael, holds little interest for me.

It is possible that a gay person, not you, but some gay people might react positively to a male painted by Raphael. And there might be gay painters with whom a gay spectator would have very little sense of commonality. I don't want to set up exclusive categories. What counts here is that we respond to images in a very visceral and emotional way when they embody our fantasies or make visible the archetypes that are meaningful to us.

> I understand that. But when I mentioned Raphael's name you shrugged as to indicate that you, too, find one of the great artists of Western civilization of little personal interest.

He's one of the great artists because he embodies a set of principles and ideals that are archetypally very masculine and rational—very Apollonian. I find those qualities much less appealing, personally, than the feminine, the androgynous, and the Dionysian—those things which, in fact, Leonardo is closer to, to some extent. Some art historians are now asking, How did we come to decide that Raphael was so great? Who was it who decided that the highest set of achievements within the arts would be the Apollonian, rational mode? I mean, that's compulsory heterosexuality if I ever saw it!

What part of yourself do you see reflected in the artists you study?

It depends on the individual. In Michelangelo's case, he was a very passionate man who was enraptured by male beauty and wanted to draw it. I relate to that because I started out drawing male beauty myself; it was one of the ways that allowed me to come to a realization of my own gay urges. He was also terribly frustrated and guilty, and I relate to that as well. I feel that I have some connection across time to somebody else who felt repressed, oppressed, suppressed, and blackmailed.

Do you see the homosexual artists of the Renaissance as shamanic figures of their age?

People who don't fit neatly into strict social categories like masculine and feminine are assigned a great deal of power by human society. It can be a threat, which it is to conservative religious people, but it's still a kind of power. The gay response to that in recent years has been to say, "We do have a power, and it can be a spiritual force for good."

Somewhere, deep down inside, human beings know that all of their social constructions are arbitrary. Yet most of us out of necessity fit into those categories and don't question the social order. We are all agreeing to let one another live by a social construction that serves the purposes of social cohesion. However, there are the people who don't fit very well into this category structure, who by their very existence point out the arbitrariness of the general social system. In modern society, those people are called gay men and lesbians. That's where we get associated with the metaphysical or spiritual world because once you're outside of that little box called "the human constructs of society," what's out there? Just the undifferentiated universe that hasn't been organized by rational human principles. On some level, that is our definition of God.

As for an example from the Renaissance, Sodoma comes close to the role you're talking about. His real name was Bazzi, but he was given his derogatory nickname because of his fondness for cute young male apprentices. When his horse won the annual race in Siena and the heralds asked what owner's name to announce, he told them to go through the streets praising "The Sodomite." His little revenge wasn't quite shamanic, but it certainly must have raised some consciousness or challenged some basic assumptions.

Is the notion of gay people being a third and fourth gender a useful idea or is it just more categorization?

It's certainly better to have four gender categories rather than two because at least it allows more leeway for various kinds of diverse individuals to feel that they have a right to exist. It allows for an identity and a place in the social order. But I'm not really interested in making more slices of the pie. I'm interested in allowing everybody to have whatever peculiar combination of characteristics they have as individuals and for us all to be able to simply accept that that's who they are. In other words, if there are five billion people on the planet, that's five billion genders. That's the ultimate goal.

In the meantime, what I've been spending my scholarly life doing is simply proving that there are at least four available alternatives, and that's an improvement. Anything that helps people open up from this very binary pattern of thought is a step in the right direction.

Was the channeling of homosexual desire into creative and artistic areas among the more important influences on the Renaissance?

Well, there certainly were an awful lot of those boys! If you look at the roster of major names there seems to be a real flowering in that period: Donatello, Leonardo, Michelangelo, Cellini, Caravaggio, Sodoma. It seems more than in any other.

They put a new spin on the pagan sensibilities of an earlier era and created what our notion of Western culture is. This was recognized and talked about in the late nineteenth century by homosexual scholars and writers like Walter Pater, John Addington Symonds, and Oscar Wilde.

Those gay art historians all got interested in the Renaissance as a historical precedent for the revival of Greek culture, which means the revival of positive precedents for homosexuality. One of the effects of the Renaissance interest in

Greek antiquity was an increased awareness of an alternative view about sexuality, one that had little sexual guilt and none around the issue of hetero versus homo. I don't think anybody in the fifteenth century said, "I'm gay and I'm going to go hunting for historical precedent," because they couldn't have said that. But in the late nineteenth century they could, and they did.

Pater is particularly self-conscious about his historical search for a common temperament, a sensibility between himself and other people. He means gay, although he never uses something so overt. He's a good Victorian and so can't speak out loud about these things, but he's building a cultural tradition. Pater has a very spiritual tone to the way he writes, as if we're being put in touch with something mystical. It all has to do with "wayward love," one of his code-name phrases for being gay.

What he was saying, first and foremost, is that we must understand our own aesthetic and emotional responses to the world. And we have to validate them. Never mind if they fit into somebody else's scheme of what is appropriate and right; just go with your feelings and explore them, see where in the past you find other people who are like you. It's a way of helping you understand your own aesthetic and erotic longings, and from that point on art becomes very much more subjective. It's a romantic view.

Are you a romantic, too?

I've been called that. If the Romantics are basically to be identified with Dionysian emotional immediacy, I would like to try to be in that camp rather than in the very restrained, very systematized Apollonian camp.

Isn't any culture created out of a balance between the two?

I'm always a little afraid of statements that epic. But in Western culture there certainly is a tension between the whole ideal being symbolized by the Greeks and the ideal symbolized by the Jews or the Christians. It's not as neat as Apollonian versus Dionysian, however, because the Greeks had both. But it does have something to do with a pagan attitude versus a very rational, legalistic attitude. Perhaps it's really the battle between unity and dualism. One interpretation of Greek culture is that it manages to include everything and find a balance. The Judeo-Christian ideal is to separate things into varying, diametrically opposed categories and then rank them. One side is better than the other. Good is better than evil. Therefore, be only good and shun evil. A person is a pure spirit and the physical body is this embarrassing accident that we should strive to overcome. Instead of saying, we are all a combination of spirit and body, so what's the big problem?

What is the big problem?

The problem is in insisting that one or the other is the answer to everything.

From your vantage as an art historian, what are some of the archetypes that seem to hold a particular resonance for gay men—those we tend to paint, sculpt, or otherwise portray. Why has the image of Ganymede being carried aloft by an eagle been historically associated with homosexuality, for example?

Clearly the myth of Ganymede is an archetype. It has to do with the younger being swept away by the older and more powerful figure. On the emotional level, it's about an enraptured relationship that brings one closer to heaven or the spiritual world, since the older figure is a god. Obviously that can be a dynamic for straight people, too, but this is our version.

When Michelangelo did his drawings of Ganymede, it is not clear whether he is the eagle or the boy or maybe both. Because he was in love with a younger man, you might say he literally sees himself as the older figure. But on another level, Ganymede stands for anybody who feels in some way loved by the universe, or who is overwhelmed emotionally by a powerful other figure and is thus brought closer to some awareness of cosmic divine principles.

This is another way in which gay people are brought into conflict with the uptight elements of the dominant culture. We're saying that our sexual relationships are meaningful, and in the physical and emotional rapture that comes with them we have some glimpse of the cosmic forces in the universe. In Western society, sex is this great problem because it's identified with the body, which is bad. So this Dionysian force is boxed into very Apollonian categories: sex is only about reproduction or fulfilling marital duties. Ecstasy got lost somewhere. And gay people insist on ecstasy, which is outlawed because it helps one to see beyond society's limitations. The world is a big sphere, but human culture wants us to live in a little box in the middle of that sphere and not venture outside into any of the uncharted areas, since they're hard to control.

The eagle is taking Gaynmede out of this world. The word *rape* comes from the same root as *rapture*. The whole idea behind the image is that here comes a force that is so overwhelmingly powerful that it comes and plucks you up and away from socially defined reality. That force is our homoeroticism.

You're saying that gay men are more attuned than others to seeing the link between the erotic and the spiritual?

It's easier for straight people to fit into society than not to fit in, so they do. But we have to deal with the distance between what we want and what society allows with a little bit more self-consciousness. And that has to do with Eros as much as anything else. Straight people aren't any less erotic than gay people, but it gets channeled into such socially acceptable things as marriage and parenthood. We're always aware of our marginality in a way that many straight people are not, and so sexuality becomes something that we really have to ponder.

You talk about the unfathomable depths and dimensions existing outside the neat box called reality that humankind has organized around itself. Maybe the elements of that outer sphere are, in some way, reflective of the contents of our inner being. What is soul for you, and how do you care for and nurture yours?

I'm not sure I have a definition for soul. Spirituality has to do with the relationship of the individual to the whole universe. But to the extent that I feel that I have a soul, I'm an atheist.

I would put it this way: If the universe as a whole is the big circle, then within that there's this box that is logically organized society, and within that is another little circle that represents the individual soul. The soul is local and it's within me—it's my core identity. I believe there is some connection between the little circle in the middle and the big circle at the horizon—they're both totalizing rather than logical and organized.

Part of what I would like everyone who is gay to be able to realize is that you, too, are a child of the universe. It produced you. And some people with their little rational boxes will try to make you feel that either you aren't who you think you are or you are who you think you are and that's bad! Ultimately what we should be trying to do is to come to the realization that we are exactly who we are, and it's okay.

*What other well-known images in art have an archetypally gay
quality about them?*

Narcissus, but not for the reason that most people think. Narcissus has
been identified with gay people because we're supposed to be selfish. That's
straight people defining us and saying we're so absorbed in our own aesthetic delight that we're not filling our social obligations—that our self-absorption is
somehow pathological. That's not the point of the image at all.

Narcissus is a very powerful gay archetype because it's about self-exami-
nation. We have to be self-examining because nobody else is going to tell us who
we are. When I was a kid, for instance, everybody knew I was gay except me. But
they wouldn't tell me what they thought; they just whispered about it among
themselves. And of course, they made sure I would not see any images reflective
of myself or of people like me—the theory being that if you don't ever see it, it
doesn't exist, and therefore you can't become it.

They were calling me by their ultimate negative word, since artistic ability is associated with effeminacy and therefore with being gay. Yet I was trapped
in a double bind, trying to be good at creative things while proving to other people and to myself that doing that didn't have to entail being a fag, second-class, or
second-rate. It totally confused me because there was no other role model available in the late fifties and early sixties. The only things I saw that suggested a gay
life were a glance in the YMCA bathroom or a grope in an elevator—and I rejected that kind of sordid experience.

*What effect did the paucity of positive gay images and the denial of
your homoerotic nature have on your sense of self?*

I remember thinking a lot of the time that I must be undersexed, which is
a humiliating self-image. Since I didn't respond in the way that other people did,
the only logical answer seemed to be that I didn't have much of a drive. Which, of
course, transfers into the feeling that one is not much of a Man with a capital *M*.
But once I came out in my midtwenties, it was possible for me to think, I may not
be much of a man by traditional definition, but that's a horrible definition to have
to live up to. Once I realized that, I felt enormously liberated.

*One image that gay men have seen themselves positively mir-
rored by is the Double, images of hero twins such as Gilgamesh*

and Enkidu, Castor and Pollux, among others, in history and myth.

What's fascinating to us is likeness or similarity, whereas for heterosexuals, to some degree, there's always going to be a sense of differentness about the other person. A husband is never his wife's twin. But two gay men can, in a way, be twins. This is revealing of the fundamental difference in the way that gay people look at the world. In a heterosexual relationship it's easy to fall into a binary pole: male-vertical-sky, female-horizontal-earth. It tends to polarize experience. But in a gay male relationship, whatever could be said about one could be equally true of the other.

Cross-dressing is one literal way of uniting opposites within oneself. Is this why you occasionally put on a dress?

A lot of drag queens don't necessarily see their cross-dressing the same way I do, but to me it's about taking a lot of very rigid social expectations and turning them upside down or booting them out altogether. It's a way of not being caught in polarized ways of thought and of trying to find some way of connecting with both the rectilinear and the circular. Why can't I wear a dress? Why shouldn't I pretend to be certain famous women of history? Why is it that I can only pretend to be famous men of history? If there's a quality in Marie Curie or Catherine the Great that I find appealing as a kind of archetypal role model, why shouldn't I impersonate them? I mean, we all know it's a fantasy, a psychic or spiritual exercise.

Cross-dressed men get some people terribly upset, and I can never figure out why because to me it's all play, or carnival. It's a way of expressing and getting in touch with those parts of me that are there. And if they happen to be called feminine by some people, so what? Being involved in cross-dressing is a way of laying claim to all the possible archetypes of the universe. It's all about symbols, right? I'm not really a girl; I've no interest in being a girl. In the divide between women and men, I like being right on the fence, to be able to sense the experience of both sides and to implicitly point out that the divisions are artificial.

Do you feel that gay men serve as a transformative element within the collective because of their intuitive understanding of and ability to transcend rigid categories, as with your cross-dressing? Does that somehow put us closer in touch with the kind of deep wisdom that comes from listening to that inner voice which our society calls the irrational?

We tend to have that possibility if only because we're always put in positions where we can't fall neatly into categories, and we therefore have to question and look beyond them. In a way, getting into drag is about those things. I question all the categories. Who says men can't wear this particular item of clothing? Or this color? Or makeup? Why not? It's another way of getting beyond social convention. And I'm nothing compared to the queens of the Imperial Court—or the Cockettes, they should rest in peace. That kind of utter genderfuck does shade off into a wacky spirituality, like the Sisters of Perpetual Indulgence—those are the nuns I'd have wanted if I'd gone to Catholic school.

The trouble is that people insist on an either/or, binary system of perception. Most gay boys growing up in our world have to contend with those very loaded words—feminine and masculine—and the problems they create. It would be better to use words like yin and yang, active and passive, or rational and intuitive. But whatever language is used, I believe that many gay men are more in touch with the so-called feminine aspects of their psyche than most nongay men. One thing that's interesting to me about drag is that gay men do not generally dress up as housewives from Peoria. If you're going to do this, you tend to dress up as somebody larger than life.

Do you suppose this has something to do with gay men being labeled as "queens"?

It probably comes from the notion that we somehow have feminine identity. But we're not going to be just any old female; if you're going to live outside of normal social rules and regulations, you might as well upgrade. Aim high! This is part of turning yourself into an archetype. For a lot of people, the usual frame of reference is pop culture, so they pick Bette Davis. But I'm a historian, so I pick Elizabeth I. They have similar characteristics, you know: larger than life, imperious, and somewhat gender-ambiguous. Bette even played Elizabeth—she made a great drag queen.

How much does the world owe to its creative others, to the types of people that today we call gay or lesbian?

There are more of us in creative history than people used to be willing to admit, but I wouldn't necessarily want to claim that there are hugely disproportionate numbers of us across the board. In Western Euro-American culture of the last couple of centuries, we have carved out certain niches for ourselves in creative areas. But I'm not sure whether that's because more of us tend to be artistically creative or because artistic creativity is one of the safe places to dump people who are socially deviant. Society is willing to tolerate the exception as long as it's within the world of the artificial and the aesthetic, the amusing and the entertaining, because most people don't take those spheres very seriously. It's all right for us to dominate flower arranging and hairdressing because those are not centers of power.

That raises the question: Is there such a thing as a gay sensibility?

No, and I have one. By that I mean there's no *one* gay sensibility. There may be a number of qualities that preponderate in gay people. There certainly are a number of different avenues to gay identity or gay cultural cohesion in this society. And you might even be able to draw certain continuities between these and the past. Maybe bikers today are similar to the Theban Band, and the crossdressers are similar in some ways to the berdache in other cultures. But I'm not sure we should try to force them into something called a gay sensibility. There are many strands of sensibility. It doesn't especially interest me to try to trace the cross-dressing desire from ancient New Guinea to the Imperial Ball of New York and make it something continuous and connected. Those are different places, different times, and what it means now is quite different from what it meant in New Guinea. After all, a drag queen imitating Bette Davis has very little of a spiritual dimension as I would define it. Where a berdache, of course, is defined by his culture as a spiritual mediator.

Do you think queer folk have a certain social role and function to play in human life? Or do you prefer not to ascribe any meaning to our being here at all?

Human beings ascribe meaning to everything. So I'm sure we're going to keep trying to look for the meaning of being gay. What is the significance of the fact that we exist? The gay cosmic joke may be that we'll find out through scientific means that it's all a matter of random chance and which hormones got washed through the womb at which month of pregnancy. Maybe we'll find that we don't have a great evolutionary purpose; maybe our purpose is pure play. I would rather like the idea of a mythology in which gay people represent the play principle, in which our role is simply to be the agents of increasing spontaneity and aesthetics and fun. And you know, after all that's been said and done, that really wouldn't be so bad.

Ram Dass

A LIFE BEYOND LABELS

If eyes are the windows to one's soul, then Ram Dass's are shatterproof. At first, they are all you notice, suspended in space, lambent and unflinching, a world unto themselves, until slowly the surrounding features assemble. It's like watching a portrait by a sidewalk artist take shape: first the eyes, and then, in a few deft strokes, the rest of the face is drawn.

The face itself is generous and kind, inset with permanent lines of amusement. But it's the liquescent, penetrating gaze of the man that so clearly impresses, momentarily jolting me out of superficial pleasantry. We finish our handshake, and I renew my introduction. Ram Dass nods jovially. I try to feel reassured despite my nervousness.

It's this quality of being stripped so clean, so zero to the bone—a vast but potent emptiness that Ram Dass reveals with one effortless look—that leaves me unnerved. I've come to his front door armed with questions and theories, a lifetime of assumptions left intact. With uncanny ability, he absorbs my projections and hands them back to me. The interviewer, in the end, must answer to himself.

I've long considered Ram Dass a wise gay elder, a conferral that comes as a surprise not only to Ram Dass but to others as well. While the author, speaker, and spiritual activist has made no attempt to hide his homosexual past—it is discussed at random, usually in passing, among the pages of his seven books—the fact that he is gay is not commonly known. And while he counts among his followers many who are gay, he has left little imprint on the gay community itself.

"Gay sexual autobiography," he quietly muses to himself after we've settled down to talk. We're sitting in a high-ceilinged room that has one wall covered with shelves holding hundreds of tapes of his lectures. A bowl of figs and other fruit sits on a small table between us. He continues to reflect while fingering his mala beads; the raucous laughter of children in a nearby schoolyard fills the silence. It's almost as if he's flipping through the various tapes in his head containing past life experience. Finally, he looks up, smiling. "It's interesting," says Ram Dass. "I've never been interviewed about this topic, so this is fun for me."

I'm surprised to hear this but, of course, allow its truth. After all, much of Ram Dass's life for the past thirty years has been about unloading the weight of personal history, chucking away and burning in the bright, pure flame of spiri-

tual enlightenment all that is not needed. Sexual identity has undoubtedly been part of that consumed baggage. Judging from the spartan, business-like trappings of his home, Ram Dass seems to need or want very little these days other than the opportunity to perform compassionate service in the world.

When asked anything about his personal life, he casually mentions a longtime male relationship: "We've had a very close and dear friendship for fifteen years," he says. "We don't define it, and it's extremely satisfying to me as a fellow human being."

Ram Dass was born in 1931 as Richard Alpert, son of a wealthy and influential Jewish lawyer. A bright scholar, he studied psychology, eventually earning a Ph.D. from Stanford. From 1958 to 1963 he taught and did research at Harvard University. His study involved explorations of human consciousness, which eventually led Ram Dass to conduct pioneering research, in collaboration with Timothy Leary and others, with LSD and other mind-expanding agents. Amid a firestorm of public scandal, both professors were fired on account of their psychedelic investigations.

Ram Dass continued his research privately until 1967, when he traveled to India and met his spiritual teacher, Neem Karoli Baba. Under his guru's guidance he studied yoga and meditation, receiving the name Ram Dass, which means "servant of God." He returned to the United States the following year and quietly began to talk about his transformative experiences in locating the true self that exists beneath ego-driven personality. Candid in talking about his own previous dissatisfaction and lack of fulfillment, Ram Dass attracted a growing number of listeners. In 1971 he published Be Here Now, *a spiritual guidebook that has since gone on to sell over one million copies.*

Over the past two decades, Ram Dass has devoted himself to many causes working to bring about social change. His Hanuman Foundation has developed diverse projects, from helping the spiritual growth of prison inmates to providing support to the dying, including those with AIDS. His latest book, Compassion in Action, *recounts the evolution of his commitment to service and offers advice to others who would also like to alleviate suffering in the world.*

The human fate of suffering—on both the physical and spiritual planes—is the one universal condition that Ram Dass seems most apt to address. Suffering is "grist for the mill" (to borrow the title of his classic 1977 work), the propellant of conscious awakening if one only employs it as such. Sexual needs of whatever persuasion and material wants, such as fame and fortune, are fueled by the personality-possessed "me" part of our minds. Desire creates suffering and keeps our innermost selves from finding life's ultimate fulfillment: the state of being at one with God. Given this quintessential Eastern view of life, I can understand Ram Dass's objections to labeling people based on their sexual predilections. Gay or straight—what's the difference if we are meant to transcend attachment?

Still, as appealing as this philosophy may sound, we live in a Western world deeply entrenched in its prejudices and roles, a you-are-what-you-own attitude. Modern gay identity has been spun out of those elements, but some of us cling to the belief that there remains an inexplicable mystery about our being that exists far beneath the constructed surfaces. According to Ram Dass, the answer lies in examining the clinging itself.

To rigid Westerners, Ram Dass may seem like an anomaly living a contradiction. But after a few hours in his presence there's no doubt that here is an individual who acts and speaks from the integrity of an awakened soul. The eyes alone communicate that. Yet to be fully human is also to be imperfect and seeking. Appropriately enough, at the end of our afternoon together comes Ram Dass's startling admission that, concerning homosexuality, there is inner work left for him to do.

Later, while driving toward San Francisco, I think about what Ram Dass has to say regarding the artifice and unnecessary containment of labels. That evening, while strolling through the city's gay ghetto, I study the faces of the gay men and lesbians passing by. It's Friday night in the Castro district, time to have fun and be oneself. Here, among the crowded streets of this newest of old neighborhoods, I wonder what essential elements of the human soul are being allowed to breathe free and what parts are being stifled. The last words of our conversation ring in my mind.

"It's been nice being with you," he says, as I begin to depart. "I really respect where you're coming from, what you're trying to do."

Being HIV-positive, I allow, means doing a bit more of my work while I still can. "I don't assume a thing," I shrug. "I may live to a ripe old age, but who knows?"

"You may give 'em light before you die," he quickly replies.

"Yeah, I may give 'em light before I die," I say, taking my first steps down the stairs.

"So you will have died before you die, and then it won't matter any-way," Ram Dass concludes.

I'm almost gone before his final words reach me: "Take care, dear."

°

In Compassion in Action *you freely relate past homosexual experiences, something you have not often done. Have you been uncomfortable in talking about being gay? When did you first know?*

I had a late latency, and not until I was fifteen years old did I start to really become sexually awakened. Up until then I hadn't differentiated, I had no labels; I was just so floored by sex. By the time I was seventeen I started to have relations with boys and realized I enjoyed that. But it was still within the category of teenage folly. You see, I grew up at a time when homosexuality was far deeper in the closet than it is now.

I became engaged to be married when I was in college in Boston, but then I started to go out cruising. I'd pick up people or get into sexual encounters with men in parks and bathrooms. So I was confused. Later, when I moved to California to do postgraduate work at Stanford, I started to get more involved in gay life in San Francisco. I've only roughly estimated, sometimes to just blow people's minds, but I'm sure I've had thousands of sexual encounters. It was often two a night. Then I returned east as a professor at Harvard and continued to have this incredible sexual activity. But I always had a woman as a front to go to faculty dinners and things like that.

As many did, and continue to do, you were leading a double life.

My life was completely duplicitous for thirty years. I had an apartment and would have guys in overnight, but I didn't live with anybody and didn't make any real liaisons. I gained a reputation at the health service for how sensitive I was to people with gay problems. The psychiatrists kept referring all the homosexual cases to me, but they had no conception of who I really was. This was 1958 until 1963, the year I got thrown out of Harvard.

That's a famous incident. What really happened?

Tim Leary and I and a lot of friends had one of these big community houses. We got into a situation where Harvard started to get so freaked about the drugs we were using that they asked us to stop doing our research using any undergraduates. We could use graduate students, or outside populace, but we couldn't use undergraduates because it was too risky. But I had all these relationships with young men whom I really wanted to turn on with. And it had nothing to do with our research; it was my personal life, so I went ahead. It turned out there was another student who was very jealous of this, an editor of the campus newspaper, and he created a huge exposé.

So it was gay eros and not LSD that got you thrown out of Harvard.

It was a combination of all those things. In a way, LSD had given me the license to be what I am. It looked at me inside and out and said what you are is okay. And that gave me a license to start to say I didn't want to hide anymore. The American Association of University Professors wanted to defend me, but I realized that that would just be such a mess—the hell with it! I wasn't interested in going back to Harvard anyway; I was too far on the drugs. I wanted to go on that trip much, much more.

Most gay men, particularly of that time, have had to deal with over-whelming emotions of guilt and shame. How did you cope with your feelings of internalized homophobia?

The guilt was toward all sex in life. There was no differentiation because nobody even thought about homosexuality in my upbringing. So after that, I didn't feel called upon to define myself in any way at all. I mean, why define myself? I can fill many roles in life. So I didn't join "being gay," I didn't become a clubbie within the gay community—I just wasn't drawn to it. Instead, I became very involved in consciousness and spiritual work.

There was a moment when there were four of us making this pilgrimage around southern India in a Volkswagen microbus. One of the fellows in the car was an extremely attractive young man, and one night he and I ended up having a sexual affair together. The next day we sat down in front of my guru, whom I knew knew everything even though I had never discussed this kind of thing with him. He looked at me and he looked at this guy, and then he said to me, "You're giving him your best teaching." I thought, Okay, if you say so. I'll buy that. But then he said we shouldn't have any more sex—and we didn't.

There was a long period when I really saw my homosexuality as deeply pathological. I was growing up in the zeitgeist of Western psychology. I had been trained as a Freudian therapist in the analytical institute, and that's the way it looked. Men and women were made to go together, and everything else seemed like something had gotten fucked up somewhere along the way.

I saw my mother as a prime contender of that because she had taken my power. She was such a deep love for me. The reason my puberty was so late was because I kept trying to stay a child to stay in intimate relationship with her. It was clear that if I became a man, she'd reject me. And so I got fatter and fatter, eating everything she gave me as my form of intimacy with her. At one point, in prep school, where I was horny all the time, I hugged her and got an erection. She pushed me away and said there's milk and cookies downstairs.

This is a more common dynamic between gay men and their moms than would be supposed.

Oh, I understand! So I ended up having a hard time in my relations with women, in getting my own pleasure. The women that I ended up having sex with were women who were quite aggressive, who really demanded it of me. I mean, they were just scratchers and yellers. I got to the point where I would take huge amounts of acid and look at these slide pictures of women to try to see where my fear was because I saw that there was a block where I just turned off women.

As you were growing up, what was your relationship with your father like?

I was sort of an appreciator of him. He was a very successful and up-wardly mobile person, so he didn't have too much time for the family. He was a somewhat remote figure. When he was around we did a lot of things together, but I never felt he heard me.

In Compassion in Action *you state: "As the result of being a Jew, I felt that I had been imbued with three things: first, the sense that behind and within the multiplicity of forms there is One, seamless*

and radiant, and that loving that One, with all my being, is a path.
Second, a love and respect for knowledge as a path to wisdom. And
the third great gift I felt I had received was an awareness of suffer-
ing and the compassion that arises with that awareness." I'd like to
know how being gay has also shaped your spiritual journey. What
gifts have been endowed to you from that?

As a result of being caught with another fellow in prep school, I was completely ostracized—nobody would speak to me for about a year. I'd walk into a room and all the kids would stop speaking. I couldn't tell my parents, so it cast me way back inside myself; it drove me inward.

That deepened, first of all, the quality of my compassion toward other human beings who are ostracized. But I also think it served me in good stead later on when I started experimenting with psychedelics. I have always felt like I was an outsider.

The added burden was that I had small genitals, and in this society that is a major crime. I was ostracized a lot for that, too. I was laughed at, and I'm sure it affected my behavior a great deal because it was the double whammy of not only being gay but having this feeling of deficiency. But after I had done a lot of deep work with psychedelics, genital sexuality wasn't a dominant issue. The areas of my gratification had shifted. It didn't matter to me that much.

Maybe being gay has less do to with how you have sex, or even if
you have sex at all, but rather with something else.

I don't know which way you want to put the essence of the label. I mean, there's probably a differential use of the brain, a differential tenderness in gay men. In my own life, I feel very much more like the mother of a system than like a father. I feel very matronly in my embrace of pain into myself. At times during drug experiences I've turned into a very large black woman with huge breasts just reaching out and almost vomiting in the midst of drawing a world of suffer-ing into myself. So that's deep—primordially, mythically, archetypically—in me. But how do I start to label what is a gay quality and what is not?

I have very close relationships with a lot of men who are truly heterosex-ual. I find the same deep reservoir of psychic qualities in them—this tenderness, softness, and compassion. These are things I look for in people whether they're gay or straight.

Perhaps within the kinds of people we today label gay there is a particular matrix of archetypal forces at work. Some of the archetypes that seem prevalent in the gay male psyche are the Trickster, the Wounded Healer, and the Double, which is the archetype of the sames. These influences vary in our lives, of course, depending upon our personal history, who our parents are, our cultural upbringing, and so forth. Does this ring a bell with you? Certainly I see some of those archetypes quite dominant in your personality.

When I am responding to you, I'm attempting to place gayness in the same central position that you place it in, which is quite alien to the way I think. You see, I don't regard being gay as a central, defining charactistic even though I could build a case either for the psychogenic or somatogenic or reincarnational point of view. There's space for all of those interpretations. It's all the speculation of the mind, it seems to me, as to which way you want to place being gay in terms of causality. Everything can be an effect of a cause because we're beginning to realize the way the mind and the body are just one thing. I can certainly put all the pieces together under your theory, but I can't feel a predilection for that theory over any other at this moment.

Rather than discuss ideas and theories let's talk about something that is very real in the lives of gay men—the issue of being wounded. I have talked with hundreds of gay men over the years, and not one has escaped being ostracized, or being called a "sissy" or a "faggot," or having some other kind of deeply wounding experience.

I would say that's true. But being "wounded" refers to the personality—not to the soul. I'd say I've been deeply wounded in my personality. Absolutely, deeply wounded. And I don't think I've ever gotten over it. I still feel wounded by it. I still feel unwelcome in this culture. Because I live among so many straight populations, I've started to talk more about being bisexual, being involved with men as well as women. Most of the audiences with whom I do that are people who already love me so much they couldn't care if I turned into a frog. Allen Ginsberg, who's an old friend, goes and confronts people with his gayness. I don't see any reason to do that—it's not my trip. I never deny it, but I don't push it because it's not part of my active identity.

You've been more open in recent years. Why the candor now?

I trust myself more. Before, the candor would have been a bid to try to seduce people, to get young men to come near me. Like as an initiation or something like that—come up and see my holy pictures! I don't think I trusted myself because I think my desires were so strong.

Do you still have strong desires for young men?

I delight in the beauty of the male body, of youth and all. But I don't have any craving to do anything about it.

You've written that within you there still lay some remnants of the little boy who desires to be good, who needs to achieve and accomplish, and that these desires may stem from a sense of inadequacy.

My whole personality is built on a root of inadequacy, which I don't think is unique to me, by the way. I think most personality is built on that, actually.

But what can happen, and often does happen, in the lives of everyone is almost certain to happen in the lives of gay men. The fate of being the best little boy in the world, the boy who has been psychically wounded and left with a deeply compromised self image, is all too common to us.

If I want to venture a psychogenic description of my gayness, I would say that it's about the absence of my relation to my father and the love affair I had with my mother, which I was never willing to give up. If anything, gay people are to me better lovers because they took their first love and wouldn't let go, which was the love of the mother. Because I'm a Freudian, that would be a way I would interpret it. I experienced that I didn't want to let go of the nurturance and intimacy I had with her. But I didn't experience the wounding in my childhood; the wounding came later in my adolescence.

How do we use the wound for our own awakening?

Well, the question is: Who's used by it and who can use it? I would say that for many years I was used by it, and then I started to shift my consciousness and started to use it. Anybody who is awake to the human predicament of being lost in separateness starts to yearn for the truth that they are not separate, since then they are back home—they are in harmony with things rather than always being alienated and outside. Once that awakening occurs, then it's a set of inevitable steps before you get to the point where you see your incarnation as a curriculum. You see that the ways in which you're suffering are good things to work on in yourself. In other words, you begin to understand that suffering is grace.

That's a major shift. Suffering stinks, and then suffering becomes grace. It still stinks, but it's grace. You'd rather not suffer, unless you're a masochist, but if you do suffer, you work with it and experience what it's showing you, which from the Buddha's point of view is where your mind is clinging. Because you always suffer where there is clinging.

If I have a model that society should act a certain way toward me and they don't, I suffer. If I don't have that model, I don't suffer—they act the way they do, and I'm responding like a tree on a river. The tree doesn't have a model for how the river should be. So I really hear the second noble truth of the Buddha: the cause of unsatisfactory conditions is the way the mind clings.

Suffering is a clue that there is clinging in the mind. It gives you a place to look to begin extricating yourself from identification with the thought that is creating the suffering. If you can draw your awareness back so that you're not identified with thought—so you enjoy thought but you're not busy being caught in the thoughts—then there will be no more suffering.

Is there a thought about death? I mean, until the last moment it's just another moment. The anticipation of death, the fear of loss of life, and the attractions and aversions of all that cause you to suffer. The phenomena themselves are just phenomena.

Like many gay men, I've been caught up in thinking about death a lot these days because of AIDS. But that aside, it seems to me there's still an enormous amount of suffering around being gay in such an intensely homophobic culture.

I think there is, too. But for gay men, the work is to work on their own minds. They may be doing social protest, or be part of the Radical Faeries, or whatever, but let them do it from a place where they understand that it's all work on themselves. Because as long as their minds are the way they are, they're going to keep suffering. Ostracism and the judgment of the culture feed on very deep inadequacies in the individual that they're still clinging to in the mind, and these judgments play upon them. They resonate with those thoughts that are not quite excoriated, extirpated, expiated.

Do you think gay men have a special role to play in society today, a role that would encompass special aptitudes for compassion, empathy, and insight? And, if you do, then what is your advice for actualizing that potential in the world?

When you read the obituaries you become aware that an extraordinarily disproportionate amount of beauty brought into the culture was created by gay people. But how to interpret that? I would be hard-pressed to say that those qualities aren't available in everybody, but the cultural roles everybody found themselves in made it easier for gay men to express themselves in this way. It's like, the Jews became moneylenders because they weren't allowed to do anything else. People who have identified either androgynously or in a way not as male in the cultural sense of maleness have accessible to them qualities of creativity and sensitivity and appreciation that they would be well to capitalize upon and use.

You've got to stand back far enough to see the stages of transformation in a culture. If you watch the women's movement, for instance, you see it go through many stages: from a kind of militant, male identification in which women want what the man has, to then finding themselves having lost something that they wanted because they were so busy getting something else, until finally you start to see women who are not imitating outward strength but are really developing inner strength as beings. At that point, they're more willing to accept differences and celebrate them rather than to deny them.

What is your view of the gay movement? It's made great social and political strides in the last forty years, but from your vantage point what's still left to be done?

It's at an early stage of its maturing process—a revolutionary, militant, us-against-them, exhibitionistic kind of flamboyance. There's a harsh quality to the gay movement that underestimates what the human spirit is about. I just think the game is more interesting than that. One of the things that human beings want is to feel at home, to be able to be who they are, to feel safe in the universe.

But any identification with any institution, any identity at all, is a limiting condition. Even when you've got everybody respecting you for it, it's a trap because you're stuck in a definition. And what we are is not defined—we are much more than any definition.

Defining yourself as gay is just like defining yourself as an American, or a Jew, or whatever. You may play within a subgroup, but you'll never feel fulfillment as long as you define yourself that way. Your fulfillment in the universe is on many, many levels. What is group membership about anyway? It's usually a way of having power, which means that one feels powerless in the face of other powers, so one bands together.

That's why there's a gay movement, so that individuals who were beaten up or shut out, just like you were, can have a safe harbor, a place to mend, to take stock, and hopefully to go on.

I want to be really careful in what I say; I don't want to be glib about it. Yes, I also think gay people come together in order to breathe together through the pain and the wounding. They come together to feel comfortable, safe, and playful among people of like mind. However, I'm not convinced that the gay community comes together to grow. I don't think that model, or that metaphor, is a dominant theme. Instead, it's more like, "We are what we are and we're proud of it." That's fine, but I just don't want to join any clubs. I'm a universalist.

I would agree with you that in certain respects the gay community is in a stuck place. Do you have any wisdom and advice for taking the next steps?

First of all, we can't have this discussion without bringing up AIDS. It has changed the nature of the gay community in some very profound ways. Yet, in some ways, it hasn't. The question of what does the gay community do now has to take into account that issue.

One of the most profound metaphysical issues of life is the relation of sex and death. And HIV has brought that right to the forefront, although it is interpreted by different segments of the gay population in different ways. For the younger, more immature group it's like surfing in water where the waves are a little too high—they're playing with death through sex. A lot of young people are becoming HIV-positive out of a cynical, "I don't give a damn" attitude. They're playing with the edge without really understanding what they're playing with. Death isn't real to a teenager.

A lot of the gay people I work with today have AIDS symptoms. There's a percentage of them who stay deep in their anger, self-pity, and feeling put-upon by God. And then there is a segment of more mature gay men who have gotten lighter and clearer and will say, "Boy, I'd rather be here than in all the shit I was in when I was so busy being this sexual operator." They've seen the superficiality of a lot of their past relationships and so are now seeking for deeper truth in the way they connect with other human beings. That's the beautiful side of it, that's where the really exciting part comes. We're meeting each other in a whole different way. Compassion is a much more dominant theme, and I had never found the gay community particularly compassionate before. Part of it was that I was trick-or-treating all those years. I mean, I was in the hard part of sex, too. I wasn't having partnerships and long-term relationships. I didn't want them, I didn't feel comfortable.

That said, I'm very impressed with the way the gay community has kept pressure on the culture to bring its prejudices to the surface. There's a rhythm of change in a culture where you push, then you pull back a little bit and they adjust, and then you come forward again. You never stop the pressure, but you don't keep escalating it because then you force a confrontation. What happened in the sixties was that we forced confrontation, assuming the other side would fall before us. When you have that, nobody wins. That's an immature stage of a revolution. So I would encourage the gay community to keep the pressure up but to do it with wisdom. See it as a long-term game. Give society a chance to come along rather than demanding they come along, since the price of demanding is going to cost the gay community in the long run.

Finally, I would say that sex and social relationship is not enough—that eventually you will be driven into spiritual awakening. I figure my game is the only game in town. It's inevitable.

There are many spiritual seekers to be found within the gay community, of course.

Oh, many. The predicament is that the deeper your spiritual practice, the more you are aware that everybody is androgynous. That's why when you say "gay soul" there's something in me that grabs, since I don't think of souls as either male or female. I think souls have karma that determines the way they manifest, gay or straight, female or male. But I don't think souls themselves have any sexual identity at all.

I agree that AIDS has opened a lot of hearts and minds. Still, gay men have built a culture based largely on desire—the commercialization of sex and physical attractiveness. The gay sensibility is very Dionysian. So how do we learn to strike a new balance? Is pursuit of sexual fulfillment really antithetical to spiritual enlightenment? Can both exist harmoniously?

There's a sequence: You grow up very invested in the physical and the psychological. Then you feel the finiteness of those things. And then you awaken through some process only to realize you've been trapped. After that, there's a tendency to go into a kind of renunciative fervor to get into the place where you feel at one with the universe and spirit. That often creates what are called horny celibates—it's a certain kind of rejection of the physical/psychological plane.

But in a still later stage you realize that the aversion is keeping you from being free—and you want to be free, not just high. So you start to come back into who you are, passionate and nonattached. You are fully in life, joyfully participating—sex is a celebration. It's all wonderful, and at the same moment, it's all empty. That's a very evolved stage of spiritual maturation.

I don't find the gay community as a group very spiritually ripe or eager to go beyond. I think they're too caught up enjoying the power and the desire systems. In some ways it feels like a certain kind of hell realm to me because it's not going to be enough.

How do we move out of that? How can being gay be used as "grist for the mill" of inner development?

Only when you have gone through your rebellion against the culture for cutting you out of the juice, then getting the juice, having what you want, and seeing that that is just another state. Once you get a partner, a bed without hiding, and freedom to walk down the street holding hands, then what are you going to do? But you can't shortcut the process. If somebody wants a Cadillac, you can't say, "Don't have it," because they'll be busy not having the Cadillac, and they're not gonna get free. They'll be somebody without a Cadillac.

*One of the deepest issues plaguing gay men is inner-directed hate.
People can go out and march in gay pride parades all they want,
but that still doesn't mean they've dealt with low self-esteem or
their own internalized homophobia.*

There are corrupting psychological correlates to being gay in our society—I'm not necessarily saying of being gay, but of being gay in our society. There's tremendous frustration, self-hatred, and fear that's rooted in power issues—a good coating of masochism. Those things color the way a movement proceeds. You can make those things into icons to be worshiped. I mean, there's a lot of masochism expressed in the gay community. There are clubs for it.

What do you think about all of that? Does it bother you?

I like Genet's writings. You know, I've spent so much time in seedy places with that stink of decadent lust. It's so thick, it's like being in another realm. But I don't feel anything about it. I go to something like a Hollywood opening with all my Hollywood friends, and it stinks the same way! It's a slightly different odor, but I don't see that it's a hell of a lot better. I mean, if somebody gets fisted in a club, is that different from somebody getting an Oscar? I'm sorry, I'm supposed to be morally dignified, but I'm not, you know. It's not my way.

*Many people have tried to ascribe a moral meaning to AIDS. How
do you see this devastating crisis?*

What's happened is that AIDS has cast everybody into the advanced course of dealing with death, loss, and grief—emotions that the gay community was not long on. Dealing with suffering well was not their long suit. They bitched and moaned and got caught in the drama of it, but they didn't really let it in. And it demanded it get in, this time. So AIDS is forcing the gay community to confront their deepest spiritual being. From a spiritual point of view, AIDS is an incredible grace.

*You have said, "Trust that the universe is unfolding exactly as it
should." But that's a tough lesson, particularly if you're in a shit-
stained bed in an AIDS ward somewhere. How do you help people
in that situation see what you mean?*

Most people try to get ready-made answers through fundamentalism, or through rationalism or humanism, and those answers are never good enough.

The people with AIDS I work with are at the edge of the human condition; AIDS has cast them into the mystery. Whatever I do or say to them is coming out of a balance in me, a balance of realizing suffering stinks and it's grace. I'm watching with awe the way the universe is working. It's just so incredibly, mysteriously beautiful—the suffering, fear, and all of it. They hear me as an empathetic person who feels their pain. And then as they feel safe enough they relax, and we start to meet in this other place, which is in ecstasy and bliss and equanimity and delight in the play of the universe, including what they're going through.

Tell me a little bit about the Living Dying Project.

As a result of all the drugs I took and the experiences I had in the East, it became clear to me that I had a different attitude toward death than most of the people around me. Death seemed perfectly fine to me, like a natural process. And as with myself, I realized that for all humans the deepest fear is death, and somehow I wanted to keep working with that edge of my being. So I found it very advisable spiritually to hang around dying people because my lack of anxiety created a space for them to get beyond their own anxiety. At the same moment, my being with them helped me deal with the issues I had about fear of pain and the suffering of death. The real healing is the inner healing when we learn that we are on this other journey, and dying is just part of it.

I began to see that some of the people who were dying were busy trying to live and others were using that whole process as a vehicle for awakening. So then I thought, If there are people like me who want to take care of dying people in order to awaken, and there are people who are dying who want to awaken, why don't we put them all together? We'll have ashrams where some people are helping others and some are dying, but basically everybody's there to awaken.

What do you mean exactly when you use the word awaken?

There are many planes of awareness, many levels of consciousness. William James really expressed it the best. He said, "Our normal waking consciousness is but one type of consciousness, while all about it, parted from it by the filmiest of screens, there lie other types of consciousness and we spend our entire lives not knowing of their existence. But apply the requisite stimulus and there they are in their completeness. . . . Whatever their meaning, they forbid our premature closing of our accounts with reality."

So I would say that awakening is the recognition that there are many planes of consciousness and that you exist on all of them. You are limiting yourself incredibly to define yourself only in terms of the physical/psychological planes, as if they were absolutely real. So it's an awakening into the relative reality of the world you thought was absolutely real. It's awakening to realize that you're in a prison you've created by your own thoughts—that your conceptual definitions of reality are imprisoning you from what reality is, which is something that has no concept. You've reduced yourself into a shadow of who you are, in a reductionistic way, through clinging to concepts, instead of understanding that the true nature of being is not knowing you know, it's simply being.

We got trapped in separateness. When we awaken we realize there's a spiritual dimension to life, that there is a wisdom that lies within the mystery that surrounds life. The answer is that there is something else going on, and realizing this is awakening.

So, if we let go of the certainty of being gay . . .

It doesn't make you any less gay. The art form is to enjoy being gay without being trapped by it.

In your own life, what fears and areas of resistance are you particularly aware of right now?

Gee, that's tricky. There are some bizarre ones, like trying to be at peace with the emptiness of it all. I would say trying to continually let go of models about existence into the richness of the moment. I still cling to somebody doing something, going somewhere. But I don't cling very much to it. I can see this correlated with gayness at some level. I have a tremendous perfectionistic streak in me about myself. And because I don't live up to it, I have a tremendous judgment of others as being not perfect enough. I find that a very unappealing quality, and I have to work with it. I'm horrified by my imperfections because I so want to be free. But I think that's a cop-out. I'm very fierce, at times, and the fierceness isn't coming necessarily out of love; it's coming out of judgment, out of my own pain.

How does your perfectionism correlate with your being gay?

That perfectionistic quality is very deep in many gay people I know. I think it comes from unworthiness and inadequacy, a sense of wanting to be perfect so that you can be loved enough. If I do something perfectly, I can love my-self. I get the gold star. And that's hard when you're a human: you just can't do things perfectly enough.

You know, this conversation has brought to the surface in me a lot of uncooked stuff that I haven't fully integrated into my being—things I've just put into little compartments in my head.

Like what, for instance?

Different stages of life, different attitudes toward the gay community. Talking about these issues with someone who has given them as much thought as you gives me something to work on. I mean, what have I got to learn here? What have I got to learn about my own prejudices? I just took a course last year on hidden racism from a Latino man who was showing me my own oppression, my own subtle racism. I'm probably imprinted so deeply from my generation that I don't know if I will ever get out of thinking that gayness is a pathology. Even though I'm delighted that other people don't, and I would like not to, it's so deep in me.

I experience being gay as a wonderful blessing, an opportunity—anything but a pathology. But I've come of age during a different time than you. I'm making my assumptions with a different set of cultural references in hand. People who have defined themselves as gay are at a point in their collective journey where they don't need to throw the definition away, but rather keep evolving it.

I would say that if gay people who read this are willing to really sit down and examine their own minds in a systematic way, they may experience the freedom to take more delight in life and in their gay expression of it. And they will see that who they are isn't gay, and it's not not-gay, and it's not anything—it's just awareness.

I really challenge them to make that exploration on their own before they write the script of their lives in stone too much. Because if they have picked up a book that's called *Gay Soul,* they're asking for it. And if they're asking for it, they should be able to get it. Somebody should say, "Look, don't get trapped in that. Get on with it." There's no need to label yourself at all.

JOSEPH KRAMER

BODY AND SOUL

The room is redolent of sweat and massage oil. On my left, a nude man lies weeping, his body quivering in almost uncontrollable sobs. The man on my right laughs with equal abandon, one spasm of giggles following another as if the joke is too much, or just too private, to share. I feel curiously calm, letting the neighboring waves of emotion crash and ebb against the tiny island of foam cushion and warm sheet that I occupy, nearly oblivious to any sensation but the great cloud of tranquility that has descended on my being.

Around me lay about twenty-five other men of all ages and descriptions. We have just completed the "big draw," an exercise involving sustained rhythmic breathing and the release of tightened muscles, which results in an emotional catharsis. The effects of such measured breathing, clenching, and letting go vary in each individual. And so, here we are, each of us experiencing our own private epiphany in the same room; the energy of profound release is palpable, as if some strangely scented breeze has suddenly refreshed the chamber.

In the center of this cacophonous whorl of naked feeling and flesh stands Joseph Kramer, an articulate, energetic man of stocky build, who has led the group to this moment. It is the climax of a two-day workshop designed to recharge the "body electric," to recover it from the stultifying effects of modern life. Combining his own lively brand of wisdom with tantric ritual, deep-breathing technique, and genital massage, Kramer has gone around the world teaching men—mostly gay—how to love themselves and each other more completely.

Born in St. Louis, Missouri, in 1947, Kramer was raised in a middle-class family of Irish-Catholic heritage. Bright and capable, he seemed indistinguishable from the other boys of his neighborhood. But even at an early age, Joseph knew that he was somehow different—that what he felt about his body and the bodies of other males around him was not deemed socially acceptable. Like many, he learned to cover up and sublimate his desires. Years of education in a Jesuit high school were followed by seminary. It was the best kind of training for a life of the mind and, surprisingly enough, in the ways of same-sex love. Joseph came out in the arms of a fellow Jesuit and has been singing the love of dear comrades ever since.

Kramer left his life as a Jesuit scholastic in 1975 and set off for New York City. There he lost no time in exploring the hedonistic pleasures of gay life in the fast lane. It was one way of bringing body and soul into closer union, although few then were attributing spiritual gain to sexual excess. The bountiful, sometimes harsh, lessons of the period were not wasted on Kramer, however, who eventually moved on to the West Coast where he completed a master's degree in sexuality and spirituality from the Graduate Theological Union in Berkeley.

Professing the view that "conventional Western sex is necrophilia," Kramer entreats us to become fully alive: to wake up our bodies by any means available and to rid our minds of the shame and meaningless fantasies that keep us from fully experiencing intimacy with ourselves and one another. His byword is ecstasy, the type of all-barriers-down, full-throttle inhabitation of the body that most people experience rarely if at all. Kramer feels that gay men have a particular role to play in educating others about such healthy eroticism. But it's a function, he cautions, that can be realized only when gay men themselves learn to overcome the inner shadows that he, as a rigorously trained Catholic, perhaps understands better than most.

Now, after nearly a decade of leading gay men into a more integrated vision of who they can be through his Body Electric School workshops and teachings, Kramer is once again departing into untried territory. He recently passed ownership of the school into new hands and started EroSpirit, a research institute producing gay video and audio educational materials about erotic spirituality.

We begin our conversation one January afternoon in his home in Oakland, California, and conclude it a year later in Los Angeles, the day after a major earthquake has rocked the city. The ground continues to heave as we speak, the violent aftershocks a reminder of the living, dynamic body beneath our feet. Despite the unnerving temblors, Kramer exudes a dauntless enthusiasm about the ways in which we can bridge the divide between our bodies, our souls.

o

How old were you when you began to recognize that something was different about you?

I remember taking afternoon naps when I was three years old and loving to put my hands down in my underwear, cupping my tiny genitals and rubbing. One day, my mother was tucking me in and she said, "You shouldn't be doing that. God doesn't like when you touch yourself." And I knew from that moment I had a problem.

I always dreamed or had fantasies looking at the Sears and J. C. Penny's catalogs. I didn't look at the little girls' underwear ads; I looked at the boys' underwear ads. I knew no one around me who had this interest. No one.

How did you survive your high school years?

High school years were the blossoming. I'd just reached puberty, and it was like that moment in *The Wizard of Oz* when the picture goes from black and white to color. I went to an all-boys Jesuit school, and that's where I recognized the importance of homosexual sensibility. Certainly the vast majority of Jesuits are homosexual. Many of them who taught me were in their twenties, and so it was in this ideal environment that I was educated in my emotions, in my way of interacting with men. I didn't have to fear being close to other boys at all. For a Catholic institution, that was really extraordinary. I loved my high school years so much I didn't want them to end. So I decided to be a Jesuit.

I went into the novitiate in rural Missouri. It was a place of silence—we got to speak one hour a day. When you spoke other times you were supposed to speak in Latin, so it kept communication to a minimum. I was with fifteen other men, most of us seventeen to twenty years old. And now I know that twelve of the fifteen were homosexual. We were gay but didn't know it at the time. So here were gay boys coming together to live and be educated by older homosexuals, men who were there for our best good. This was the best I could have found, unless the Radical Faeries had snatched me away.

When did you have your first sexual encounter with another man?

I was probably eighteen. There was an older brother in the seminary to whom I just opened my heart, and he kind of took me under his wing. Eventually that flowered into a night of wrestling and play, eroticism and ejaculations. I've known him ever since then; he's a wonderful man. At least half of the students who were there had sexual encounters with one another. But none of this was compulsive; it was the expression of a deep connection—spiritual, emotional, and physical. We were so close in so many ways that it seemed right for our bodies to touch and to sear. We were the Body of Christ.

How has your training as a Jesuit informed the work you're doing today?

Many of my Jesuit teachers, without acknowledging it, were wizards. They understood the transformative power of intentional community. I was guided in the ways of the weaver. I was taught to bring people together in an environment where everyone was invited to unleash their full potential. This process generated massive amounts of creative energy. The Jesuits taught me the skill of containing this energy, then circulating and directing it. This is a foundational skill that I use in all my erotic-spiritual work. Human synergy is one cauldron where evolution occurs.

In the Jesuits I learned about the heart-head connection. There are a lot of big-hearted men in the Jesuits and some extraordinary brains. But the Jesuit energy is largely disconnected from cock. And even when it is connected with cock, cock is never acknowledged.

The great gift of Jesuit education is that Jesuits teach you how to think. In doing that, they surrender forever the power to tell you what to think. So they set you free. The Jesuits educated me and Fidel Castro, Alfred Hitchcock and Voltaire, Jerry Brown and Pat Buchanan. Jesuits want you to think for yourself.

You're known around the world for helping gay men get in touch with their full erotic selves, to express their gay nature in healthy, positive ways. Yet the seed of your belief and energy for doing this has come out of the heart of the Roman Catholic church, which of course, is one of the foremost enemies of gay people. There's a real irony here.

Many of the gay leaders of this country have been educated by the Jesuits. And the education they received took them beyond the container called the Catholic church. It's a way the homosexual community has been gifted by the Catholic church.

The hierarchical-political level of the Catholic church—what I call the Imperial church—is very oppressive of gay people. But the community-based levels of the church—where real men and women live, work, and pray—can be incredibly nurturing of gay people.

You eventually left the order to go live in New York, where you became very involved with the sexual mystique of the city's docks, gay bars, and backrooms. Was your search born out of compulsive need, loneliness, or was it a kind of an existential quest?

I didn't find it a lonely or compulsive acting out in the least—it was a quest. I felt I was stepping into my tribe. I wanted to make as many connections as possible, to celebrate those connections, to fully breathe with the men I was interacting with, to look in their eyes, and to laugh. I had sex with strangers, I had sex with friends, and at the same time I was involved in the most significant love relationship of my life. I was looking at myself in all these men as if they were a mirror. It was very pleasurable but also profound. At age twenty-eight, I was waking up my body. It seemed the whole culture was dancing and waking up. There were core themes reflected in the disco tunes of the time: "I Need A Man," "I Will Survive," "I Feel Love." Those were the mantras of that era.

> *You are describing very positive experiences from that period, but that was not universally the case. A lack of self-love has deeply affected many gay men and their relationships with others. How do we best purge homophobia from inside ourselves?*

What I recognize in myself is layer upon layer of homophobia. During the initial stages of coming out in New York, a certain layer was peeled away and healed. That was relatively easy with the help of lovers, friends, therapists, and all kinds of body work. Then after a while I got to the layer of Catholic-induced homophobia. And then I got to some deeper levels, maybe culturally induced levels of homophobia. Right now I'm looking for guides who've gone beyond where I am in ridding themselves of the homophobia that I still feel deep within me.

> *What form do these traces of homophobia within you take?*

I find that the degree of intensity of my emotions has a limit. High levels of feeling activate an uneasiness, even a paranoia, that I attribute to homophobia.

> *Most people would say homophobia is an unconscious attitude, a product of society's negative programming, and that with enough therapy it can be brought to the surface and let go.*

Most psychotherapy is dead. It is a mode of healing that fragments the human person. We are energetic beings, and so I believe my wisdom is within my body. My experience is that there are different gateways into being. The major gateway that I've gone through is the physical. Some people are visually or audially oriented—I'm kinesthetic. That's probably why I became a masseur and deal with breath work and sex; my body is my way of sensing the world. I think there are some places in the body itself, maybe deep in the spleen, where homophobia resides. The Taoists say that emotions reside in specific locations in the body.

Can you define your practice in more detail?

Internalized homophobia is fear of our own power and authentic selves. To be in that power changes the way you live your life. My teaching to men is that they can access their power in the present moment through breath work and erotic massage.

Do you view what you do as a shamanic practice?

The image I like to use for myself is that of a body-based sex magician. I feel the movement of erotic energy within my body and around my body and even in groups of people. I'm interested in how to intentionally focus that energy for transformation and healing. Many shamans are and were sex magicians— they have an understanding of the uses of sexual energy.

Some would say that the shamanic path is a traditional gay role.

Being an outsider, I had a double vision: I had my own vision, and I learned the vision of the larger culture. My spirituality developed out of the conflict between the two. I do see myself as a bridge, as somebody who wanders between peoples, who translates between cultures, who guides others in integrating sex and spirit.

I like the idea that gay men have some cultural role separate from the raising of children. Perhaps it's the weaving together of people to spark evolution. It's a tremendously generous act to have a child and to follow through and raise that child. But I think there's equal generosity in following the shaman's path or the weaver's path. A shaman-weaver connects disparate parts of an individual into a whole; other members of the weaver clan weave individuals into community. When I'm doing massage I feel I am doing shamanic weaving. And when I lead groups my intention is to weave a community where everyone can experience wholeness. Most of the shaman-weavers I know are gay.

The magician is an archetype . . .

The transformer. And here's how I've done it. What I learned in the Jesuits was to listen for the request from the outside world. What are people asking for? What is this individual asking for? When I go to gay gatherings—parties, parades, bars, baths—I open up my empathic sensors and silently ask, "What are you truly seeking? What is your heart's desire?" I let the responses come into my body. I feel both the collective and individual desires of the gay men's community. Out of this information, this ongoing "market survey," I create structures that allow an individual or group to experience their heart's desires. A common comment I hear in my classes or after an individual session with a man is, "This is what I have dreamed about. This is what I have always wanted but didn't know how to get." This is part of my magical process.

Some people have challenged me by saying that I am just participating in the best-little-boy-in-the-world archetype, that I am merely a people pleaser. This criticism concerns me. I call part of my path "sacred service." I call my compassionate response to others being a Good Man.

The great gift that gay magicians have to offer nongay magicians is contact with cock, so that cock isn't shadow. Cock is the biggest shadow for nongay men. That is why they rape and sexually abuse. That is why businessmen call their women peers "corporate nuns." That is why bikers with tattoos call their women "cunts." That is why homeboys relate to their women as whores. Men have not learned to honor cock. Men are terrified of cock. Men are overwhelmed by cock as shadow. Queer magicians turn cock—only known as sword—into wand, scepter, staff, and root. When I look at the World Trade Center in New York, I don't see cock competition but rather proud, cooperating erections.

Have you always expressed your sexuality so strongly?

Always. But my parents instilled a guilt in me from childhood for my desires, my passions, and my erotic curiosity. They could not comprehend the naturalness of my desire. This is the source of emotional and energetic abuse by nongay parents of their gay children. We are outside of their frame of reference even before we are explicitly sexual. Gay erotic innocence terrifies parents.

When I was three, I became shy. I realized instinctively that who I was was not acceptable to the people I was relying on for food, shelter, and clothing. I became shy—went inside until I could construct a false self that was acceptable to my parents. I buried my sexuality and my erotic gifts because my very life was threatened by my parents' reactions to my special way of being and loving. My desire was my parents' enemy and thus became my enemy.

This has been the greatest abuse in my life. I was taught that my life force—the power of the divine in me—was my enemy. This is what we call the closet in America. My authentic self was terrified to express itself until I traveled to New York City at age twenty-eight and met men who were kindred spirits.

That's an extremely perverse message.

That's the major wounding: that I'm separate from God, parents, and myself by activating the level of being we call the erotic. My eroticism is the soul glue that weaves me all together, weaves me together with other folks. It's the "adhesiveness" Walt Whitman spoke about and that I use in my work to call forth wholeness.

Some would say the work you do is only skin deep; how can it possibly manifest in deeper and more soulful ways? What would you say to those critics and naysayers?

First of all, I believe that my spirituality is skin—and deeper. That it is about the body as gateway. I don't have a spirituality that is based on some distant idea. Jesus didn't say, "This is my mind, these are my thoughts." He said, "This is my body, this is my blood. If you want to be in communion with me, eat my Body, drink my Blood." My spirituality is right here and now. And it's not just skin deep; it's as deep as the earth. So my spirituality is focused there, too. The Lakota phrase "all my relations" has influenced me greatly. I am all my relations. When I honor this, when I honor my authentic self, then I'm very aware I'm connected with everything in the past, the present, and the future.

At Fire Island in 1976, everybody I knew had sex all the time, and I thought, Ah! My tribe. As I say, I'm a sex magician, and I really honor life force in the sexual form. But I found I had made a mistake, a misperception, when I was thirty: All gay people are not into sex. My core tribe are those men and women, gay and straight, who honor eroticism as the life force.

Maybe God is this astonishing vibration, the greatest possible orgasm of all, sustaining everything, vibrating all the time. And as I vibrate higher, I resonate with that Orgasm. For me, breath is one path toward that Orgasm; sex is another.

Spirituality for me is the basic question, What is life? What is the meaning of death? And that can boil down to, Why do I breathe? That gets pretty heady at times, but what if your life has no other meaning than to just breathe? To merely be in harmony with oneself and one's surroundings, not to be in conflict. To just sit quietly?

In your experience, what are the problems that gay men have in awakening to their erotic-spiritual potential? Is there one thing that seems to be a stumbling block above others?

Awakening takes place in certain environments. I don't think our society—our school and religious systems, for instance—is organized for people to wake up, to go beyond. It's certainly not set up for gay men to come into their own power. That's why I went to live in a ghetto where I ate, breathed, slept, dreamed, and touched men who were like me but more evolved in their gay identity. I learned how to dance and have sex, how to laugh and be witty, how to feel and care deeply—to unleash all the blinders that had been put on me.

I developed Body Electric as a greenhouse growth experience for pioneering gay men to explore the erotic frontier. The highpoint of my work as an erotic weaver was the Sacred Intimate Training in 1992. Fifty men, committed to service, gathered at a mountaintop retreat for sixteen days of erotic ritual. We were committed to waking up one another and challenging one another. The themes were truth-telling and being heart-centered lovers of one another. None of the men who were there have been the same since. We all need to be in environments that are constantly supportive of who we are and wake us up. We all need to create contexts for our growth.

The question is: How do we get in alignment with ourselves? I feel orgasm—not ejaculation, but orgasm—is a major aligning process. It's a vibration that's so powerful that we get pulled in and we're fully present. It takes something extraordinary to bring the different facets of ourselves together. And for me that's prolonged, full-bodied orgasm.

The men were awakened, but then they had to go back home. What then? What's the next step? Anyone who is truly awake has an infectious quality, the ability to deeply affect others. But that's a tough job if nobody's listening.

There are places of light, of consciousness, of waking up, and I wanted to show other people how to create those environments—a cauldron in which magic can take place. Sex magicians take the energy of the universe and transform it so it can be used in very tangible ways.

What motivates you, Joseph, to do this type of work?

There's a part of me that's a be-er; I know that just being in the world has its effect. The doer part, however, is how I can be of service. I am a magician creating a world that doesn't exist. For me to be happy, safe, and fulfilled that world has to exist—so my work is to create it.

One of my models of service is mentor-magician, a "fluffer" of gifts. When I see someone's charisma, their innate gift, I push them to feel it in their body. Sometimes I see and name someone's special gift even before they recognize it themselves. As an alchemist, I do not turn lead into gold. It is just that some people perceive themselves as lead, and I perceive them as gold and so banish their illusion that they are lead. The major techniques I use to awaken a man's charisms—his gold—are erotic massage with intensely nourishing breathing.

Are gay men's innate gifts more in the realm of the erotic than other men's?

The very quality of our lives demands that we transform the sex negativity of modern culture. But I do feel that there are gay men whose life vocation is sex work.

What do you fear the most in the work you do?

I fear interacting with toxic, shame-based people. Often their shame activates residues of shame within me that take a great deal of time and effort to clear.

I am aware of the Heisenberger Effect in quantum physics: that the experimenter always influences the outcome of the experiment. Similarly, I am aware that I cannot create a container for a man to have a transformational experience without influencing that experience. I constantly challenge my motives in my work of influencing other men's lives. I fear not being conscious of my motives, not being in integrity. A central meditation of Jesuit spirituality is called the Two Standards: the Standard of Jesus or the Standard of the World. Because of this Jesuit imprint in my dualist mind, I create a standard for myself that is higher than the standards I demand of the men I work with. I help them go to the "promised land," but I remain behind. I let go of the Body Electric School in order to let go of this dynamic.

I also fear martyrdom for speaking the truth about cock. This fear has not stopped me from speaking, but I have chosen carefully where I speak and to whom. I've also had the tendency to believe that all my insights are for the community; sometimes I just have to say the insights are for me alone.

Are you saying that you have not been personally nourished by all that you have given others?

The Catholic in me says I made a trade-off of being there for the community rather than of taking care of myself. That's what a lot of middle-aged men do. I know I don't need to be Mother Theresa. I don't need to sacrifice health or self for the world.

But, actually, I love my life and my work. American culture separates us from our eroticism and our erotic power very early. Relearning to make love to ourselves and passing this on to others so they can heal their bodies, open their hearts, and make better relationships is extremely important. It's one way of healing the barriers that exist among men. It's how I've healed myself.

GUY BALDWIN

RECLAIMING THE EXILED SELF

Guy Baldwin has long been an enigma to me. But ever since the autumn afternoon in 1984 when my friend Geoff Mains said that Baldwin was a man to look out for, I have looked. Geoff had delivered his pronouncement while perched on crates of empties stacked along the blackened back wall of the Ambush, a hangout bar for the leather-clad bohemians who live in the industrial jumble of San Francisco's South of Market district. Geoff had just published Urban Aboriginals, *a now classic examination of the gay male leather world, and told me that he would soon visit Baldwin, a psychotherapist in Los Angeles working almost exclusively with gay men "into S/M." His groundbreaking practice aside, Guy himself was an active player in the scene.*

The world of "tops" and "bottoms"—games and rites involving some form of administered pain or relinquishment of power—is foreign to most people. Sadomasochists, tainted as they are by scary myths and misinformation, are certainly among any community's most unwelcomed members. But within queer urban enclaves, men with S/M proclivities, or leatherfolk, have emerged as being among the gay community's more active and hard-at-work advocates. Yet for every gay man living out the urge to adventure beyond sexual norms, there exist dozens more shackled by shame. In the ten years since I first heard his name, it's become obvious to me that Baldwin—therapeutically speaking—has had his hands full.

Over the past decade, the close-knit fraternity of gay leather men has seen its ranks disproportionately suffer due to the devastating effects of AIDS. Geoff is among the legion now gone, but Guy continues his work, becoming an ever more powerful and articulate spokesman for his tribe. He's crisscrossed the country numerous times, candidly addressing the promise—and problems—inherent in the leather lifestyle. A recent book, Ties That Bind, *offers his collected advice and insight to those wanting to further chart a course on the "crimson map" of radical sexuality.*

Despite his eloquent and impassioned voice, Guy Baldwin has remained a pleasant mystery to me. Like any true voyager, he appears as someone infinitely complex, a puzzle box to go figure. On the day of our interview, the question of what facet to pull out first is daunting. But we begin, and as I shortly discover, his many parts make up an engaging, conscionable, and sometimes fearsome man.

○

When did your interest in sadomasochism become evident to you?

I had my first homosexual experience when I was thirteen. By my nineteenth year it was clear to me that the kinds of sexual expressions mainstream gay men engaged in were less and less interesting to me, and it was at that point that I began finding my way—slowly at first—into what I would now call the S/M leather-fetish world. In Denver, Colorado, in 1965, there were not many ways to be gay, and so the opportunities to connect with men who were out on the more butch, more masculine, end of the homoerotic spectrum were small. But that's where I gravitated to.

Why do you think different types of loving have been so marginalized—consigned to shadow places?

We live in a sex-negative culture, so any inquiries about human sexuality are automatically surrounded by an atmosphere of nervousness, suspicion, and fear. The more the sexuality under investigation departs from what mainstream America considers acceptable, then the less support there is for the investigation. When you begin to move in the direction of nonstandard erotic behavior, which I think S/M clearly is, then the degree of social anxiety about that goes up manifoldly, and thus, we are marginalized.

You describe stepping into the world of leather sex as a kind of "second coming out." Do you think that coming into leather also represents a kind of spiritual occasion as well—an initiation into a deeper part of Self, perhaps?

It certainly may be so for some people. But I don't think that it is seen in those terms frequently, if at all, by most leather men. My guess is that most people find their way into the kind of sexuality that we think of as leather sexuality and engage in much of what they do in a pretty unconscious way, for much of their lives. But you know, people tend to run their sex lives pretty much the way they run other parts of their lives. If you're a cerebral, reflective person who is circumspect about the nature and quality of your experiences, then it's likely that you're going to be willing—guilt notwithstanding—to turn your mind upon your own sexuality to divine whether or not there's more there than meets the erotic eye.

I would like to believe that walking into a church can produce a spiritual experience for any person who goes there. What I know to be true, however, is that there are lots of people who go through lots of churches and don't have anything like a spiritual experience. I would like to believe that there's something special about leather sexuality that leads people to a spiritual path. But the more I come to visit with people about their erotic lives the less clear I am about that.

You describe participating in S/M rituals and practices as playing with "holy fire." What do you mean by this?

Well, for me, the S/M experience is a kind of crucible in which I place myself, where I hope that my own impurities and illusions are somehow burned away. The experience is often—but not always—the opportunity for me to alter my own state of consciousness and have a higher kind of awareness about the way the world is, my place in it, and the relationships between all things. So for me the S/M experience can function as a lens through which existence becomes focused, clarified, refined, and revealed.

Would you call that a spiritual experience?

I certainly would. Absolutely, it's a spiritual experience. In fact, I think it would have been difficult for me to stay as connected to the S/M leather scene as I have, for as long as I have, had that element not been rather consistently present in my S/M leather experience.

You've said that by truly surrendering within the context of an S/M scene, a psychic portal can be opened in which healing and transformation can happen. Tell me what happens when you face the abyss, that "black hole" you write so convincingly about.

When I am with a partner with whom I can achieve a nearly perfect synchronous dance, my "self" becomes stripped of all of its external trappings. I stop becoming identified with he who is male, he who is forty-six, he who is losing his hair, he who is Caucasian, he who is American, he who is a leather man—all of those identities fall away from me. What I am left with is an ecstatic contact with Self. There are no words passing through my mind; there are no cerebral events

It's certainly possible to have that without knowing that you have it. From my point of view, it wouldn't matter whether people knew they were having spiritual experiences or not. I don't spend a lot of time really talking or thinking about spiritual experiences much. However, I can think of some things that would serve to make our gay environment more conducive to having a soul-filled relationship with oneself, with one's soul, if I can put it like that. And of course, the very first thing I would do would be to wish homophobia gone. But it's hard for me to imagine a world without it right now.

Homophobia, the hatred and rejection of anything queer, is one of the prime factors in shaping gay male lives. But this is largely an external reality put upon us by society. Is there some indwelling, constitutional difference between the type of men that today we label gay and those who are not?

At this time in human history, homophobia is the single most defining element in what I think we could call gay consciousness. Homophobia is almost certainly the only experience that we have in common. It is a tragedy of unimaginable proportions and consequences for everyone on the planet. The answer to your other question is more complex for me. The answer is yes, I think there are some things that make our experience different. But I don't see them in absolute terms. If we look at human sexuality through the lens of the Kinsey scale, for example, we find that there's not just one gay sexuality. There are the gay sexualities, plural. There is a tremendous amount of variation in terms of style, content, frequency, partner choice, and so forth. Just as there are many ways to be straight, there are many ways to be gay.

What I'm driving at here is that I believe there is a continuum for each point on the Kinsey scale. The influences that produce a person's erotic psyche are presumably infinite in number. At some point those influences arrive at a kind of critical mass, and the person's sexual and erotic polarity gels. It's very seductive to think of the gay psyche in absolute terms, but when it comes time to really sort what the elements of that might be, I think it would be very difficult.

It's important to pay studious attention to the things that we have in common with humanity rather than the things that make us different. Because to the extent we are willing to focus on the things that make us unique, in some way we engage in or support the dynamics that are inherent in homophobia.

taking place. I suppose some in Eastern spiritual traditions might call that nirvana or some kind of single one-pointedness. I believe that this experience is the goal of most Eastern and probably some Western Christian traditions as well.

When that happens for me, I lose all sense of time and space, I lose my sense of mass—in other words, having body weight. Sometimes it is impossible for me to mobilize my muscles or my voice. Sometimes I lose sensory input altogether; even though my eyes may be open in a lighted room, I lose the capacity to see. It depends on what role I'm in. When I'm on top, I don't lose my sensory capacities. But the ecstatic, transformational event can occur for me on either end of the top-bottom, master-slave, sadist-masochist dynamic.

There is virtually no doubt in my mind that one essential part of this experience is based in our organic reality. By that I mean specifically what goes on in our heads at the biochemical level. Research has revealed these wonderful substances produced in our brain chemistry called endorphins, which make us feel extraordinary when they happen, and that there is a connection between what happens to our bodies and/or minds and endorphin formation.

There are lots of ways to produce the endorphin flood. One is through physical stimulation overload, carefully orchestrated, but another is through a kind of mental stimulation overload. Classically, one of the ways bottoms get high is by the physical confrontation that they have with stimulation. The tops get high—I know I do—when they confront their own internal impulses to the infantile. In the sense that the infant, as a primal force, wants what it wants when it wants it—without obstruction or objection.

Children are spontaneously destructive: they will build with blocks and then destroy the edifice gleefully just because it feels good. At some level, deep in our primal consciousness, there is an impulse to destroy. Freud commented on it, and certainly Jung did. So at some level tops have the opportunity to wrestle with the part of themselves that would be destructive, that would be totally self-indulgent without regard for the other. And it is that conflict within the self—the need to destroy versus the need not to destroy, the war between the id and the super-ego, if you will—that forms the platform which sadists and tops, dominants and masters, walk on the edge of. The ritualized S/M scenario is the crucible in which this battle occurs.

Now there's a different battle that occurs in the head of the bottom. Bottoms have to wrestle with their essential vulnerability—the confrontation that goes with their survival. They end up going through rites of passage and transformation by ordeal, and they come out on the other end triumphing over their own vulnerabilities.

I have seen the motion pictures taken during the fifties of nuclear tests that suddenly blow buildings to bits with a huge shock wave. That's a good way to describe what occurs when the superficial realities of our personae are swept away in an S/M experience. There remain only the two elemental selves of the players merging in a kind of ecstatic fusion when the cathartic portal opens. The top in that situation is the navigator—both top and bottom are passengers.

Are you saying that this kind of psychological annihilation has to occur before one can really have the cathartic, transformative experiences you're talking about?

In order for the S/M experience to deliver players to this place that we are now speaking of, certain elements must be present. One is that the bottom must have a real experience of his vulnerability. Bondage can make the experience of absolute vulnerability—inability to protect oneself—clear. Some people need more than simple bondage in order to have that vulnerability revealed to them in crystalline terms. They may need a hand at their throat. They may need to feel themselves broken under the assault of heavy physical or mental stimulation—a whip comes to mind, or they must feel deep submission. And the top must experience as real the fact that his bottom's life is in his hands and feel his own urges to push the bottom's vulnerability.

Why do so many choose not to go through that portal? What are they afraid of?

The top is afraid of his own impulses to destroy, of destroying another person and thereby himself—his morality, his self-respect. The bottom is afraid of being destroyed, of nonexistence.

What you're talking about seems to go beyond erotic play—it deals with the soul. Do you see the core reality of S/M experience, as you've just described it, relating to other kinds of initiatory or soul-making rituals available in other cultures? Does the human need for this kind of experience run so deep that perhaps modern S/M ritual is one way to compensate for the lack of real initiatory or

soul-making tests in our own society? After all, we seem to be peculiarly a culture of vicarious thrills—in other words, events watched but not actually, physically lived out.

It's been interesting for me to watch the recent interest in the fad of bungee-jumping, and before that of skydiving, where you have the experience of falling to your destruction. It's a very easy way to come face to face with your mortality in a heartbeat. But these experiences have been seen as the province of adventurers and exotics, of sports aficionados and warriors. So these have been activities in contemporary American culture where people could pursue the kind of powerful experiences I'm speaking about, but tend, as a rule, not to.

In many other societies, analogous kinds of rituals exist. In order to marry in certain Australian aboriginal tribes, for instance, a young man must undergo three physical ordeals at different points in his life. He must first have his penis circumcised, then later at puberty it must be sub-incised, and then when it comes time to marry, his intended bride's father must remove the boy's right from incisor. These are three very painful rites of passage for a young man in those particular tribes.

We could go through countless so-called primitive cultures and find of passage across the board. Even in Christian, Roman Catholic societies are the penitents, who will crawl on their knees across cobblestone court make painful pilgrimages in order to arrive at the pilgrimage site in a sta gious, ecstatic rapture. Some sadomasochists and leatherfolk have har mechanics of the S/M activity to similar kinds of objectives.

As gay men, how great is our need for this type of transfor activity? And are we receiving enough of it? Does S/M re kind of solution or path for this lack in modern life?

Some people need it, or are aware of needing it, more people will tell you they don't have much of a spiritual life lives suffer much from that. They move through their lives way and can give and receive love. So I suppose you could is not spiritually deficient. Your presumption is that a he sential for a happy life?

Yes, in the sense of feeling in balance, in tune

Once you start down that road, you are courting more of the illusion of duality in the universe. And that is a dangerous path to tread—well, perhaps just less interesting.

Are you saying that we're no different from so-called straight people except for what we do in bed?

Well, I know that we feel different. My experience of being in the world as a gay person feels to me like there is a profound, fundamental distinction between myself and the world of heterosexuals. I feel a kind of satisfying harmonic resonance with gay people when I think of them in abstract terms. Yet, what I also know is true is that there are some gay people in the world with whom I feel no connection whatsoever. We are at polar opposite ends of any scale that you could put us on—politically, aesthetically, spiritually. There are many straight people with whom I feel more of a closeness than many gay people. And I'm sure the same is true for the vast majority of other gay men.

The feeling that we are different may be merely a consequence of the fact that the single defining influence in today's human environment on gay people is homophobia. One could persuasively argue that the reason we feel different is that we are socialized to feel different. Speculations about our having some special "gay sensitivity" may be nothing more than the accidental consequence of a homophobically created stereotype. Mainly because our attitudes about homosexuality were given to us by homophobic heterosexuals.

I would like to think that we are special because everybody likes to think that they're special. But the social scientist in me—my early background is in anthropology—is deeply suspicious of that. From a spiritual point of view, I take a certain umbrage at the suggestion that somehow we are better than heterosexuals or are elevated or gifted in any special way. The larger and more interesting question is what makes any person sexual in the way that they are sexual? Because any theory that talks about homosexuality has also to be able to talk about heterosexuality and the development of any erotic configuration.

Let's return to questions about soul. Do you think gay men are paying enough attention to the care and nurturing of their inner life?

Some men do, some men don't. My guess is that the reason more men don't is that they mature in an environment that is toxic to the process of developing a relationship with one's own soul. If I had to guess what the most common culprit would be in the lives of gay men, it would be homophobia. Whatever it is in contemporary society that makes people soul sick, gay men are exposed to the same thing, and we have homophobia on top of that as well.

> *You've written that there's a "beast," a primal, powerful, instinctual force living within the soul of every man, and that men into S/M seem to have better access to theirs. What does your inner beast look like? What are its appetites? Has a more conscious knowing of it served you better than if you'd kept it locked away?*

I think that at some level we all share the same inner beast, in an archetypal sense. The way that mine manifests itself may be functionally different than the way yours manifests itself, but it's the same energy. I don't have a visual representation of it, but I certainly feel it.

> *Do you become it sometimes?*

Yeah, I have become it. And that's a very—that's a very terrifying moment for me.

> *And for the person you're with?*

Oh yes! It's almost as though we are beamed into an arena along with another guy who looks exactly like me, who is dangerous, powerful, destructive, unscrupulous, skilled, deadly. "I am the destroyer of worlds." In other words, a part of myself becomes manifest as a contrapuntal whole, and he becomes a counterpoint to the rest of myself when he appears in the room with me—in the arena with me. My consciousness moves back and forth alternately between his head, if you will, and a head in which I am all of the opposite things: I am protective, I am benevolent, I am generous, I am paternal, maternal, fraternal—I become the creator. And so we have the Creator and the Destroyer. We have Good and Evil.

> *Is this other self the same thing that Jungians would call your shadow, or is it different than your shadow?*

I think it is the shadow, and I suspect that one reason the Jungians call it the shadow is because it remains in such obscurity for most people. That doesn't mean it doesn't operate or influence or direct. My beast is a shadow figure.

Most people project their shadow—that part of themselves that remains unconscious—onto other people and situations in often harmful ways. It's indiscriminate; people can't usually see it. But you seem to have acknowledged that part of yourself, given it a form.

I can look in the mirror and see it, him, looking back at me. But he can come out very spontaneously and in the most common and mundane of environments. Still, at some level, when the S/M experience that is spiritual works, the top and bottom walk along the razor's edge of good and evil and are able to glance indifferently from one side to the other, reveling in our ability to find a peaceful, serene unity within those two polar opposites.

It has been observed that boys play but men work. And staying conscious about life—who you are, what you really want—is work. Yet so many gay men whom I know, both outside and within the leather community, seem to hang on to a kind of boyish, "I don't want to grow up" mentality. They don't seem to be able to make a commitment to do the inner work necessary for finding their own power, looking instead for definition and identity from a source outside themselves. Is this too harsh a judgment on my part?

I'm reminded of a wonderful Hermann Hesse story called "The Rainmaker," in which the apprentice shaman becomes aware from watching his mentor that all things in the universe are connected to one another and that to fully understand one object or one phenomenon is to fully understand all of its connections to other things. He realizes that there is a giant web of connections in the universe and that they lead to a center and that a man standing at that center could see all, know all.

It's my personal belief that not to keep one's life moving more or less toward that center ends up reducing life to a frivolity. And I think many gay men run their lives as though they were a frivolity. I don't know if the experience of homophobia causes more of us to live meaningless, frivolous lives than we might. Still, I do know that homosexuals haven't cornered the market in frivolous lives.

Do you think there is something within S/M experience that suggests a possibility of remedy for this frivolousness?

Anything that takes people closer to themselves as they are, anything self-revelatory, is going to be a remedy. And to the extent that some men and women use S/M as a lens through which they can get a clearer view of themselves, then yes, absolutely.

Has this been the case for you?

Oh, very clearly. Everyone needs some kind of a lens through which to get a clearer focus on the self. And it doesn't matter whether it's someone practicing Japanese floral arrangements or corporate law. The thing that does this most consistently for me is the exercise of my interest in S/M leather sexuality. So, from a certain point of view, you could say I look at the world through black-and-blue colored glasses. I suppose I could have picked up any number of other kinds of glasses—I could have been a cleric, I could have been more of a poet than I am— but S/M happens to have been the way I've done it. I mean, I don't believe that S/M sexuality can do that any better than any other path that a person might choose; it just happens to be the one that I fell into and like and that few others understand.

Gay men have seemingly developed this particular form of sexual-
ity to a high art—or at least craft. Would you say that we are
among its most skilled practitioners?

Who can really be surprised about that? Given the fact that homophobia is the most defining element in our lives, then what that means is that we spend disproportionate time thinking about our sexuality and experiencing our primary identity as erotically different from the rest of the world. When the rest of the world is busy pointing at you and saying, "You're different," it's very hard not to be influenced by that fact. You would expect, therefore, that such a subculture would pay very much more attention to its own erotic interests by virtue of every-one else's interest. Impossible not to. So it's no surprise to me that most world-class sadomasochists are to be found among gay men.

Certainly not all gay men who've had some form of S/M experience
have had these profound cathartic experiences you speak of.

For those who are coming from a mentally unhealthy place with it, where they are being punished for real or imagined sins, where they are busy trying to undertake some kind of atonement or acting out of homophobic rage, then it is unreasonable to expect that they are going to be able to have a spiritual experience. There are a lot of people out there who are doing S/M for reasons that I don't approve of, in the sense that I don't think they are engaged in S/M for life-enhancing purposes. Some have harnessed self-destructive impulses to their sexuality and found a way to manifest that in the S/M scene.

What lessons about life can leather men share with those who are not necessarily interested in this path?

Most of us have learned that when we encounter one another from a mindset that includes rage, condescension, elitism, and the like, the cathartic portal remains closed. When we approach one another with love and respect and a mutual desire to experience a journey toward Self, the portal is much more likely to open. I think that those of us who journey through S/M with these transformational and ecstatic objectives in mind learn the value of reclaiming the exiled self. That by embracing the disowned parts of ourselves and developing honest relationships with them, there is a diminishment in our tendency to project those disowned parts onto other people and have them influence our relationships accordingly.

In the moments of ecstatic fusion that occur in S/M scenes, there is no place to hide from anyone or anything. The exposure is absolute. And that's why as a setting it is so useful for undertaking ecstatic transformation. The British writer Nigel Kent once observed, "If you beat the shit out of a man, he will learn all about you." I didn't understand it when I read it, but I sure do now.

ED STEINBRECHER

SEX WITH GOD

One day a man from Time magazine came to see me. He said he wanted to discuss gays and religion, from orthodox to New Age, for a piece his publication was researching. So we sat in my office for a couple of hours and talked. I concluded by expressing my beliefs about the potential gay men have for expressing themselves in deeply spiritual ways, a "receptivity" of the soul commented on by Jung and many others.

"Potential," the newsweekly editor abruptly replied, standing to make his departure. "I don't believe in potential."

It's funny how the thing so easily dismissed by one man can exist as another's central truth. For Ed Steinbrecher, the very notion of potential—a latent quality capable of being but not yet fully realized—serves as the bedrock for his life and work. An astrologer for over thirty years, Steinbrecher views his ancient practice as one of the best means available to comprehend and realize the intangible forces of nature that reside in each of us. As for gay men, "their spiritual potential is incredible," he says. "They form one of the most important communities on the planet right now."

Even though the sixty-three-year-old author, teacher, and lecturer is widely known in his field, "I'm a very strong skeptic for what I do," he admits. "It helps keep me grounded." Born in a suburb of Chicago, Steinbrecher grew up in a family of primarily Bohemian descent where astrology—a language of symbols—was the common tongue. His mother, as well as her brother and sister, all practiced the seemingly arcane art. "My aunt lived with us, so it was like I had two mothers," explains Steinbrecher. "My real mother took care of my physical and emotional needs, but my aunt was my spiritual mother. She always encouraged me to be myself."

Today, Steinbrecher lives in Los Angeles. He directs a meditation center and conducts his thriving practice in a house located just a few steps away from the city's bustling Sunset Boulevard. Once inside the tree-shaded center, however, all sounds and impressions of a frantic outer world quickly pass away. The quarters are shared with several close colleagues—all men—and the serene quality of monastic-like life permeates the air.

The second-generation astrologer has distilled much of his knowledge into The Inner Guide Meditation: A Spiritual Technology for the 21st Century. The book is a blend of Jungian analytical psychology and Western metaphysics taking place. I suppose some in Eastern spiritual traditions might call that nirvana or some kind of single one-pointedness. I believe that this experience is the goal of most Eastern and probably some Western Christian traditions as well.

When that happens for me, I lose all sense of time and space, I lose my sense of mass—in other words, having body weight. Sometimes it is impossible for me to mobilize my muscles or my voice. Sometimes I lose sensory input altogether; even though my eyes may be open in a lighted room, I lose the capacity to see. It depends on what role I'm in. When I'm on top, I don't lose my sensory capacities. But the ecstatic, transformational event can occur for me on either end of the top-bottom, master-slave, sadist-masochist dynamic.

There is virtually no doubt in my mind that one essential part of this experience is based in our organic reality. By that I mean specifically what goes on in our heads at the biochemical level. Research has revealed these wonderful substances produced in our brain chemistry called endorphins, which make us feel extraordinary when they happen, and that there is a connection between what happens to our bodies and/or minds and endorphin formation.

There are lots of ways to produce the endorphin flood. One is through physical stimulation overload, carefully orchestrated, but another is through a kind of mental stimulation overload. Classically, one of the ways bottoms get high is by the physical confrontation that they have with stimulation. The tops get high—I know I do—when they confront their own internal impulses to the infantile. In the sense that the infant, as a primal force, wants what it wants when it wants it—without obstruction or objection.

Children are spontaneously destructive: they will build with blocks and then destroy the edifice gleefully just because it feels good. At some level, deep in our primal consciousness, there is an impulse to destroy. Freud commented on it, and certainly Jung did. So at some level tops have the opportunity to wrestle with the part of themselves that would be destructive, that would be totally self-indulgent without regard for the other. And it is that conflict within the self—the need to destroy versus the need not to destroy, the war between the id and the superego, if you will—that forms the platform which sadists and tops, dominants and masters, walk on the edge of. The ritualized S/M scenario is the crucible in which this battle occurs.

Now there's a different battle that occurs in the head of the bottom. Bottoms have to wrestle with their essential vulnerability—the confrontation that goes with their survival. They end up going through rites of passage and transformation by ordeal, and they come out on the other end triumphing over their own vulnerabilities.

I have seen the motion pictures taken during the fifties of nuclear tests that suddenly blow buildings to bits with a huge shock wave. That's a good way to describe what occurs when the superficial realities of our personae are swept away in an S/M experience. There remain only the two elemental selves of the players merging in a kind of ecstatic fusion when the cathartic portal opens. The top in that situation is the navigator—both top and bottom are passengers.

Are you saying that this kind of psychological annihilation has to occur before one can really have the cathartic, transformative experiences you're talking about?

In order for the S/M experience to deliver players to this place that we are now speaking of, certain elements must be present. One is that the bottom must have a real experience of his vulnerability. Bondage can make the experience of absolute vulnerability—inability to protect oneself—clear. Some people need more than simple bondage in order to have that vulnerability revealed to them in crystalline terms. They may need a hand at their throat. They may need to feel themselves broken under the assault of heavy physical or mental stimulation—a whip comes to mind, or they must feel deep submission. And the top must experience as real the fact that his bottom's life is in his hands and feel his own urges to push the bottom's vulnerability.

Why do so many choose not to go through that portal? What are they afraid of?

The top is afraid of his own impulses to destroy, of destroying another person and thereby himself—his morality, his self-respect. The bottom is afraid of being destroyed, of nonexistence.

What you're talking about seems to go beyond erotic play—it deals with the soul. Do you see the core reality of S/M experience, as you've just described it, relating to other kinds of initiatory or soul-making rituals available in other cultures? Does the human need for this kind of experience run so deep that perhaps modern S/M ritual is one way to compensate for the lack of real initiatory or

*soul-making tests in our own society? After all, we seem to be pecu-
liarly a culture of vicarious thrills—in other words, events watched
but not actually, physically lived out.*

It's been interesting for me to watch the recent interest in the fad of
bungee-jumping, and before that of skydiving, where you have the experience of
falling to your destruction. It's a very easy way to come face to face with your
mortality in a heartbeat. But these experiences have been seen as the province of
adventurers and exotics, of sports aficionados and warriors. So these have been
activities in contemporary American culture where people could pursue the kind
of powerful experiences I'm speaking about, but tend, as a rule, not to.

In many other societies, analogous kinds of rituals exist. In order to
marry in certain Australian aboriginal tribes, for instance, a young man must undergo three physical ordeals at different points in his life. He must first have his
penis circumcised, then later at puberty it must be sub-incised, and then when it
comes time to marry, his intended bride's father must remove the boy's right front
incisor. These are three very painful rites of passage for a young man in those particular tribes.

We could go through countless so-called primitive cultures and find rites
of passage across the board. Even in Christian, Roman Catholic societies, there
are the penitents, who will crawl on their knees across cobblestone courtyards to
make painful pilgrimages in order to arrive at the pilgrimage site in a state of religious, ecstatic rapture. Some sadomasochists and leatherfolk have harnessed the
mechanics of the S/M activity to similar kinds of objectives.

*As gay men, how great is our need for this type of transformational
activity? And are we receiving enough of it? Does S/M really offer a
kind of solution or path for this lack in modern life?*

Some people need it, or are aware of needing it, more than others. Some
people will tell you they don't have much of a spiritual life and don't feel their
lives suffer much from that. They move through their lives in a fairly easygoing
way and can give and receive love. So I suppose you could say that such a person
is not spiritually deficient. Your presumption is that a healthy spiritual life is essential for a happy life?

Yes, in the sense of feeling in balance, in tune with life.

It's certainly possible to have that without knowing that you have it. From my point of view, it wouldn't matter whether people knew they were having spiritual experiences or not. I don't spend a lot of time really talking or thinking about spiritual experiences much. However, I can think of some things that would serve to make our gay environment more conducive to having a soul-filled relationship with oneself, with one's soul, if I can put it like that. And of course, the very first thing I would do would be to wish homophobia gone. But it's hard for me to imagine a world without it right now.

> *Homophobia, the hatred and rejection of anything queer, is one of the prime factors in shaping gay male lives. But this is largely an external reality put upon us by society. Is there some indwelling, constitutional difference between the type of men that today we label gay and those who are not?*

At this time in human history, homophobia is the single most defining element in what I think we could call gay consciousness. Homophobia is almost certainly the only experience that we have in common. It is a tragedy of unimaginable proportions and consequences for everyone on the planet. The answer to your other question is more complex for me. The answer is yes, I think there are some things that make our experience different. But I don't see them in absolute terms. If we look at human sexuality through the lens of the Kinsey scale, for example, we find that there's not just one gay sexuality. There are the gay sexualities, plural. There is a tremendous amount of variation in terms of style, content, frequency, partner choice, and so forth. Just as there are many ways to be straight, there are many ways to be gay.

What I'm driving at here is that I believe there is a continuum for each point on the Kinsey scale. The influences that produce a person's erotic psyche are presumably infinite in number. At some point those influences arrive at a kind of critical mass, and the person's sexual and erotic polarity gels. It's very seductive to think of the gay psyche in absolute terms, but when it comes time to really sort out what the elements of that might be, I think it would be very difficult.

It's important to pay studious attention to the things that we have in common with humanity rather than the things that make us different. Because to the extent we are willing to focus on the things that make us unique, in some ways we engage in or support the dynamics that are inherent in homophobia.

Once you start down that road, you are courting more of the illusion of duality in the universe. And that is a dangerous path to tread—well, perhaps just less interesting.

Are you saying that we're no different from so-called straight people except for what we do in bed?

Well, I know that we feel different. My experience of being in the world as a gay person feels to me like there is a profound, fundamental distinction between myself and the world of heterosexuals. I feel a kind of satisfying harmonic resonance with gay people when I think of them in abstract terms. Yet, what I also know is true is that there are some gay people in the world with whom I feel no connection whatsoever. We are at polar opposite ends of any scale that you could put us on—politically, aesthetically, spiritually. There are many straight people with whom I feel more of a closeness than many gay people. And I'm sure the same is true for the vast majority of other gay men.

The feeling that we are different may be merely a consequence of the fact that the single defining influence in today's human environment on gay people is homophobia. One could persuasively argue that the reason we feel different is that we are socialized to feel different. Speculations about our having some special "gay sensitivity" may be nothing more than the accidental consequence of a homophobically created stereotype. Mainly because our attitudes about homosexuality were given to us by homophobic heterosexuals.

I would like to think that we are special because everybody likes to think that they're special. But the social scientist in me—my early background is in anthropology—is deeply suspicious of that. From a spiritual point of view, I take a certain umbrage at the suggestion that somehow we are better than heterosexuals or are elevated or gifted in any special way. The larger and more interesting question is what makes any person sexual in the way that they are sexual? Because any theory that talks about homosexuality has also to be able to talk about heterosexuality and the development of any erotic configuration.

Let's return to questions about soul. Do you think gay men are paying enough attention to the care and nurturing of their inner life?

Some men do, some men don't. My guess is that the reason more men don't is that they mature in an environment that is toxic to the process of developing a relationship with one's own soul. If I had to guess what the most common culprit would be in the lives of gay men, it would be homophobia. Whatever it is in contemporary society that makes people soul sick, gay men are exposed to the same thing, and we have homophobia on top of that as well.

You've written that there's a "beast," a primal, powerful, instinctual force living within the soul of every man, and that men into S/M seem to have better access to theirs. What does your inner beast look like? What are its appetites? Has a more conscious knowing of it served you better than if you'd kept it locked away?

I think that at some level we all share the same inner beast, in an archetypal sense. The way that mine manifests itself may be functionally different than the way yours manifests itself, but it's the same energy. I don't have a visual representation of it, but I certainly feel it.

Do you become it sometimes?

Yeah, I have become it. And that's a very—that's a very terrifying moment for me.

And for the person you're with?

Oh yes! It's almost as though we are beamed into an arena along with another guy who looks exactly like me, who is dangerous, powerful, destructive, unscrupulous, skilled, deadly. "I am the destroyer of worlds." In other words, a part of myself becomes manifest as a contrapuntal whole, and he becomes a counterpoint to the rest of myself when he appears in the room with me—in the arena with me. My consciousness moves back and forth alternately between his head, if you will, and a head in which I am all of the opposite things: I am protective, I am benevolent, I am generous, I am paternal, maternal, fraternal—I become the creator. And so we have the Creator and the Destroyer. We have Good and Evil.

Is this other self the same thing that Jungians would call your shadow, or is it different than your shadow?

I think it is the shadow, and I suspect that one reason the Jungians call it the shadow is because it remains in such obscurity for most people. That doesn't mean it doesn't operate or influence or direct. My beast is a shadow figure.

Most people project their shadow—that part of themselves that remains unconscious—onto other people and situations in often harmful ways. It's indiscriminate; people can't usually see it. But you seem to have acknowledged that part of yourself, given it a form.

I can look in the mirror and see it, him, looking back at me. But he can come out very spontaneously and in the most common and mundane of environments. Still, at some level, when the S/M experience that is spiritual works, the top and bottom walk along the razor's edge of good and evil and are able to glance indifferently from one side to the other, reveling in our ability to find a peaceful, serene unity within those two polar opposites.

It has been observed that boys play but men work. And staying conscious about life—who you are, what you really want—is work. Yet so many gay men whom I know, both outside and within the leather community, seem to hang on to a kind of boyish, "I don't want to grow up" mentality. They don't seem to be able to make a commitment to do the inner work necessary for finding their own power, looking instead for definition and identity from a source outside themselves. Is this too harsh a judgment on my part?

I'm reminded of a wonderful Hermann Hesse story called "The Rainmaker," in which the apprentice shaman becomes aware from watching his mentor that all things in the universe are connected to one another and that to fully understand one object or one phenomenon is to fully understand all of its connections to other things. He realizes that there is a giant web of connections in the universe and that they lead to a center and that a man standing at that center could see all, know all.

It's my personal belief that not to keep one's life moving more or less toward that center ends up reducing life to a frivolity. And I think many gay men run their lives as though they were a frivolity. I don't know if the experience of homophobia causes more of us to live meaningless, frivolous lives than we might. Still, I do know that homosexuals haven't cornered the market in frivolous lives.

Do you think there is something within S/M experience that suggests a possibility of remedy for this frivolousness?

Anything that takes people closer to themselves as they are, anything self-revelatory, is going to be a remedy. And to the extent that some men and women use S/M as a lens through which they can get a clearer view of themselves, then yes, absolutely.

Has this been the case for you?

Oh, very clearly. Everyone needs some kind of a lens through which to get a clearer focus on the self. And it doesn't matter whether it's someone practicing Japanese floral arrangements or corporate law. The thing that does this most consistently for me is the exercise of my interest in S/M leather sexuality. So, from a certain point of view, you could say I look at the world through black-and-blue colored glasses. I suppose I could have picked up any number of other kinds of glasses—I could have been a cleric, I could have been more of a poet than I am— but S/M happens to have been the way I've done it. I mean, I don't believe that S/M sexuality can do that any better than any other path that a person might choose; it just happens to be the one that I fell into and like and that few others understand.

Gay men have seemingly developed this particular form of sexual-
ity to a high art—or at least craft. Would you say that we are
among its most skilled practitioners?

Who can really be surprised about that? Given the fact that homophobia is the most defining element in our lives, then what that means is that we spend disproportionate time thinking about our sexuality and experiencing our primary identity as erotically different from the rest of the world. When the rest of the world is busy pointing at you and saying, "You're different," it's very hard not to be influenced by that fact. You would expect, therefore, that such a subculture would pay very much more attention to its own erotic interests by virtue of everyone else's interest. Impossible not to. So it's no surprise to me that most world-class sadomasochists are to be found among gay men.

Certainly not all gay men who've had some form of S/M experience
have had these profound cathartic experiences you speak of.

For those who are coming from a mentally unhealthy place with it, where they are being punished for real or imagined sins, where they are busy trying to undertake some kind of atonement or acting out of homophobic rage, then it is unreasonable to expect that they are going to be able to have a spiritual experience. There are a lot of people out there who are doing S/M for reasons that I don't approve of, in the sense that I don't think they are engaged in S/M for life-enhancing purposes. Some have harnessed self-destructive impulses to their sexuality and found a way to manifest that in the S/M scene.

What lessons about life can leather men share with those who are not necessarily interested in this path?

Most of us have learned that when we encounter one another from a mindset that includes rage, condescension, elitism, and the like, the cathartic portal remains closed. When we approach one another with love and respect and a mutual desire to experience a journey toward Self, the portal is much more likely to open. I think that those of us who journey through S/M with these transformational and ecstatic objectives in mind learn the value of reclaiming the exiled self. That by embracing the disowned parts of ourselves and developing honest relationships with them, there is a diminishment in our tendency to project those disowned parts onto other people and have them influence our relationships accordingly.

In the moments of ecstatic fusion that occur in S/M scenes, there is no place to hide from anyone or anything. The exposure is absolute. And that's why as a setting it is so useful for undertaking ecstatic transformation. The British writer Nigel Kent once observed, "If you beat the shit out of a man, he will learn all about you." I didn't understand it when I read it, but I sure do now.

ED STEINBRECHER

SEX WITH GOD

One day a man from Time magazine came to see me. He said he wanted to discuss gays and religion, from orthodox to New Age, for a piece his publication was researching. So we sat in my office for a couple of hours and talked. I concluded by expressing my beliefs about the potential gay men have for expressing themselves in deeply spiritual ways, a "receptivity" of the soul commented on by Jung and many others.

"Potential," the newsweekly editor abruptly replied, standing to make his departure. "I don't believe in potential."

It's funny how the thing so easily dismissed by one man can exist as another's central truth. For Ed Steinbrecher, the very notion of potential—a latent quality capable of being but not yet fully realized—serves as the bedrock for his life and work. An astrologer for over thirty years, Steinbrecher views his ancient practice as one of the best means available to comprehend and realize the intangible forces of nature that reside in each of us. As for gay men, "their spiritual potential is incredible," he says. "They form one of the most important communities on the planet right now."

Even though the sixty-three-year-old author, teacher, and lecturer is widely known in his field, "I'm a very strong skeptic for what I do," he admits. "It helps keep me grounded." Born in a suburb of Chicago, Steinbrecher grew up in a family of primarily Bohemian descent where astrology—a language of symbols—was the common tongue. His mother, as well as her brother and sister, all practiced the seemingly arcane art. "My aunt lived with us, so it was like I had two mothers," explains Steinbrecher. "My real mother took care of my physical and emotional needs, but my aunt was my spiritual mother. She always encouraged me to be myself."

Today, Steinbrecher lives in Los Angeles. He directs a meditation center and conducts his thriving practice in a house located just a few steps away from the city's bustling Sunset Boulevard. Once inside the tree-shaded center, however, all sounds and impressions of a frantic outer world quickly pass away. The quarters are shared with several close colleagues—all men—and the serene quality of monastic-like life permeates the air.

The second-generation astrologer has distilled much of his knowledge into The Inner Guide Meditation: A Spiritual Technology for the 21st Century. The book is a blend of Jungian analytical psychology and Western metaphysics *utilizing astrology and images from the tarot. Steinbrecher's well-honed tech-niques and exercises offer a practical, concrete way of gaining insight about one's life problems and potentials. Central to his vision is the discovery that "we each have an inner Guide, someone who's been with us all our life, who will teach us if we ask him to, and who makes working by oneself in the unconscious safe." Knowing this inner Guide is important, emphasizes Steinbrecher, "because the unconscious is not a playground. It contains all of the energies that are creating outer personal reality—including atom bombs and death. All the gods and god-desses live down there, and if you invite them, they come."*

Uppermost during our talk in his book-lined study is a mutual concern for the spiritual well-being of gay men. "They've been handed an incredible gift," says the sage metaphysician, "only they don't know it."

°

I'd like to know what you can tell us about the kinds of people we today call gay. Are they influenced by any particular archetypal forces? If so, what are they?

Being gay means you are born different. In simplistic terms it's often ge-netic, in that the brain is patterned differently. But also one's projection system is different from average humanity. If you are born a straight male, you will auto-matically project the feminine aspects of yourself outside of yourself, generally speaking, and assimilate the masculine aspects. The opposite happens with a straight woman. Something different happens with gays and lesbians—I prefer the wider term "metasexuals," which includes some celibates and all virgins. In this group both male and female aspects tend not to project. Both of these aspects remain within the individual and have the potential to more easily come into con-sciousness. The American Indians call this group "two-spirited." Both the male and female aspects of spirit indwell. This group doesn't have to wrestle to bring the opposite sex aspect back within themselves. Both aspects are already there, even if one is more conscious than the other. This gives metasexuals an incredible access to universal power.

As a result of this potential, society instinctively reacts against gays as a threat to themselves and their established reality. In my definition, most gays usually stay "virgin." In other words, if they never have sex with a member of the opposite sex that includes penetration and orgasm, they never "ground" in the electrical sense. This virgin state gives gays access to an incredible amount of power that could change the status quo were it ever to become conscious. The Catholic church recognized this at one time and put them away as priests and nuns to utilize this power for the church's ends.

The metasexuals are designed for the shaman role, but they're usually not aware of the consciousness problem within themselves. Gay men have to make a resistant feminine part of themselves conscious and bring it into equality with their slightly more conscious masculine principle. If this isn't done, the unconscious feminine takes over and compels the individual to seek the unconscious masculine in other males again and again, but it can never be found outside. If you're not centered—having your masculine principle within and allowing your heart to direct your life—you're driven to look outside of yourself for what is perceived as a vital missing part of your life. You look for this part in another being, the partner who will complete you. But you never find him—outer relationships won't work. One after another they disappoint you. It's only when you turn within and unite the male and female aspects of yourself that truly satisfying outer relationships can occur.

Could this be one of the reasons why there is a high degree of promiscuity within the gay community?

Yes, it's a desperate emotional search for this masculine principle that is really inside. The male ego is driven by the unconscious feminine principle to look for that which will complete and balance her, not understanding that it resides within. We are ignorant of the psycho-spiritual physics at work.

In your book, The Inner Guide Meditation, *you say that while sexual orientation is totally irrelevant on a spiritual plane, "sometimes being gay has certain advantages." Like what?*

What I just spoke of. While many people have to struggle for years to get the opposite sex part of themselves back inside, the gay and lesbian is born with it automatically inside. Automatically inside doesn't mean automatically conscious, however. Here you have this incredibly powerful group of beings that have been given at birth what every spiritual person is seeking, but nobody has told them.

Gays more than most people have a sense of their power, you know. They're different. They can tell that by the way society reacts to them. But it's more than merely being different—it's that they are dangerous.

Dangerous how?

Dangerous to consensus reality, to the status quo, to reality as we know it. This power is sensed. They're unique. They're not like everybody else. They have the powers ascribed to sorcerers and witches. But no one has ever said how valuable their uniqueness is or could be.

> *Most people's knowledge of astrology is limited to what they read in a newspaper column, or through sensational revelations about public figures such as Nancy Reagan, who apparently relied upon it to guide her husband's career. You see it as a kind of blueprint or scenario for a person's life. Can you explain?*

A horoscope is a picture of an entire reality from one person's point of view, and it contains everything in that reality. For instance, what your brothers and sisters are doing now or what your parents are like. I don't believe in astrology. I use astrology and find it works. The same way I don't believe in electricity, but if there's juice in the wires and I flip a switch, something happens. Astrology is the only map I have found that is able to demonstrate to someone that reality is, in fact, a oneness—and that if they change, all reality changes. We can't change something unless we are willing to change ourselves. If we change, everything changes.

Everything is connected to everything else. Physicists know this now. But astrology is ignored and has a really bad reputation—and I can understand why—because there are so many astrologers that really don't have this awareness of oneness. Any tool depends on the consciousness of its user; the more conscious someone is, the more useful it will be to others. Astrology offers us a map for working on ourselves.

> *How do astrological signs relate to the symbols on the tarot deck and other archetypal images of transformation?*

The twenty-two main cards of tarot represent the twelve signs of the zodiac, the eight planets (excluding earth), and the sun and the moon. They relate to each other in very specific ways and to the unique energy patterns we have inside us. Tarot cards also have four suits, which represent the four bodies that each of us have. They correspond to fire, earth, air, and water. The physical body has to do with the earth quality. The emotional, or astral body, is water. The air body contains all our thinking—the three modes of thought: logic, comparison, and gestalt. And the last body, the one that vibrates the highest, is the fire body, which contains our abilities to give love, create, and be alive.

These bodies interpenetrate one another. The way I use the tarot is to retranslate a horoscope in terms of these energy picture terms. The twenty-two main cards of the tarot are pictures of very specific archetypes, energies that are the same in everyone. They create and sustain our experience of reality.

An archetype is a principle of spirit and nature. For instance, the archetype of the moon, which in tarot is called High Priestess, is the mother archetype of the universe. It has to do with anyone's receptivity and nourishing ability. It has to do with containment, the protective part of us. You see it in the way a city is organized or in how a thing called *house* is made into a home by giving it specific meaningful spaces. It's the High Priestess principle operating in different ways.

Evidently whoever designed the tarot was able to take the energy called God and break it up into twenty-two very specific energy components. These are the archetypes. They are the male and female, androgynous and hermaphroditic aspects of deity. Shake them all together and you get what some call God. It's an inconceivable entity, you know, so beyond us.

> Here you are, a mile from West Hollywood, one of the great gay gathering points on the globe. What do you see when you look into the faces of all the gay men who've come from throughout the world to live in or visit this gay village? What would you most like to say to them?

Stop looking outside. You're not going to find what you're looking for outside of yourself. You're not going to find it at all unless you go within and do the work of consciousness. Change is work, and it's scary. You're always moving into the unknown.

> Certainly, in recent years, we're seeing gay men get more in touch with their anger and frustration. Isn't this a good thing?

The only good thing is consciousness—doing the inner work with an expectation about a result. If you're doing inner work and everything around you doesn't change, you're doing something wrong.

What's the best way to do this inner work?

Find your inner Guide and just start getting acquainted with your own archetypal energies. They're already creating and sustaining your reality. If you're miserable, go after the part that's making you miserable and change it by changing yourself.

> *The sadness that a lot of gay men feel is related to the germ of homophobia, which has been planted within their psyches at a very early age. This results in low self-esteem, problems with despondency, addictive behavior, and a host of other problems later in life.*

Within gay men, those symptoms tend to be symptomatic of an unconscious feminine principle. As soon as it's worked with and brought into a sort of inner sexual union—in Jungian or alchemical terms—with the masculine principle, a healing and freeing occurs, leading to centeredness and strong self-esteem.

> *But it seems to me that gay men, as a general rule, are very attuned with the feminine. They're usually more in touch with their feelings than straight men. And what about those who are caught up with strong feminine icons, like Madonna or opera divas, or who like to dress up in drag?*

This is because the unconscious feminine principle tends to be in control and identifies with the outer feminine. Anything unconscious tries to take us over. But as soon as one's feminine principle comes into equal partnership with the masculine principle, something else happens—more freedom of choice occurs and compulsions fall away.

What happens?

You become your own prototype. Suddenly life comes into balance; you get on with your uniqueness.

> *Let's say a gay man has been reading this interview full of challenging ideas. Now let's invite him to put the book down for a moment*

*and undertake a meditation that could help him to understand
more clearly what you're talking about.*

Try this: Begin by visualizing yourself in a cave—any kind of cave. The important thing is to be in your body, to be looking out of your own eyes. If at any time during this visualization you find yourself watching yourself, get back in your body by imagining what you sense. Feel the cave floor under your feet. What is the temperature? Is it moist or dry? Once you're in the body, even though it's in your imagination, move forward and to the left in this cave until you find some kind of door or opening that leads you out into a bright landscape. Again, take the time to feel what the ground is like out there. Is the wind blowing or is it calm? Is it warm or is it cool? See what's around you. Are you on a mountain cliff or in a meadow? What is the landscape like? Even if you think, "I'm just making this up," it's all right.

Then call with your mind for an animal to come to you. Accept the first animal that shows up. Give the animal permission to lead you off to your right, to your true inner Guide. When the animal stops, don't look up, look down at the ground, and describe the man's feet you see there. And then just move slowly up his body. One of the interesting things about the true Guide, as opposed to a false guide, is generally you can't see his face very clearly. You can see the rest of him, like his hair and what he's wearing, but you can't see his face. That may take months of doing this meditation to achieve.

Then ask the figure to take both of your hands in his. Are they warm or cool, hard or soft? Once you have his hands, give him permission to let you feel his feelings for you. If no love comes to you from this man, it's not your Guide. But if you're with a false guide, the true Guide is very close. He's always been with you. So feel where love is coming to you from and look toward the source of that love until your true Guide appears. And then ask him, "Are you my true Guide? Do you have the power to protect me on the inner planes?" Once you're with the true Guide, have him take your right hand if you're right-handed, or let him take your left hand if you're left-handed, and ask him to bring the Sun figure. This is the living archetype of spirit within you, and we invite it to come as a male because it's a yang energy. Then ask what the Sun needs from you to work with you, to be your friend, and to be a conscious energy in you? Second, ask what it has to give you in the form of a symbolic object that you will need. Say it gives you a heart-shaped object. Well, what does this heart do? What effects can this symbol produce in your everyday, outer life?

Thank the Sun figure, let him go, and then next ask the Guide to bring the High Priestess, which is the core energy of the soul, or the feminine aspect. Ask her the same—what does she need from you to work with you, to be your friend, and to be a truly conscious energy. And what does she have to give? Then have the two come back together and ask them—what do they need from each other to begin working in harmony as energies within you? And second, how must you change to allow them to continue working in this manner? And then thank them, let them go, and have your Guide take you back to a meeting place that he chooses—it may be right outside the cave, it may be somewhere totally different: a place that you can visualize coming to whenever you want to be with him, to talk and work with him.

It's a fairly simple meditation—in fact some people have difficulty with the simplicity. How humanity lost something this important and easy to do is hard to fathom. Your Guide is your teacher. He will teach you your path to spirit if you ask him to. He cannot volunteer information. True guides never judge, and they never give information unless asked.

Tell me about your own gay life.

I've had gay experiences, I've had straight experiences. But in 1972 the *kundalini* awoke in me. When the kundalini awakens it changes how you want to use your sexuality. I was in bed alone, sort of reviewing my day, and suddenly this energy awoke in me. All I can say is it was like having sex with God. It was eight hours of constant physical orgasm. I know that that's impossible. But it was me as God's phallus, creating galaxies and dinosaurs and Model-T Fords—continuous, unending creation. Once you've had sex with God, everything else sort of pales, and you don't want to do anything that will sabotage your having that experience of union again. People ask, "Well, Ed, isn't giving up sex hard?" There's nothing to give up. I became celibate at that time.

Can you define what kundalini is?

Kundalini is a Sanskrit word that defines an energy that sleeps around the tailbone. It translates as "serpent power." It awakens as a side effect of any meditation practice, but very rapidly with the particular meditation I had been doing, and still practice, since 1968. Kundalini, as understood today, is an evolutionary energy. It is pushing us into our next evolutionary step and is awakening now in more and more people. LSD or any of the hallucinogens often awaken spontaneous kundalini experiences. In the West we call it the descent of grace. It requires the union of the masculine and feminine principles.

Anyway, after this experience my sexuality became like money in the bank. How was I going to spend it? Sexuality to me now would be useful only if it had to do with helping someone to grow spiritually. Otherwise, why do it? All needs to partner with another person fell totally away with that awakening. You want the union to happen inside.

I prefer the term *metasexual* to *gay* or *lesbian*. That is, someone who is using his or her sexuality in a different way from most people. Whether it be a gay man or a Jesuit priest or a hermit alone in the woods, they are not in the sexual norm. Nor are they grounding; they are not having sex with a member of the opposite sex that includes penetration and orgasm, and therefore the kundalini energy is able to circulate safely in them.

What is soul, and how does it differ from our notions of spirit?

To me, spirit is the yang, masculine energy, symbolized by the sun. Soul is the yin, feminine energy, symbolized by the moon. Spirit as a concept is easy for the gay man. Soul is difficult. Spirit is the giving of love. Soul is the receiving of love and the feeling of compassion for others. Gay men seem to have, in my experience, more compassion than straight men. Even if their feelings are unconscious, they still tend to feel the pain of others. But the soul problem comes from the ego identifying with the feeling aspect and not with the spiritual aspect. God becomes "other," not ego. Then this other is projected onto and sought in other men.

But you just said that gay men need to do more work to bring soul into consciousness.

Gay spirit is not the problem. Gay soul is the problem. Until the feminine soul aspect is seen as an impersonal inner archetype, made conscious and directed toward union with the masculine inner spirit, wholeness and integration are impossible. Ego identification with it must be released. When the soul problem is solved, any problem with spirit solves itself. This inner partnership must be made before you can partner with the world in any kind of centered way.

What you're talking about is potential. In other words, bringing something to a higher awareness.

Soul and spirit must unite. And once that happens, you get this new being. I get so sad when I'm in West Hollywood—frustrated is more the word. Many gay men there are looking for something outside themselves when they should be looking within themselves and creating this incredibly satisfying inner union.

Here's a deck of tarot cards. I'd like you to select certain cards and discuss them in terms of their archetypal relevance to gay men.

The card closest to a metasexual archetype would be the Fool—it symbolizes the freedom aspect of gay people. Counterpoint to that is the image of the Hanged Man, which represents the victim role of gay people.

Looking at the image of the Fool, we see a young man about ready to step off the edge of a cliff. There's a barking dog at his heel, and behind him there's an image of a radiant white sun.

The white sun is the symbol of the sun of the galaxy, not of the solar system. So the gay man and woman and an avatar—anyone with awakened kundalini—are operating beyond the bounds of the solar system in a galactic kind of way and in a truly cooperative humanitarian way, where they really see that we're all in this together. It's an accepting, impersonal kind of love that comes from them. The Fool is everyone's friend and doesn't discriminate against anyone on any level. It's the symbol of the Uranian, which has to do with our body's electrical system. This is the electricity that short-circuits projection and allows us all to be ourselves without modification by our psychic projection/expectation energies. It's the energy that frees people to be who they truly are.

Are there other archetypes that seem ascendant in the gay male psyche?

My experience has been that gay men have much more access to their feeling side—they can't say no to an appeal to their feelings. Straight men often don't even know they have feelings, and that's a basic difference. So there's more awareness of the archetype of the High Priestess, although that doesn't mean it's necessarily more conscious. You can be aware of this strong emotional part of yourself, and it can still push you around.

The archetype of the High Priestess means dealing with feelings and emotional communication?

The strong feminine aspects in the tarot are the Empress and the High Priestess—Venus and the Moon—and these archetypes tend to be sealed within the gay man. But because they're pushed down into unconsciousness, they have this tendency to try to take over and run things. If you have the Moon down in the darkness, what you're going to draw from life is not what you're going to like. It will correspond to the darkness of that archetype within you. It's like a constant magnet that's pulling that darkness to you. So the gay man has to work with his own feminine, the Empress and the High Priestess archetypes, first to release them more into consciousness and then to balance them—the High Priestess with the Sun, for instance. The ignorance of spiritual physics in the gay community is as rampant as the ignorance in the rest of the world, you know.

It's obvious as we approach the end of the twentieth century that there is a great deal about life in America that is staying in a stuck place—not just for gay men.

That's about to change.

But aside from embracing high-tech consumer marvels, much of society seems resistant to change. Change when it does occur is imposed by external forces, like a faltering economy, rather than being something that is consciously, inwardly willed and sought out. What role do you see gay men playing in society's positive transformation?

We're coming into a cycle in America that we last experienced from 1963 to 1977, where masculine spirituality infuses us. Then it goes away and our conservative elements come in to sort of handle all the change we've made. Last time, because we wouldn't allow it to happen any other way, God came in the form of a pill called LSD. Who knows how spirit is going to visit us this cycle? We are now so overdeveloped in terms of logic and information that we're psychotic. We're out of touch with the psychic and the intuitive, so we have nothing to balance our common sense and logic—we need to bring the former two back. I believe all of humanity is going to be pushed into a time when we're more willing to cooperate with one another and not be as afraid of differences.

Gay men and the other metasexuals are designed for leadership. If they are able to first bring the feminine to consciousness and then merge it with the masculine, they'll have an easier job of it than the rest of humanity. They have the same potential that an avatar has, the difference being that an avatar has worked on himself to make these two energies conscious and in balance. But they have the same power available. They just have to be disciplined and brave enough—because it takes bravery—to change and to bring these energies into a conjunction. Gay men are going to be forced into leadership because of their psycho-spiritual design. But will they be ready for it?

Some say that being gay is a gift. You seem to agree.

Yes, but it's a gift where the package is almost never opened. You have this gift, but you never quite know what's in the box.

So you're saying that it's time for gay people to get down and unwrap the gift, especially in a time of such tremendous cultural turmoil.

We are in a new era. This cycle started in 1943, when wars stopped working because of a new heightened consciousness. It's an age when things no longer polarize into black and white. The "good guy/bad guy" division is blurred. Things now are all shades of gray. Americans are currently experiencing the first president ever to be born in this new time. So a whole different breed is suddenly in power. It's truly of the new.

Is the emerging gay presence in society an integral part of the new age you speak of?

Humankind is struggling with understanding what sexuality is all about. And gays are a very predominant sexual specialty in terms of the power they carry. Yet gay men have still to wake up and go inside. They've got incredible power, but they have to let it come to consciousness. They have to because the world is in a mess. To gay men I say: Just stop whatever you're doing and go inside. Find your inner Guide and wake up. There's nothing more awesome than sexual union with God.

ROBERT H. HOPCKE

THE UNION OF SAMES

Near the end of his scholarly work Jung, Jungians, and Homosexuality, *Robert H. Hopcke takes a surprising turn. After a long and careful survey of references to homosexuality in the writings of Carl Jung and his followers, Hopcke turns his attention to another kind of literature. "Revenge of the Captive," "Father Blows Best," "The Coach Taught Me," and other gay male erotic stories are analyzed with the same profundity that Bruno Bettelheim applied to his study of fairy tales in* The Uses of Enchantment. *In fact, says Hopcke, stories such as "Brothers Do It" hold the same meaning and importance in gay men's adult lives as classic folk myths did during their childhoods. In both instances, the stories are instructional, usually initiatory, pointing the way toward some new stage of inner development.*

What homosexual erotica explicitly reveals is gay men's need to grasp the archetypal masculine and to be initiated into its mysteries. A story like "Cop Brothers," in which the young protagonist, Brick, is introduced to the joys of gay sex by two sets of brothers of different generations, serves its one-handed purpose well by arousing the prurient thoughts of the reader. But on a deeper level, in the realm Hopcke travels, gay male erotic stories assist in connecting men with a part of themselves that is often found missing in modern life: the full, two-sided nature of their masculinity.

Like all of the psyche's enduring symbols, the archetype of male Eros has a dual quality; the aggressive, competitive aspect so prominently displayed in our contemporary culture and the receptive, feeling side kept at a distance by most men. Gay men, because of their propensity for integrating the solar and lunar sides of the masculine—as illustrated and abetted by the kind of stories Hopcke cites—actually have a more well-adjusted relationship with their masculinity than many of their heterosexual peers who disparage homosexuals as "nellies," "sissies," and "queens."

"Within male-male Eros the masculine is contacted, lived, and embodied both in fantasy and in real relationships of flesh and blood," writes Hopcke. "To assign this rich masculinity to the realm of the feminine is both logically fallacious and notoriously pathologizing. Isn't it time to acknowledge that [male homosexuality] is the shadow of heterosexual masculinity, which attempts to contain this fearsome male Eros by projecting it onto gay men rather than owning it as its own?"

In talking about the mythologies of gay male life, Hopcke underscores a central psychological truth: what appears one way in daily life is, more often than not, its opposite in the underworld of the human soul. Psyche offers the ultimate mirror image of ourselves: what can't be found in waking reality presents itself in our dreams; what our ego-ruled consciousness fails to perceive is made relevant through the symbols of the unconscious. Through his copious writings and practice as a Jungian-oriented psychotherapist in Berkeley, California, Hopcke entices all people—but especially gay men—to become fellow travelers on the path toward wholeness.

In Jung, Jungians, and Homosexuality *and* Men's Dreams, Men's Healing, *among other works, Hopcke shows how that path takes a different course for those who soulfully unite with someone like themselves—the same—rather than with their opposite. Raw erotic tales of brothers as lovers, father-son couplings, and comrades held tight in each others arms, exemplify the union of the sames at its most potent: a relationship no less satisfying or sacred than any other. Furthermore, by not focusing on the opposites of gender, same-sex love is more capable of integrating the other myriad oppositional forces that exist within every individual and that, each in their own way, call out for harmony and balance.*

Mediating conflict and arriving at some new accord is more than just a professional skill for Hopcke—it is an innate knack he has applied throughout his life. Born on March 15, 1958, in New Jersey, Hopcke was adopted at birth by a family "who was pretty much the pillar of the local Lutheran church," he says. As a young boy, Hopcke seemed unusually energetic for his buttoned-down, reserved German family. "I was definitely not shy, in fact quite the opposite," he recalls. "I was very Italian—which is my actual ethnic background—very extroverted, artistic, and musical."

Hopcke grew up as the classic overachiever: straight A's in school, self-taught on the organ and piano, the author of seven novels before completing college. "I was the most intelligent person in all my classes," he states matter of factly. "And so that set me apart. When I subsequently realized I was gay, it wasn't all that traumatic because I was always somewhat different anyway." The prodigious student's sexual awakening happened in the seventh grade: "It hit me when I had this huge crush on my Italian English teacher, who was gorgeous and really sweet. I realized then that my feelings toward him were the same as all the girls'."

Such anecdotes are the stuff of which gay erotic stories are made. But I begin our conversation by asking Hopcke about his examination of another myth that has long held gay men's fascination, The Wizard of Oz.

○

You say that Dorothy's journey is representative of a gay man's inner journey, his path toward individuation. Why?

My interest was aroused because there's so much reference to *The Wizard of Oz* in the gay community. What do gay men respond to in this movie? After all, Dorothy's journey is a journey that many gay men feel is their own. She's kicked out of her home; she has to find her own standpoint, her ruby red shoes; she must integrate various pieces of experience, her new friends, that weren't given to her to integrate at home; and then she has to find some kind of relationship with the transcendent, the Wizard of Oz. Gay men resonate to that. The story embodies a particular kind of conflict around masculinity that feminine gay men feel is very much their own. That's where the Wicked Witch of the West comes in. Gay men have to wrestle with the negative feminine in this culture, which has often been projected onto them, and defeat it before they can get to the "Emerald City," before they can get to the place that brings them back to themselves.

Many gay men's relationships to the negative feminine are very pronounced. We see this in our fascination with the doomed queens of opera, the bitch goddesses of popular culture.

To the heterosexual way of thinking, gay men are seen as embodying the feminine because of their love for other men. We know that's kind of cracked, but nevertheless as you're growing up as a gay boy you're identified as feminine. Defeating that projection of femininity and seizing hold of masculinity is the essential first task for gay men's wholeness. And that's what *The Wizard of Oz* is about: Dorothy defeats the negative feminine and integrates various masculine qualities—the Tin Man, the Lion, and the Scarecrow. And she must come into contact with a certain kind of archetypal masculinity—the Wizard of Oz—before she is allowed to return home. That's what a gay man's inner journey must entail, too.

When I say negative, I don't mean negative in an absolute sense; I mean those aspects of the feminine that heterosexual men find threatening or unacceptable. That's where Glinda, the Good Witch, comes in. Dorothy has to have contact with the "positive feminine," as do gay men. They have to go past the negative feminine, which is really only negative from a heterosexual man's point of view, in order to find a certain kind of power, wisdom, experience, and embodiment that is a positive part of the feminine.

That's why gay men are not afraid of figures like Bette Davis, Joan Crawford, Katharine Hepburn, and Judy Garland—women who are very powerful. Gay men see those things that other men call "bitchy" as actually positive aspects of women's power. It's the desire to integrate those qualities that accounts for many gay men's wishes to be like Bette Davis. It's the deinternalizing of the perception of those things as negative that gay men see in *The Wizard of Oz*.

It has been suggested by some gay thinkers that the type of people whom we today call gay are uniquely suited for the role of cultural mediator—artists and healers. Do you agree with this assessment, and if so, does this mean we're somehow more connected with our soul business than others?

Being gay is a mystery I haven't quite gotten to the core of yet. The best way I can state it, archetypally, is that it requires outsiderhood. To fulfill the mediating function in a particular society requires that you be an outsider. You cannot be inside the society and act as a mediator. You have to have a perspective on it. People two hundred years ago whom we would currently label as gay would still fulfill that kind of function because they'd be outside the general way of thinking about themselves.

So what makes them outsiders?

It could be any number of factors. Certainly their sexual behavior, that's one. It could be a particular kind of giftedness or talent. Certain acts that they've committed would also place them beyond the pale, perhaps even leading them to being scapegoated and thrown out of the community. Those people are transformative forces. Gay people, archetypally speaking, are outsiders.

*What are the archetypes we embody more than others that result in
us being outsiders? The berdache archetype, perhaps?*

It seems to me that the berdache is a particular variation of the Androgyne, the archetype of the union of opposites. Historically, the Androgyne has
been understood as a union of masculine and feminine opposites. But what if our
conventional thinking about the Androgyne has been conditioned by heterosexual ways of perception? It's possible to think of the Androgyne in another way
than just the union of masculine and feminine—it could be the union of any opposite. We're saying andro-gyne, and we might want to call it something else than
that. Truly androgynous people marry two different aspects of masculinity as
well as two different aspects of femininity. They exhibit soft masculinity and aggressive masculinity, as well as soft femininity and aggressive femininity. There's a
way of thinking about the Androgyne that isn't quite so heterosexual and is more
of a union of any kind of opposites around sexuality.

*Is this archetype of opposites united a predominant characteristic in
the psyches of the people we today label gay?*

Oh, clearly. The current set of gender roles does not really account for
our experience. And so partly from their outsiderhood, gay men are given a different view of masculinity that essentially helps them to find the two different aspects of the masculine. And because we're so often identified as feminine, that
enables us to have an understanding of what the feminine is, which most men in
this culture don't have. Heterosexual men don't feel the feminine is theirs; they
feel they can marry it, or they can be with it, but they usually don't feel it's within
them or could be within them. Gay men naturally bring together things that are
seen as opposites through our experience of being outsiders.

What would some of our other predominately felt archetypes be?

One that I've had the most experience with in conventional ways of
thinking about archetypes is the Trickster. Any outsider is a Trickster figure: Coyote, Hermes, Loki, the thief. There's a certain kind of trickster function that gay
men and lesbians serve in this culture.

The Trickster's function is to grab people from inside the circle and pull
them out, to help people become outsiders and therefore gain spiritual enlighten-

ment. That's why Hermes is identified with thievery, with stealing. He's the one who does not respect boundaries. The entire universe is his.

Drag queens are tricksters, aren't they?

Clearly. It's so easy to see them as being androgynous that you miss the kind of clowning aspect that they bring to this culture. There's an aspect of play that Western culture, particularly American culture, lacks—it's so work-oriented. There's a quality of play that tricksters bring, and I feel like gay people and lesbians embody that archetype for this culture.

Why are these particular qualities you cite more ascendant in us?

I've taken to thinking that the universe and the process of creation is pretty cyclical. There's a certain quality of building up and consolidation as well as a certain quality of dissolution and breaking down that need to occur. Culture in general is the building up and consolidating piece, but if a culture is going to survive there has to be built into it a dissolution and breaking down piece. The outsiders, the tricksters, the androgynes, the people who break the boundaries— in other words, gay people in our culture—serve a very vital function in that second half of the cycle, in the breaking down and dissolution.

That's why lesbians and gay men are in the forefront of creative pursuits, since we are the people who break down and let something new come in. That's the function we serve and that's why we're here. That's also why it's very easy to identify us with death and decay.

And obviously this, too, is a source for our oppression.

It's why the identification of gay men and AIDS is so paramount in people's minds despite the fact that it's a disease that affects far more populations of people than just gay men. We dissolve the various myths in our culture. That's why Jesse Helms targets us, since he perceives quite accurately that we are revolutionary, so to speak. The natural world is a process of building up and decaying and breaking down. That breaking down piece is essential.

How do you define the difference between soul and spirit?

They're hard to differentiate. Spirit seems a little higher, more mental, less embodied than soul. When you say "spiritual," you think of transcending the material world. Soul is gaining that kind of enlightenment without transcending. It's the enlightenment that comes from living the experience, as opposed to going beyond the experience. Archetypes of the soul tend to be those things that sort of grab us by the neck and drag us down the path.

Would you say that the kinds of people we call gay are carriers of soul for society as a whole?

Definitely, because of the way in which in this society our salvation has come through owning our body, owning our embodiment. We understand the material world in a transformative way as opposed to a literal, materialistic kind of way. I think that's why gay people embody soul, perhaps more than spirit, in this culture.

Out of your considerable experience dealing with soul sickness, is there one thing more than others that gay men need to be mindful of? In other words, what is our central psychological dilemma, and what is the way toward resolving it?

Because enacting homosexual sexuality is often forbidden or discouraged, the one thing that accounts for a lot of gay men's unconsciousness is the conflict around their sexuality—either they don't enact it and continue to repress it or they act it out all over the place in an unreflective kind of way. Gay culture in general supports a very literalistic way of thinking about sexuality, as opposed to a more symbolic or deeper way. In a certain sense what happens, then, is that gay men don't fully appreciate the power of sexual action. And it comes around and bites them on the ass. Or they're so afraid of the power of sexual action that they put a lid on it and their soul dries up. Many gay men have fallen into the trap of the dominant culture's way of thinking about sexuality as something very frightening or as simply mechanistic.

Do you think your interest in matters of the soul is connected to being gay? Do you feel that being gay is a gift in the same way that perhaps your musical talent or ability to write is?

As I became more conscious of being gay and integrated it more deliberately into who I am it became more clearly a gift. It is a way of seeing the world that is very different from that of the majority. It gives me access to a deeper way of understanding other people and relationships, the kind of understanding that I think heterosexual people have to go through another process to reach.

What way is that?

Growing up gay, you really don't see portrayals of gay people or relationships, or at least I didn't when I was growing up. You realize that everything you've been told, everything you've been given, and everything you've seen has another whole level that actually speaks to your personal experience. And so you have this awareness of a dual level—the homoerotic level of relationship that has been forbidden but that you realize nevertheless exists. Being gay is very different from a heterosexual's experience, in which everything they see, hear, and have been told confirms their own experience. Whereas for gay men and lesbians, their experience is at odds with what they're told. And so you have this sense—like in *The Wizard of Oz* myth—that everything isn't really what it seems. That's gay people's gift. That's the gift I feel I have.

> *But it's a gift that society, more often than not, does not seem to want. You've examined homophobia, suggesting there are five underlying reasons for society's intolerance of gays. Two of the reasons, in particular, seem linked: the repressed envy from heterosexuals over the perception that childless gays seem to have an easier life, and the fact that gays awaken in the unconscious of others an intolerant fear of death because we leave no generation to succeed us.*

There's this myth that links heterosexuality with creativity, fecundity, and longevity—and anything that's the opposite of being heterosexual is not linked with those things. Yet we as gay people know that's false. The presence of gay men in all the arts throughout the ages speaks to the particular kind of creativity that's really identified with being a social outsider. We see things differently, and that's the purpose of art. There's a certain kind of creativity that gay people have that does provide for longevity and progeny and transformation, and always has, throughout Western civilization and probably beyond.

To take that myth of heterosexuality too literally is to shove homosexuals into the shadow, but I think that's changing. The myth doesn't even really make sense because there are so many gay people today who have literal children.

Everyone has procreated, period. What heterosexuals don't cop to is how burdensome that myth is to them. I see that in my work with family men in particular. They're saddled with the provider role and feel all kinds of restrictions on their ability to be who they are. That's what that envy is about: gay people are perceived as having more freedom. In fact, perhaps we do, since we're free from this myth.

> *But are we really? We may have more freedom in a physical sense, but don't you think the myth still operates in negative ways on our self-perception and ability to love? This strikes me as a problem that is perversely difficult to detect and deal with. In your experience as a therapist working with gay men, how big is the problem of internalized homophobia?*

It's a huge problem. Even the most "well-adjusted" gay man that I see struggles with it. I struggle with it myself. Having been identified from a very early age as gifted, I developed a certain kind of narcissism that helped protect me against self-hatred. But, still, it's there.

> *How do you detect it? What do you do with it?*

For me, it's actually wider than just homosexuality; it's more about sexuality in general. In my case, the atmosphere at home was not sexually repressive, but sex wasn't anything that was really talked about. It was very German and very Lutheran. There was a certain kind of decorum that was always maintained. And so, for me, it's more like sexophobia as opposed to homophobia. Sexuality has been the entryway into a greater spirituality as well as the Charybdis of my shadow. I have to struggle constantly with how much eroticism is appropriate, how much isn't, and where it is, and what it is—as opposed to anything necessarily about my gayness.

> *Gay men are wounded by homophobia, which usually first takes form when our fathers distance themselves from us. But haven't we also been wounded by our mothers?*

Our mothers have been trained to think about their sexuality in a particular heterosexual way that leads them to look to their sons for erotic mirroring. But a gay son does not do that. A gay son might feel very warmly toward his mother and be very connected, but there's a certain kind of erotic mirroring that he's not going to be giving her. The wounding we receive from our mother is the revenge of the rejected suitor; the mother feels rejected by the gay son and takes revenge.

What form does that revenge take? What form did it take in your own life?

There's a certain quality of my mother's consistent rejection, in both overt and subtle ways, of my homosexuality that is a piece of her revenge. It's like: If you're not going to mirror me erotically, don't expect me to mirror you. I'll be polite, but don't expect me to be with you emotionally or be very support-ive—you're on your own. Boom, the door is closed. I've learned to live with that closed door. I wish it were open. But it won't be.

When does this rejection set in?

The mother's rejection doesn't really occur until the child comes out, since up to that point Mom's still holding out the hope that she can seduce her son into mirroring her erotically. And then the son says no.

Does this seduction account for the almost inseparably close bond that exists between many gay boys and their mothers? Well into adulthood, many gay men still labor under the weight of having to be the best little boy in the world.

That's the myth of the seductive mother, the close-binding mother of our youth. It has to do with the mother's attempts to seduce the gay son into mirror-ing her, and the son's close bond to the mother has to do with wishing Mom would mirror him and not ever getting it. So their relationship becomes, in a cer-tain sense, compulsive.

Is this a fairly common experience with gay men?

Yes. However, if you have a mother who is sufficiently mirrored by her husband and who is confident enough about herself and her own sexuality not to expect a great deal of mirroring from her children, this is a dynamic that's absent. But it's the rare mother who is able to celebrate her child's sexuality regardless of what it is.

As an adult gay man, I have a closer relationship with my father. He doesn't expect that kind of mirroring and so doesn't have any investment in exacting revenge. My father's more open to who I actually am than my mother is. You would think Dad would be more threatened, but that's not really true.

Has this compulsive dynamic between gay men and their mothers left most of us narcissistically wounded—ageless boys, afraid of growing up and finding our adult masculine power? What is referred to, in Jungian terms, as being a puer aeternus?

That's a homophobic way of thinking about gay men, derived from the dominant culture's repressed envy. We have gay men of all psychological types, but the puer is the thing heterosexual people focus on because it supports their preconceptions.

We learn to love ourselves through being mirrored in love by another person. If you're gay, and you grow up in a heterosexual family, you're just not going to get the kind of mirroring you need to really learn to love yourself on a very deep level. That's the type of narcissistic wound that homosexual men and women are prone to. But that doesn't mean you can't receive that mirroring at another time in your life or work at creating that mirroring. That's certainly what love relationships and friendships are about, that's what teaching and therapy are about.

Does the narcissism develop through intense self-gazing?

Or from a certain kind of emphasis on our homosexuality that might not occur if we'd been mirrored rightly. This is why the dominant culture is always saying we're making too much over being gay or we're flaunting it. What that's really about is us attempting to get the kind of mirroring we should have had. I don't think gay men and lesbians are necessarily more narcissistically wounded than other people, but it's of a particular type. Heterosexual people are wounded narcissistically, too. It's just that our sense of self, our psychological development, occurs on a separate track.

How does our sexuality intersect with our souls?

In my adolescence and early adulthood there was absolutely no question to me that eroticism was a divine gift. The most important relationship I had in high school was with the Italian-American captain of the soccer team, whose brother was a priest and who had grown up in a town where Padre Pio, the Capuchin friar who received the stigmata, lived. Vince had been baptized by Padre Pio. My relationship with him was clearly erotic and yet sacred at the same time.

When I bring my eroticism into a relationship with a man, whether he's gay or not, there's a kind of transformation that gay eroticism brings to that person that pushes him past what he thought he was or what he was even comfortable being. We're bringing something new and transforming to that person that certainly accounts for a lot of the myths around sacred male-male relationships throughout the ages. Gay sexuality, gay eroticism, is as transformative as any transformative sacred event.

Could the fear of this transformative power be another source of gay oppression?

Absolutely. Once you've come out you're beyond heterosexuality, and so you are free to start playing with the transformative powers of eroticism in a way that you're not ordinarily given permission to do. That's why gay people, in particular, are the carriers of that kind of transformation in this culture. But it's not just cultural, it's archetypal.

One of the great insights of Jung was to define Eros more widely than Freud, who, when he said Eros, meant genital sexuality. Jung talks about Eros more as the life force of the universe and goes back to the more classical use of the term: that Eros is a god, responsible for a whole variety of human behaviors and impulses, not just the genital sexual impulses. Eros is Aphrodite's son. So there's a certain kind of puer quality of creativity, newness, and rebirth—as well as a certain kind of violence—that's inherent in Eros. So when I say eroticism, or Eros, I mean it in that much wider sense.

Gay men and lesbians know that there's a certain kind of salvation through the body, through owning who you are as an embodied person, which we've all directly experienced in our coming out process. For us, those two elements—the material world and the spiritual world—are not dichotomous. They're one.

Tell me a dream, one of your dreams or some other man's dream that has been told to you, that somehow best exemplifies the promise and joy of being gay.

Here's a dream that I used toward the end of *Men's Dreams, Men's Healing*. It's from a client who gave me permission to use it. He was in bed with a woman, perhaps his girlfriend, and the bed split in two. So now he was in bed with the woman and he was in bed with another man. He stroked the man's navel and the man's belly began to undulate. The dreamer realized the man was giving birth.

I think this dream incarnates the joy of being gay. There's a sense of all possibilities being open, a sense of both masculine and feminine as well as male-male relatedness. I love the idea of male birth; it's a very archetypal symbol, a sacred symbol. It's not an image that is ever given to us in conventional culture—that our gayness is fertile.

What is being given birth to? Extend the dream.

I want to say a male child, but my other association is a dream that my lover had in which he gave birth to himself. There was the same imagery: he was pregnant and went through the birth process. Who he gave birth to was himself. I feel what we, as gay men, are giving birth to is a new sense of masculinity as well as giving birth to ourselves. Our relationship with another man and being impregnated by his masculinity allows us to be who we are.

Is the self you're talking about with a capital S the archetypal Self?

It's both the little *s*—ourselves—as well as the big *S*, the Self as a reflection of the divine. To be fully who you are is to be part of the divine.

And this is possible through romance with another man?

Oh, yes. And not just romance, but I think through erotic connection. Gay men don't think about their sexuality as particularly impregnating, but it is on a symbolic level. I think that is why sexual enactment requires a great deal of consciousness. Joseph Kramer's work around tantric insights is his way of talking about the same sort of thing: how to contact the divine through sexual expression, how to impregnate another man symbolically, emotionally, if not literally.

You believe, then, that there is a profound, sacred aspect to our homoeroticism.

It's very difficult for most gay men to see that, and that's a result of society's homophobia, its sexophobia. Sexuality, any sexuality, is understood literally as opposed to symbolically or emotionally. Gay men have to work past that.

The great tragedy of homophobia, then, is that it keeps gay men from knowing their innermost selves.

Absolutely. That's the intention. Members of the dominant culture, without even articulating it, are aware of how powerful that connection is and don't want that to be enacted.

But it's so tragic all around: we're kept from connecting with our authentic selves and society is kept from receiving the contributions that spring from that discovery.

Homophobia doesn't just hurt gay people, it hurts heterosexual people. Heterosexual men are cut off from sources of male impregnation through their homophobia, and it's tragic. What we get are legions of men without any friends, with a profound fear of other men, who have been cut off from their own masculinity in a way that's alienating. And they're the ones who suffer from it, not just gay people in terms of external oppression. Heterosexual men themselves suffer grave psychological consequences from homophobia that they aren't even aware of. It's kind of amazing to me. It's almost like heterosexual men suffer from it more than gay men nowadays. Gay men have a community and a literature and they can go someplace and be out. Heterosexual men have very few places to work through their homophobia.

You advance the idea of the male anima as being an important part of gay men's psyche. I thought the anima was supposed to represent the archetypal feminine within a man. So how can there be a male anima? It seems like a contradiction of terms.

Jung originally called that archetype Soul Figure, without any gender identification. It's the figure in your psyche, in your dreams, that is the symbol of your soul. He noticed that in the majority of cases the Soul Figure was contrasexual: that is, if you're a man, it's a woman; if you're a woman, it's a man. And that got codified because it's very consonant with our way of thinking about gender in general. But I've noticed that for gay men it's often a male figure. What we're really talking about is a symbolic figure of the psyche that isn't bound by our gender constructions.

We're bound within a two-gender system, but couldn't there be three or four genders?

Absolutely. And more. And something in between. I would say in the majority of gay men's cases the most powerful soul figures are male, are identified as male. In their dreams they project their soul figures onto men rather than women. This Double/Soul Figure is a really important piece of gay men's experience, and acknowledging it as a living reality can widen the dominant culture's consciousness of how false the gender dichotomy actually is. The psyche is a far more fluid place than Jesse Helms would have us believe.

A union with the same precedes the ability to unite with the opposite. If you don't have a union with yourself, you cannot unite with someone who's different. And so a male-male or female-female union precedes male-female or female-male union. Unfortunately, that twinship, that doubling, is not encouraged at all—quite the opposite. It's outrageous.

Doesn't this, in effect, keep all people out of touch with their inner selves—their souls? It seems to me that any culture would suffer as a result of this attitude.

Western cultures all pretty much think in the same dichotomous ways. The indigenous cultures that haven't gotten into literalistic, technological, materialistic, dichotomous ways of thinking, that think more holistically, seem to be a little bit healthier psychologically. The danger, of course, is idealizing these cultures in some way. We're really only talking about one aspect, a more holistic way of thinking about gender and sexuality. On that issue, it feels like indigenous or aboriginal cultures are a little bit more together.

If we could go back to ancient Mesopotamia or Greece, would we be able to recognize the types of people we today call gay?

It's very easy to see other historical ages through our lenses, but that isn't necessarily accurate. Still, something is certainly going on that has an archetypal foundation in human experience. There's a certain union with the same that I think underlies homosexual behavior and relationship throughout the ages. The union of sames is as sacred as the union of opposites and is necessary for psychic growth and health—on an individual, social, and spiritual level. There's a certain way in which uniting with the same teaches us self-love, which is an aspect of loving creation, the sacred force behind the universe.

Uniting with the opposite teaches us love for others, which is also a reflection of loving the sacred force behind the universe. Yet our modern culture has emphasized the union of opposites to the detriment of the union of sames. There are, I believe, other cultures, both ancient and modern—ancient Greece and Native American tribes, for example—that have not fallen prey to that kind of emphasis. There's a union with the same that is the fount of self-love and therefore love of the universe. It brings the wholeness that occurs from uniting with someone who's the same as you. I think that when we look back to people whom we would currently call gay, that's what we see. We see that archetypal impulse toward the union of sames and the work that that does on an individual and cultural basis.

The homoerotic is an archetypal aspect of human sexuality. In a hundred years we may not necessarily even categorize people as gay. If our culture is able to integrate homoeroticism into everyone's sexuality, there won't be a need to identify anyone as this or that.

But won't there always be people who'll be more attracted to seeking union with a same?

Yes, but we would probably refer to them as exclusively homosexual. It feels like *gay* is a concept that has been developed in order to retrieve the value and the importance of that area of human experience. If that's been retrieved and integrated into our culture, then the positive emphasis on it can drop—it's already been acknowledged. The end point of the whole gay liberation process in a certain sense is to kind of normalize it, but not in the sense of integrating it into heterosexual society. Normalize it in the sense that it will be acknowledged as a fundamental part of everyone's sexuality and no more important than that.

If you could take gay men, look collectively into their eyes, and say one thing, what would it be?

That your sexuality is sacred. The majority of gay men I have met see their sexuality in literal or materialistic terms and not in symbolic and sacred terms. Much of my work is to get them to see the sacredness of their sexuality, to perceive that it's an embodiment of Eros and not just ejaculation.

Eros is the fount of life, the primal, vital, procreative force of the universe. We must refuse to let our Eros be robbed.

MALCOLM BOYD

SURVIVAL WITH GRACE

This is a homosexual bar, Jesus.

It looks like any other bar on the outside, only it isn't.

Men stand three and four deep at this bar—some just feeling a sense of belonging here, others making contacts for new sexual partners.

This isn't very much like a church, Lord, but many members of the church are also here in this bar. Quite a few of the men here belong to the church as well as to this bar. If they knew how, a number of them would ask you to be with them in both places. Some of them wouldn't, but won't you be with them, too, Jesus?

This audacious meditation from Malcolm Boyd's much-praised collection of prayers, Are You Running with Me, Jesus?, *speaks not only for the gay everymen in the bar but of the author's yearnings as well. Bridging seemingly irreconcilable differences— the sacred and the secular, the political and the personal —has been his life work.*

As a gay man who has happened to be an Episcopal priest during the past four decades, Boyd has taken Christianity's central metaphor of death and resurrection quite literally to heart, having shed old personas numerous times in pursuit of a more authentic self during the course of his seventy-one years. And, as is his wont, this famous "disturber of the peace" has laid bare many of society's conventions that would keep others from doing the same. Whether inviting Christ down off the cross and into the underground of gay life, or seeking dialogue between the races, or preaching nonviolence in a war-torn world, Boyd has strived to unite fragmented pieces into wholeness.

The well-known author-activist-clergyman came to his avocation through a need to heal himself. Born June 7, 1923, as the only child of a well-to-do Manhattan family, Malcolm grew up feeling lonely and isolated. "A chauffeur taught me how to read the face of a clock and how to tie my shoelaces," he explains. But the gulf separating him from other children could not be attributed to class differences alone. "I've never felt in one sense like an earthling," he continues. "I couldn't share my feeling of alienation, or explain it, so I just went off by myself."

When Malcolm was ten his parents divorced, and he moved with his mother to Colorado Springs, Colorado, and a few years after that to nearby Denver. Ever the loner, the precocious youth spent Saturday mornings checking out books at the library and listening to the weekly broadcast of the New York Met-

ropolitan Opera. *The afternoon was spent at the movies, where he sat enthralled by the fictions of Hollywood's golden age. "I had a super-active imagination," he says, "so the movies deeply affected me. I always had to modify my behavior in order to get along in a social situation. I could never be myself." In a way, it was a life in training for the queer man of the world to come. "I was more worldly than the other boys—I read* The Nation *and the* New York Times, *wrote op-ed pieces for the* Denver Post *and the* Rocky Mountain News—*but in another way I wasn't," he candidly states. "I was sophisticated and very gifted, yet I played a role. I had a mask."*

Malcolm's sense of confinement continued throughout his college years at the University of Arizona. Upon graduation, he headed for Hollywood, looking for a fresh vantage and a job in communications. Boyd was hired by a top Los Angeles advertising agency and given an NBC radio show to produce. Ambitious and driven, his star never stopped rising. During the next few years, Boyd became recognized as one of the entertainment industry's brightest young players, working at studios as various as Samuel Goldwyn and Republic Pictures, and he eventually ending up as film legend Mary Pickford's partner in their own independent production company.

Still, for all of his worldly success, Boyd knew that something inside was far from resolved: his lifelong feeling of otherness, of being an actor in somebody else's script, persisted. He unexpectedly found clarity one night in 1951 at a raucous Hollywood party. The room was filled with famous faces, everyone slowly getting drunk. Standing aloof, Boyd suddenly knew that if he stayed in Hollywood, he would end up like the people in the room. The subsequent announcement that he was leaving the film industry to enter into the Episcopal priesthood made the front pages of Variety *and the* Los Angeles Times. *"People were terribly shocked; nobody believed it," he says. "They felt it was a publicity stunt, or I'd lost my mind and was having a nervous breakdown. It didn't make sense to be giving up that kind of a career." But sincerity, even in Hollywood, apparently won out. At Boyd's going away party at the glittery nightspot Ciro's, columnist Hedda Hopper reported that everybody present, including the bartenders, bowed their heads for the Lord's Prayer.*

After three years in seminary, Boyd was ordained a priest. Though he continued with graduate theological studies in Europe and the United States for three more years, he did not begin duty as a parish priest until

1957 in Indianapolis. It was a role the frank and outspoken clergyman would not hold long. The civil rights movement was gaining visible momentum, and rather than offering Sunday platitudes to a comfortable congregation, Boyd wanted to join that struggle. He spent the next several years in Detroit as a college chaplain and as a civil rights volunteer in the South working for social justice—marching past angry bigots, learning lessons of nonviolence from Martin Luther King, Jr., firsthand. The anti–Vietnam War movement was soon propelled on its fiery course, and here, too, Boyd took a stand, speaking out on campuses, in coffeehouses, and even from within the Pentagon itself. He was arrested many times for his efforts and earned the appellation "rebel priest."

In 1965 Boyd put all that he felt and had discovered into a book of plainly written prayers. It spoke directly of the zeitgeist of the time, the fury and pain and dislocation so many Americans were experiencing. Are You Running with Me, Jesus? *was hailed as a modern classic and made Boyd an international celebrity overnight. Although, in one sense, the book was a message for others to slow down and let Jesus catch up, Boyd didn't slow down at all: the next decade was filled with more books, television talk shows, impassioned opinion pieces, and public appearances. As he had been in Hollywood, Boyd was now the Episcopal church's rising wonder: a principled advocate for change, a trusted confidant of the secure and powerful. He remained true to his ability to hold the center among widely divergent forces. But despite all the changes and success, he was still trying to catch up with himself, with the inner self so acutely known in his boyhood, the one who never quite felt like "an earthling."*

Then in 1976 Boyd felt it was time, and he announced his homosexuality in a New York Times *interview. The gay movement was in its nascent stages, and he wanted to join. Neither the gay movement nor the church—nor the world, for that matter—knew quite what do with this self-outed celebrity. Too open for religion and too religious for being gay, Boyd now found that more doors had closed than were opened. He had no choice but to keep on running.*

I found Malcolm momentarily resting one balmy February night in Los Angeles in 1984. I was visiting the city for only a day on a business trip, and my employer, The Advocate, *a San Francisco Bay Area–based, national gay newsmagazine, had booked me a room at a somewhat notorious gay motel with which it had an advertising trade arrangement. I checked-in late in the day, grumpy and* tired, and I was less than pleased to find a note from a mutual friend announcing that Malcolm Boyd was also a guest of the establishment. I called and introduced myself, saying I would stop by his room for a few minutes to say hello. Shortly into our visit I learned that Malcolm was seeking refuge there, having just walked out of a relationship turned sour and with no other idea of where to go.

We were polite, yet we found each other engaging. What was meant to be a brief encounter stretched into a couple of hours. Though we never expected it, those two hours have become a relationship that has endured for the past ten years and, as far as we can see, to the end of our days. In so many ways, we could not be further apart: one from the East Coast, the other from the West; one an Episcopal priest, the other an eclectic blend of pagan-Buddhist-Jungian; one entering into his eighth decade, the other barely in his forties. Yet, somehow our life together as a committed couple works. Every person has the capacity to die and be reborn many times in a life. Malcolm has exemplified that for me simply by being who he is; I complement him in this fashion by always reminding that the work of a gay soul in the making is never done.

°

You've asked, is Jesus gay? Don't you mean was?

I have no theory about the historical Jesus. I wish that he had done an interview with Mike Wallace on "60 Minutes." But in Christ I find many gay qualities: vulnerability, sensitivity, someone who emptied himself of power, who lived as a gentle but strong person. He also broke many social taboos and found sterling qualities in a number of people who were despised by the society they lived in. He is very much a gay archetype in my understanding of what being gay means.

But one can certainly find gay men who are not particularly gentle or sensitive or kind.

Being gay for me means gentleness, sensitivity, warmth, and service to others. When I meet a gay person who is the opposite of those things, I am offended. Because that's someone who has not realized himself or herself. I'm always put off by somebody who's bitter or vindictive, who doesn't care about helping other people, who is not reflective. They're missing an opportunity to be who they really are, or at least what they have a capacity to be.

> *Increasing numbers of gay people are coming out and seeking spiritual sustenance within organized religion. Yet some critics have accused gay advocates within the church of Uncle Tom-ism, selling out and assimilating the values of their oppressor. Where do you stand on this conflict?*

My view is that the church belongs to me. It doesn't belong to somebody "over there." I have been openly gay during the past twelve years that I've worked at St. Augustine by-the-Sea [an Episcopal church in Santa Monica] and as an AIDS chaplain. I have a gay relationship, I write gay books. In other words, I live my life as I wish to live my life. And a part of my life is that I am in the church. I've never been an Uncle Tom. I've played a certain prophetic role in the church. I've accepted going to jail and been very active in civil rights and the peace movement as well as the gay movement.

Some people in the church who are gay might play an Uncle Tom role, others do not. But you can't change an institution like the church if you're outside it. And it's very important to change the church, to change the Pentagon, to change the White House, to change all sorts of institutions. I'm in the church because underneath a lot of things that I find open to extreme criticism, I'm at home in it, and I believe in its purpose to serve God and people.

> *Of all things to become, why a priest?*

I wanted to use my mind, and I wanted to use my soul. I thought life could be a multisplendid thing, and the Hollywood scene was very limiting. Mary Pickford and I talked a lot about God and about spirituality. She struggled with meanings of faith. I was studying and reading a lot about theology. I felt that the whole area of spirituality and religion was not only fascinating but held answers for me. The mystical goal of achieving union with God is a wonderful calling.

> *Did your interest in pursuing a spiritual life have anything to do with being homosexual?*

I don't think I went into seminary with the idea of meeting gay people. I went into seminary with the idea of meeting God. To my astonishment, I met more gay people in seminary than I had ever met in Hollywood. There are more gay people in the church than probably anywhere else, and you could say intuitively I was motivated by this. Because here I found my tribe. That wasn't my conscious intention, however, but if it had been it was the smartest thing I could have done. Of course, gay life was all underground. The closet in seminary was huge, much bigger than I'd felt the closet in Hollywood was.

> *How did you relate to the gay life in Hollywood during your years working there?*

It turned me off completely because I didn't know what it was to be homosexual or gay. I would have been open to an absolutely gorgeous romance with Prince Charming, but I certainly wasn't interested in abusive, cynical, snorting men who assumed that I was interested in them. I remember some friends and I were at a drive-in once, and truck drivers were going in and out of the men's room rubbing their crotch. Somebody said, "They've got a queer in there who's servicing them." That was the way I looked at homosexuality. There wasn't any other picture presented to me.

> *What is it about the church that attracts so many gay men?*

Where were gays ever going to go in the past but the military or the church? And the church dealt in mystery, beauty, music, and ritual. These are things that speak to gay men. And also the mere fact of gay men being there meant that even if you were closeted and closeted from one another, somehow you knew.

> *The church has traditionally been a shelter for broken souls in need. Is this what attracted you?*

I'm not sure that I felt sheltered so much as I clearly identified as a wounded, broken person with the wounded, broken person of Jesus. In other words, Jesus has always made complete sense to me. Here is God saying, "I've gone through the same thing you're going through—you're not alone." This has been very elemental in terms of my belief and my caring.

> *You are one of very few gay men with such a high profile to have dared to come out, even in a place as liberal as the Episcopal church. What is the price of staying closeted in the church?*

I have never seen such bitterness, vindictiveness, and cruelty as I have on the part of closeted gay priests. These are people who have chosen to live a lie and have paid a high price—a price of happiness and freedom. What do they get back? A certain prestige, which they guard with their life.

I had a brief sexual encounter with a closeted priest once that was very unfortunate. I was in need of sexual release at that time, and so I slept with him on occasion. But it was one of the most unpleasant experiences of my life. He was so unhappy. There was just no joy at all.

Having no joy is one price for staying in the closet, but sometimes there's a price to be paid when one comes out. Wasn't that the case when you announced being gay in 1976?

The gay movement was burgeoning, and I had long known I was gay. So, being a public figure, I came out in the *New York Times* and the "CBS Evening News." There was no other way, and all hell broke loose. It cost me a great deal of money, a lot of power and privilege. Many doors were closed. I certainly found out who my friends were. The church just didn't know what to do with me. I was unemployable. So I put my energy into a relationship and wrote *Take Off the Masks*. I felt like Marco Polo in China because the gay world was such a new world to me.

What basic Christian tenet or philosophy do you most closely follow in your life? What of Christianity has sustained you personally?

I have been most affected by the doctrine of the Incarnation, which states that God became human, that God entered into the ordinary life of men and women in the person of Jesus Christ. This means that there's no separation between God and people. For thirty-three years in the earthly life of Jesus Christ, God fully embraced the human condition—bled, sweated, experienced life completely, and was executed. In the doctrine of the Incarnation, there is simply no room for homophobia or racism. This has deeply affected me. It led me into the civil rights movement, for example.

What is a gay theology, a gay-centered faith? This is something you've given a great deal of thought to, yet it's hard to understand what would make a theology gay.

A gay theology is theology seen through a gay sensibility. An African-American theology is a theology seen through an African-American sensibility. A feminist theology is a theology seen through a feminist sensibility. That's what it is. And I'm shocked at how little valuable work has yet been done in this area.

It's difficult for many gay people to accept a theology of any kind, particularly when religious orthodoxy has been used as a weapon to condemn them.

The weapon wasn't used by God. And the weapon wasn't used by Jesus Christ. The weapon was used by people who have also used the same weapons of racism and misogyny. The answer is that different people come to God through different paths. We need to respect one another's traditions and where we're coming from. I do try to respect others. I ask them to respect me, too.

So you're saying that it doesn't make any difference which path one takes as long as we have a meaningful relationship with God.

I deeply respect other religious faiths and pathways to God and have personally benefited from them.

So what's the gay path to God?

I don't know if there is one gay path to God. Gay theology is mediated through whatever is one's experience of worship and spirituality. In terms of myself, I'm gay and I make peace with God in terms of my gayness. My prayer is rooted in my gay experience. My understanding of sexuality can't be someone else's understanding—it can't be heterosexual. It has to be my own. I have to relate this to God.

Worship can't really be by rote or something alien; it has to be rooted in my own struggle and yearnings as a gay person, my understanding of myself and of God. This has been my journey. If I'd grown up in the environment of being seen—and being able to see myself—as a complete whole person, it would have made all the difference; it would have saved me torture.

What is the difference between soul and spirit?

There's shit in the soul, there's sweat in the soul, there's room for cock and balls in the soul, and for civil rights and community building. The soul brings me down to the ground of my very being without any illusions—I can't hide, I can't be a hypocrite. I've got to deal with the reality of life if I'm talking about my soul. Spirit is more transcendent. If I attempted to deal with spirit by being a religious person and not deal with the soul, I would be missing the whole point.

Are gay men more in touch with their souls because they've been wounded for being different?

The gay experience is very similar to the African-American experience in terms of soul. Both peoples have been unable to bullshit the process. There's nothing to hide behind. It's all hanging out. It's frequently bloody. And we have been to hell and back at the hands of nice white people and nice heterosexuals, and "nice" is in quotes. We have suffered and are wounded. We understand soul better because we've had to in order to survive. How could we survive? Some gay people have survived by lying and not looking at reality. They have become twisted and engaged in a self-destructive process. But for the gay person who is not self-destructive and who is striving to be whole and be healed, it's necessary to embrace the soul and deal with everything that's found there.

How can gay people begin to redeem and separate out the hopeful message that perhaps does exist for them in Christianity?

The principal way is to quit concentrating on gay spirit and get involved in the muck and the reality of gay soul. Too many gay Christians have been remote, transcendent, have been involved in churchianity rather than Christianity. It's essential to discover a relationship with the radical Jesus Christ. Gay soul is the great meeting place for gay Christians and gay Buddhists, gay Jews and gay agnostics. Anybody interested in gay spirituality and theology has a meeting place in gay soul. However, we have not met there enough.

That entails coming back to the basic question: What does it mean to be gay? You can't find the answer to that unless you immerse yourself in gay soul. And soul that is gay is soul experienced through gay experience and sensibility and reality.

Some would say that if you're dealing with the soul on that very deep level, then you are addressing God.

I would say that.

How do you deal with your gay soul? What about your anger, for instance? Aside from all of the work you've done around issues of social injustice where anger can be a very righteous sword, you are also someone who's filled with a lot of deeply held personal rage. How do you deal with that on a soul level?

As a gay man, I have anger and rage. I am still wounded. I am still seeking wholeness.

But what do you do with the rage? One can't vent anger all the time, so how do you keep it from becoming a corrosive force inside?

When I'm angry or enraged, I must deal with the source of it. I can't sweep it under a rug. I can't say that the anger and rage are not real. I don't want to be destroyed by it. So as somebody working at my own healing, I try to isolate what comes out of gay soul for me in terms of my rage and my anger and deal with it on a one to one basis. If it means going to someone and either asking for forgiveness or offering it, then that's what it means. If it means dealing with envy, then I deal with it. I've turned my life around in a number of ways by trying to change anger and rage into loving.

This is very hard.

I find it one of the hardest things in the world, but I've done it.

How can we find this place within ourselves?

When we say, I will go through the pain that's necessary. I will go through the burning because I've got to go through it in order to get to this other place. A place where I am whole and not wounded, where I am realistically dealing with the issues that are haunting me and limiting my life. We can't stand back and be passive; we've got to get into the arena of soul. We've got to do the mud wrestling.

In what way does the church contribute to the kind of soul work you say needs to be done?

When the church practices the offering of forgiveness and the acceptance of forgiveness, it is doing soul work. And where it's happening, it's real. Where it is not happening, the church is refusing to engage in serious soul work. The church is split. Much of it is in heresy. Much of it isn't doing soul work. Much of it isn't doing God's work at all—it's playing games. But there are parts of the church and there are places in the church that are doing the serious work.

At age seventy-one, what wisdom would you offer to a young gay man considering vows as a priest.

One, there can be no room for the closet at all. Rule two, you cannot live a divided life; you have to be the same person in the religious setting as in the gay setting.

It's not enough to come out of the closet and lead a gay life?

What it means is wrestling in the mud. What it means is accepting the soul for what it is, not equating it with spirit, and realizing that we've got to be doing the soul work all the time.

You've said that the average gay man isn't some guy in a tank top on Hollywood Boulevard but an overweight schoolteacher living in a sort of crummy apartment. Could you explain that?

I feel some anger and rage, getting back to anger and rage, about the fact that a small group of gay people are controlling some of the media representing what is supposed to be gay life and the gay community. Probably seventy to eighty percent of gays are honeycombed into the culture or are still in the closet. The prototype of the gay male may really be a flabby, tweedy gay schoolteacher who lives in relationship with somebody in a quiet neighborhood. We've projected some very mistaken and distorted images of gay life. What's essential now is to start dealing with gay people as we are. As for the seventy percent or more that are closeted, I'm fascinated. I want to know who these people are. I want to address them; I want them to address me. These people are living a gay life. These people are grappling with gay soul.

I come back at this point to Jesus in terms of the kind of person that he was and reveals himself to be; he wasn't a "successful" type. In fact, Jesus was a failure at a human level—the cross represents that. Jesus said turn the other cheek and practice unconditional love.

That's hard to do when your loved ones are being gay-bashed in the streets or are dying horrible deaths from complications due to AIDS.

Jesus didn't say to lie down in a concentration camp and become a victim. And by telling us to turn the other cheek, Jesus wasn't saying to accept Ronald Reagan, Bill Clinton, or anybody else in terms of AIDS. That's not what Jesus was talking about. Jesus was talking about unconditional love and nonviolence, which we've never even tried. I believe that this country is doomed unless we can come to understand nonviolence and practice it. Nonviolence is not seeking the answer in violence.

Martin Luther King taught me that nonviolence is the way you pick up the telephone. I like that because it's so specific. Whenever I pick up the telephone I realize how close or how far from nonviolence I am.

Some people think that nonviolence means being passive.

Gandhi, who practiced nonviolence, was as involved in social action as anyone in the world. But it's how you accomplish social action. What are your goals? That's the point. As gay people, we have to be socially active at every level. We're asserting our own rights, we're asserting the rights of others, but at the same time I think the way we do it needs to be through nonviolence and unconditional love.

It's important that these be recognized as active, not passive. In her book *I Know Why the Caged Bird Sings*, Maya Angelou speaks of her grandmother, who won a moral victory when she was embarrassed and humiliated by young white girls who were taunting her. She did not retaliate in anger or rage, but maintained her dignity. She earned respect and her integrity was intact. Moral dignity is something that gay people need to accept. A lot of gay people, out of feelings of inadequacy or perhaps guilt, push that away and say, "I'm not worthy of that."

Moral dignity sounds like one of those truisms that are scribbled on a Sunday school chalkboard. Don't you think that one of the functions gay people have in society is to upset dignity, to be rather rude, in your face, to defy and extend social norms?

Moral dignity doesn't have to be something scribbled on a board; it's about reclaiming our self-acceptance and self-dignity.

Surprisingly, there have been no national leaders to emerge from the gay community whom one could point to as a kind of King or

Gandhi figure—someone as politically astute as they are morally forthright. Why is this?

There's a lot of self-hatred, and we project that hatred onto one another. There's a lot of non-self-acceptance, and therefore we have problems accepting one another. We tend to want to bring people down to a particular level rather than to say this person might have a certain kind of goodness and parity. We permitted Harvey Milk a certain amount of this, but it was only after his death. Self-acceptance, of course, is absolutely basic to any morality. I know it's taken me forever to deal with it, but I'm getting there.

What are some of the other elements of morality, of coming from a deeply moral point of view?

Certainly loving one another in an unconditional sense and not being afraid of that. Some people reading this might get up and start ranting at this point because they would say that love is sentimental pap, that there's no place for it. I totally disagree. Loving is absolutely essential to morality, as is hope. Hope is not the secret garden, and it's not a childish story—hope is terribly raw and real.

All right. What else?

Faith.

That's kind of ambiguous. Faith in what?

Faith in hope, faith in potential goodness, faith in meaning, faith in love. I believe this is essential for morality. It's also essential for sanity! I want to say a little more about forgiveness, too, because forgiveness is the hardest. We don't want to forgive: "Daddy hurt me, so I'll never forgive him." "I won't forgive you, ex-lover." "I won't forgive you, self." It's hard to forgive. To make it real, you've got to consent to walk through the fire. You've got to deal with the necessity for humility; you have got to deal with your pride. In our woundedness as gay people, we've chosen to make forgiveness not very viable. We've often chosen to take a bitchy road, and we've chosen to say that we don't want to forgive.

But you're saying that the ability to forgive is a prerequisite to having a true morality.

Yes. Inevitably. There's hard spiritual work that needs to be done by gay people, and too many false prophets and people out for a buck won't say it. When you add the automatic put-down of religion onto that, you're precluding a kind of dialogue, which we've often forfeited because it's painful and it offends our pride. We don't have any time for it.

We're really looking at some hard choices here.

The real choice is: Are we going to have the courage to persevere to find out what it means to be gay? And then to do the hard work to get to some new places? Or are we just going to stay wounded and unforgiving? Do we have to play the same tired roles over and over again? What we're offered is freedom. As gay people, you'd think we'd want it more than anybody because it's been so denied to us. And there is now the potential for that freedom.

You're obviously not talking about freedom just in terms of civil rights.

Not at all. I'm talking about freedom inside, freedom to develop as a person who is free of old woundings, old strictures, and old pride. It's an interior freedom I'm talking about. And unless we deal with this as gay people we're going to end up as a footnote on page 288 of world history. We won't be relevant at all. Our progress can't be measured in terms of who knows what president or who's on the cover of *People* magazine. That's totally irrelevant. What's important is the kind of life we choose to live, and if we have the courage to make it real. As I look around, I see some gay people pioneering on the path of interior freedom. I see all too many not doing it.

How are you working to achieve this freedom in your own life?

I seek mysticism in religion. I try to prepare for my own death—and therefore my own life. I don't resent anyone "beautiful." I have no time for envy. I try to be open to different kinds of gay experience. I try to enter into it, to figure out what's going on. I ask, What part of this scene might have something to say to me? I try to listen.

What you are talking about is the road less traveled.

I am. We need to get out of our own personal concerns to a far greater extent than we do and play an active role in a movement beyond ourselves. This to me has something to do with the meaning of being gay. It's not just an individual matter. It involves community. A lot of gay people who might be reading this book at some point may be sitting alone in a room feeling very individual and isolated. It's important for them to accept their place in a movement and in a world. I really do believe that we as gay people have an involved role in the world. In helping. In being a part of something greater than ourselves. I see gays as kind of a perpetual Peace Corps. We're meant for something far beyond ourselves and our own selfish concerns. This is a part of the meaning of being gay. We can find universal meaning if we find specific meaning.

What's our reward for all of this selfless service you propose?

Our reward is healing from our woundedness. Our reward is wholeness.

Did God make gay people to be wounded?

If you look at the beatitudes, blessed are the poor, blessed are those who have been persecuted. To me, the fact that God is concerned with the poor and the persecuted is very deep. I believe that God has a plan.

You do?

Oh yes. It's important for gay people to realize that we're unique. We're special. We're loved. God isn't a monster or a demon, and God has shared our own experience of human life. Shared it. All the way to and through the cross.

But to be different from others, to be queer, means that one is going to be wounded in some way.

Yes. So God then has given us gifts. The capacity to love, the capacity for a deep sensitivity, the capacity for service. How many of us are schoolteachers, shamans, priests, and ministers; how many of us are in service capacities? An enormous number, completely disproportionate. When I marched with Martin Luther King and worked in the civil rights movement, I met so many gays.

God never planned anything in terms of making gays suffer. God created. It isn't God who's ever persecuted gay people. Part of our uniqueness comes out of our sensitivity, the horror, the torture, the terror that we have lived through. I'm very grateful to have survived and to be surviving. And I love others who have survived. Our love is manifold. Our hope is limitless. Our faith is a gift. We are here for one another in acceptance and gratitude. God loves us. We can love God, and one another, and ourselves. This is survival—and victory—with grace.

MITCH WALKER

COMING OUT INSIDE

When he was seventeen years old, Mitch Walker fell irrevocably in love with the tall blond captain of his high school's football team. Sometimes, even a glimpse of his classmate's exposed ankle would send paroxysms of excitement through the infatuated teenager. But it was a secret pleasure, an obsession not to be shared with anyone. So Mitch started a journal, "the Herald love diary," he called it, in which he recorded his innermost thoughts. "It was the soul bursting forth like a blazing sun," he recalls. "I wrote pages about that ankle, the little bit of naked flesh beneath the cuff of his pants. Herald became the center around which my entire universe turned."

The journal increased in size over the next year, a mash note grown to book-length proportions. Finally, one spring night shortly before graduation, Mitch was given a lift home from a school function by his unsuspecting peer. The car pulled up before the simple, wood-framed house in the working-class community of Hawthorne, California, where Mitch lived, and with a few hastily uttered words he presented the journal to Herald. They said goodbye, and with the book laying unopened on the seat, the handsome athlete drove off whistling into the night.

The next day, Mitch knew his impulsive gesture had gone terribly awry. As he stood at attention in gym class, waiting to be checked off the rota by the coach's assistant—who just happened to be Herald—Mitch realized his anxious glances were being ignored. It was not until after class that the two youths nervously confronted one another. Yes, Herald informed Mitch, he had indeed read the journal—but then immediately burned it. "You need help," he bluntly told the rejected suitor.

Twenty-five years later, Walker remembers that agonizing moment as a pivotal experience in his development as a gay man. His open declaration of love for another just like himself initiated a lifelong search for the meaning beneath the emotion. From that afternoon on he would not hesitate to plunge into the deep currents of feeling he had always known, looking for their origin—the source of gay love itself.

After high school graduation, Walker enrolled at the University of California, Los Angeles, where he also began seeing a prominent psychologist who tried to dissuade him from homosexuality. "He told me I'd live a shitty life in the gutter or end up killing myself," Walker recalls. "But after a year and a half I fell in love with another classmate and stopped that therapy." As faulty as the experience had been, it provided Walker with an invaluable introduction to inner work, to the techniques of dream analysis, and to other tools of psychological investigation.

Walker left Los Angeles for the university's Berkeley campus, where he majored in psychology. In 1972, increasingly outspoken about gay issues, Walker became one of the first members of the Berkeley Free Clinic's Gay Men's Collective. After completing his undergraduate degree, the young activist started a master's-level psychology program at San Francisco's Lone Mountain College. The focus of his work was same-sex love from an archetypal perspective, using visionary Swiss psychologist Carl Jung's theory that archetypes are the primal indwelling sources after which behavior is patterned and images are perceived.

"One night in 1974," he recounts, "I had a revelation while watching television. The Christopher Isherwood version of the Frankenstein story was debuting, and after the doctor brings his creation to life, he unravels the bandages and the monster turns out to be this gorgeous blond hunk. Don't ask me how things fit together, but suddenly my wondering about gay love—does it result from one's social experience or are you born with it?—came to a head. Learning versus biology might be a way to describe the conflict I was feeling. Suddenly, I saw the truth. I realized that what I was experiencing in loving another guy was archetypal, not a mere accident or adaptation."

Walker's breakthrough resulted in a master's thesis discussing the then unheard-of topic of gay depth psychology. To his knowledge "it was the first-ever gay-centered application of Jungian theory to the question of what is a gay-identified person." In a 1976 essay written for the prestigious Jungian journal Spring, Walker furthered his ideas about same-sex love, identifying an archetypal configuration that he called the Double. Two books, Men Loving Men and Visionary Love, followed in quick succession, each in their way encouraging gay men to seek a more depthful comprehension of who they are.

Walker continued to develop his studies, and in 1987 he received a Ph.D. in psychology with his dissertation, "A Uranian Coniunctio: The Individuation Model of C. G. Jung as Applied to Gay Men," followed by several theoretical papers, such as "A New Theory of Male Homosexuality: Individuation as Gay" (published in the 1991 edition of Spring as "Jung and Homophobia") and "Father-Son Incest and the Oedipal Complex in Gay Men."

As profound as Walker's work has been, much of what he says has fallen on deaf ears as the gay movement has pursued its tumultuous course. The stark realities gay people face daily—homophobia, hate crimes, AIDS—sometimes don't seem connected to the intangible realities of the inner world. But the forty-three-year-old author and psychotherapist insists that without knowing the substance of our souls we will surely be caught in the cycle of unconscious actions and events that keeps most of humanity imprisoned. Gay people must "come out inside" if they are to realize the full potential of being queer in a straight-jacketed world. "Without that self-awareness gained through confronting and exploring inner psychological issues, the unconscious shadow world that exists in every mind will be activated into secret domination," Walker warns, "taking back with the left hand what the right hand puts out consciously."

For all of his inward gazing, Walker articulates a vision that is expansive, with a breadth and richness informed by the very nature of his inquiry about same-sex love. A search inaugurated by the burning of a book has taken him into the sacred heart—what he calls the "radical essentialism"—of being gay. Walker knows that gay love, the kind of love he once professed for the captain of a high school football team, is its own undeniable truth.

Walker has lived the last eleven years in Los Angeles, putting theory to work in small groups, lectures, and private practice with gay men who are trying to heal old wounds and deepen self-knowledge.

°

Nearly all gay men I know have painful childhood memories about being labeled "the other." So let's get right to the heart of the matter: How are queer boys different from nongay boys?

First of all, we are all human beings—let's not forget that. Sometimes the criticism is made that if you talk in an essentialist way, you're objectifying straights as somehow bad and awful and you're exalting, in an artificial way, gayness or queers. There are many ways to talk about being gay. But I would say that if one assumes there is a gay nature, that gay children are born with this nature, then that's as different from being straight as a woman is born different from being a man. Gay essentialists would say if you're born a woman, how can you deny that? Isn't that totally influential about who you are, impinging on your native reality, your relationship with society and family? Essentialists look at homosexuality the same way.

I believe gayness is the immutable center of an inner truth that is harbored in the genes. It's not some kind of error in the heterosexual ordering. Our sexual orientation is a genetic part of our component makeup as much as breeding is in breeders. It's a fundamental principle of organizing human personality, and it's not to be taken for granted. How could someone like [gay French philosopher] Michel Foucalt come along and misinterpret that fact by looking at sexual orientation as a social construction? What a stupid idea. It's like getting a present and waxing on and on about the box it came in, a world of boxes, without ever getting to the gift itself.

We were born with sexual orientation. How that's dealt with concerns particular historical situations. The whole social constructionist theoretical system espoused by many gays is a "step and fetch it" betrayal, accurate on the situational details but with a gaping chasm in its spiritual center. If you take an essentialist position on the question of gayness, that's radical. That's socially, intellectually, and personally radical.

This essential quality you speak of must then infuse the very core of who we are. If we're born gay, does this somehow mean we have a gay soul? Perhaps it would be more appropriate to first ask, What is your definition of soul?

I like to think of soul as the doorway to the spirit world that exists in each of us. We enter into relationship with the spirit world through the soul. That doorway can be shut up and closed down. Or it can be cultivated, developed, and expanded on. What does it mean, then, to have a union with one's soul? In shamanic terms that means a relationship with the otherworld, the spirit world.

What do you mean by the "spirit world"?

If you're born queer, you have an innate sense that your universe, your world, is as much a world of the spirit as it is a physical and material world. You live simultaneously in both those worlds at a fundamental level of experience because of that inner gay soul you are born with. It gives you a soulfulness that you inhabit, a place that's in relation to that doorway between these two worlds.

Modern depth psychology would say the spirit world is one's unconscious psyche. If we were to turn to pre-Western people to ask about the spirit world, they would perhaps say it's a universe that's interwoven with our physical, material reality of time and space but is a whole other plane beyond physical dimensions with its own rules. It's just as infinite and substantial, and we live there as much as we live here.

Is this the world we experience through our dreams and feelings?

Yes, through dreams and feelings, images and ideas—it's the world of psyche. Most of us are only aware of a little part of who we are as an inner reality. When our mind is born, it's born and lives in an inner world that it swims in like a fish swims in the sea. Waking up to that inner reality is the whole point of using the terminology of depth psychology. This way of talking in psychological metaphors is what the radicalism of radical essentialism is all about.

"Radical essentialism"? It sounds like yet another trendy movement or cause. Obviously you mean more by it than that.

I'm using it as an intellectual term of reference. We're reaching the end of the generation of post-Stonewall gay liberation, and the issues we're discussing here represent the start of a whole new social, cultural, and generational phase of that movement: coming out inside. Gay liberation in the inner world, not in the outer world. It's not about that. It's about correcting a present imbalance extrovertedly tilted; it's about liberating gay space and gay reality inside! That's radical essentialism. It's the natural progression of a modern tradition of gay-centered thought that runs from the middle of the last century through contemporary times, passed on from generation to generation of gay intellectuals. Out of that gay-centered focus on the essence comes our notion of gay as an identified ego, so you can have such things as gay-identity formation, a gay community and people, and gay civil rights.

Who are some of the figures that make up this lineage?

Walt Whitman, who during the 1860s celebrated the comrades of "adhesive" love in his poetry. About the same time in Europe, German lawyer Karl Ulrich coined the word *Uranian* to define lovers of the same sex, and Hungarian physician Karoly Benkert invented the term *homosexual*. There's a whole generation or two before them of closet queens who were pushing in this direction but who couldn't come out as much.

There's the Wollstonecraft family in England, for instance. Mary Wollstonecraft was a lesbian married to a fey gay man. Their daughter, Mary, was married to the poet Percy Shelley. People like Shelley and his friend Byron were what we would today call bisexuals, but in their time they were trying to liberate their homosexual side. Shelley did a new translation of Plato's *Symposium* in which he put back all the extirpated and bowdlerized aspects of that discussion on homosexual love. He also wrote one of the very first essays about "sodomy" and argued against the homophobia of his era. Mary Shelley's great tract on this issue is, of course, her novel *Frankenstein*. This has all been hidden history, however.

Now with the advent of gay-identified scholars, this repressed and lost material is coming to light. We see that by the end of the 1700s there was a movement forming among certain European intellectuals toward an essentialist understanding of homosexuality as an identity. They began to see that if you are what we now call a gay person, you are a real entity versus not existing at all, which is the way we were typed by our opponents at that time—and still are to a large extent. Of course, it's an attitude that is meant to dehumanize us: we're never persons to begin with; we're about nothing but twisted and illegal acts. Whether in ancient times or in modern times, this is how the ruling heterosexuals have always viewed queers.

Why has this happened? What is it about being gay that makes those who are not so inclined want to put it down?

In the course of social evolution, dominant power eventually came into the hands of what we would now call heterosexual men, especially an entire class of those who were the most heterosexual, meaning the most aggressive. Their power is based on ruthless competition antithetical to any other way of life. Women and queer-type men were increasingly demonized throughout the rise of the Roman Empire, Christianity, and modern European culture. Step by step, queers and women were excluded from any kind of power or influence by virtue of who they are. The natural gifts of wisdom they possess were quite well integrated in earlier societies; in fact, they were the fount of those societies. But no longer. Women and queer men became pariahs, each in their different ways.

What are the dynamics, the components, of a queer soul?

You don't have to be a gay-identified ego to have queerness moving in you. But when homosexual Eros is truly your inner guiding light, then you've been born into a queer universe—the energy of your psychic world is "gay." To begin to understand this, one must realize there are characters and situations in the inner world that develop just as those in our outer world do. Yet modern material reality says these things are completely ephemeral, that they have no truth in physical reality. That's why queers are marginalized, and why it's hardly possible to talk about what it is to be born queer and how that's different from being born straight.

Everyone has a soul, everyone has that doorway to the spirit world; it's not merely something queers are born with. So what makes one queer? It's when you're born into the spirit world and the physical world simultaneously through an archetypal erotic Twinship. This particular relationship makes us two-in-one in a way that heterosexuals are not. That's the distinction of queer soul from straight soul. Whether you identify spontaneously with that queerness because it's so fundamental in the inner world or your society helps you realize that inner fundament, it's going to infuse your personality at the base. In the outer social world, it often manifests as a kind of nothingness, what Harry Hay calls being a not-man or a not-woman. And it also manifests as a both/and situation, a "man-woman-other" person. Our two-in-oneness comes out in all kinds of ways.

> *The gay world is so caught up in defending its right to exist that the inner reality of being gay is usually left unexplored. Despite the modern gay movement's many accomplishments during the past four decades, aren't gay people still on shaky ground by not having a deeper understanding of who they are?*

That's why I think there need to be voices for the inner world on all these issues: What's gayness? What's gay liberation? What's gay community? What do gays really need? That's how the new wave of gay liberation is going to come. And by "inner view" I don't mean superficial psychological theory about how inner issues relate to outer life. I mean a real inner view, a present awareness inside, gained by facing yourself. That's missing not just from the gay community but from all of modern society. There's hardly any validation for establishing a stable, ongoing, conscious relationship with your own psyche and seeing what that means.

That's why the rising tide of psychotherapy has become a really important social effort because it honors the inner truth of the individual and the individual's own relationship to that inner truth. Still, how do you get through all the morass of problems around finding that inner truth? Therapy is helping us to regain a healthier connection with psyche—a connection that did exist in earlier societies. In terms of this specifically modern problem, psychology is an attempt to begin to bridge that gap. But therapy is about more than that, too. Because when you connect with psyche, you are connecting with the spirit world. I would say that anyone who goes to good psychotherapy does more for his or her soul than any amount of time spent in a church, synagogue, or other so-called place of worship.

> *If you've been deeply wounded, some form of self-recovery would seem essential. Most gay men suffer humiliation, distancing, rejection, and guilt throughout their childhood and adolescence. It's the story of your life and of my life; it's the story of just about every gay man we know. The hurt goes deep, but don't you think that hurt creates equally rich possibilities for doing inner work?*

True humanity comes from the adversities of life and dealing with those adversities, whether you're gay or straight. But without question, gays are a heavily stigmatized population. Queers experience a lot of suffering and woundedness, and so we have a lot of healing to do. What's missing from the gay community is a psychologically therapeutic kind of attitude. In gay arts and culture there's hardly any getting below the surface of these matters. Although I'll be the first to say that it's hard to establish a more mature attitude around these issues because not only do the individuals involved have to work on their own inner shadows—their own unfinished business—but as soon as they do that enough they become the enemy and are demonized by others.

> *Demonized? How? By shadow, I assume you mean the personal and collective unconscious. If someone is bringing light to these dark places, why would they be attacked?*

Because we exist in a society that only denies its shadow and therefore projects it onto others. Thus when you start to promote a way of being that addresses the issue of the shadow, shadows jump on you. Society is still so powerfully a hateful place, a dysfunctional place, that it's almost suicide to speak out about its shadow. So if you're asking what needs to be different about how gay men see themselves, we face some real quandaries. It's a very dangerous and scary time for queers in many ways. What's missing from gay life is first of all a naming of all these issues, much less what you do about them.

Is it because we hurt so much that we're in denial about these issues?

All people with shadow wounds are in denial and fight viciously against any recognition of that fact—that's what is called having "defenses." And everyone is riddled with defenses, whether they're gay or straight. That's why I would not want to focus on defining the difference between gays and straights on the issue of woundedness or the specialness of queer wounds. Centering on woundedness is a covert Christian line of thought, a disguised agenda about forgiving the antigay Father. I don't hold to that at all.

So how do we begin the naming?

What's most important is for individuals to begin doing gay-centered inner work, thus attracting others who want to learn this kind of understanding because of their own driven need to be themselves! This is the calling of our age. Human nature is an achievement, a creation, as well as something you're born with. This is what Jung meant by his idea of "individuation," that the individual becomes most fully himself or herself by actively connecting with and actualizing the deepest innate potentials, the transpersonal forces of the collective unconscious.

That gets back to my question: What is gay soul?

The best definition of gay soul that I know is this: Imagine that we're standing on a blacktop playground, and a hundred attractive men are lined up against a wall in the bright sunshine. Every single one of them is naked, and they're just standing there for your inspection. Now slowly move down that line of one hundred guys and scrutinize every single one of them. Let your eyes do the walking and talking. Then step back and pick the fifty hottest guys out of the bunch. Review them all again, and pick the twenty-five hottest guys. Then pick ten.

After that, let your feelings come out even more and see if you can't pick out the *one*. It might be difficult. Maybe there are too many good ones. Maybe it's a bad batch, and there's no one that really works the juices here. That's why I started with one hundred. Because through the course of any day we see various representatives of that one hundred, and every so often we come across an individual where we automatically go "Wow!" I don't mean a mere sexual lusting, which can itself frequently occur, nor do I mean any desexualized, clichéd romanticism. By "Wow" I mean that thing that really grabs you, not just from the cock and balls, but grabs the cock and balls as the root of a whole plant that goes up through all of your innards and shoots out the top of your head. Something your whole guts know, churningly, immediately.

If that feeling happens, then I would suggest you are now in the Temple of the true and real Holy Spirit. When one is a worshiper of that Holy Spirit all the time, whether recognized or not, that's what it means to be a queer man. But sometimes you are made singularly aware of being in that Temple by some particular representative emblematic of the great deity who sits at its head. That's the one guy over which you most go "Wow!" This is an essential experience of gay soul. And being in relationship with gay soul is the core of our spirituality. There are those who say that the core of gay spirituality are concepts of gender or abstract "otherness." But the real things that move us are archetypal—those things that come from the lusting gonads, the surging blood, and the yearning heart.

Would this one special man be the soul figure you call the Double?

That one out of a hundred is not himself the soul, of course. He's just a flesh and blood character like we are. But he's become a figure on which the unconscious psyche is projecting the soul. Milder projections of this theme occur to us constantly, but then there are these special figures. The constructionists are wrong to say that we create such projections through encountering our milieu. They arise from our deepest nature unbidden. And because the soul figure is an image of sameness, it's not an experience that a nongay person has. It's unique to homosexual orientation and is at the root of that orientation. All of our visions and understandings of gayness as a two-in-oneness come from this. Because when you go "Wow" over the hundredth guy, it is a feeling of fusion and union with one like yourself. The experience of oneness is that wowness, and that wowness itself is the touch of a transcendental deity. It's the source of whatever wisdom and understanding we later gain. It's what we mean by "falling in love." It's our initiation into soul.

Why is this experience unique to us? A heterosexual man can certainly have a similarly intense reaction to a woman.

He sure does, but the erotic relations of a hetero man to the archetypal feminine, as the fundamental source of the breeder perspective, are profoundly different than the corresponding queer experience. In the same vein, a hetero boy will experience Double projections onto other boys and adult males, but without the homosexual imperative that we feel. All the archetypes are in us all; everyone is straight and gay in potentia. If fate has caused the inner world to be informed by homosexual orientation, that's an archetype which is going to organize the inner world in a gay way from the very beginning. But in order to get to the core of that archetypal experience, you have to start with your own psyche, your own experience. It all grows from that insight.

Is this the archetype of the Same?

It's an image of reflecting selfness, but a paradox of similarities and differences together in an erotically yearning, intense way that's hard for us to talk about, especially if we're raised in male/female ways of thinking. There are many facets of duality. One alternative tradition to the man/woman, king/queen duality is that of the two brothers, which can be found in ancient myths like the Mesopotamian story of Gilgamesh and Enkidu and Egyptian legends about Horus and Seth.

What you're really talking about, then, is the transformative power of gay Eros.

It's the fundamental organizing principle of the queer psyche; from the beginning, the libido—the "energy" of the psyche—is homosexual. And so if libido itself differentiates as homosexual or heterosexual from the start, you get a whole different orientation to all the other archetypal patterns and their resulting "complexes": the mother, the father, how they relate to the development of the child, and the sense of self in the child. It's fascinating, this new theoretical understanding. There's also a practice that goes with this theory. And that's about leading a gay-centered inner life, like I do.

All right, describe how you lead a gay-centered inner life.

Your understanding of life, your loves and interests, are all coming ultimately out of this homosexual libido, which has within itself an organizing principle. In other words, its own kind of intelligence—its own personality! We might call that the "spirit of gay love." And it's the relationship between you as a budding gay personality and that inner presence which eventually results in gay identity and what we could call "gay wisdom."

What are some of the elements of this gay wisdom? How does it affect the way we see and move in the world in contrast to people who are not so inclined?

It enables us to bridge opposites. You see gays often taking on roles as mediators of all sorts, which include being teachers, healers, and priests.

Let's examine the ability to mediate, to balance and integrate opposites. How is that capacity informed by the homosexual libido?

The relationship with the one-in-a-hundred (and to lessening degrees of intensity with the other ninety-nine) is really an internal one. That's the archetype of mediation, of gay soul. When you're between the twoness, you're in the middle of all dualities. It doesn't mean you can't manifest polarities; there are very effeminate gay men and very macho gay men, for example. But there's also that presence of the two-in-oneness within the core of their being.

Theoretically speaking, at some point the libido wants to form an ego complex. How does it do that? Well, it coheres around an archetype that can be called romantic love. You fall in love with one person—there's this sense of "*I* love you." As a little child, that's how we get the ego to come out and get birthed.

Based on this instinctual preprogramming, the unconscious psyche looks around for the appropriate figure in the outer environment. For the little hetero boy, the inner godly programming looks around and picks an appropriate feminine object, most likely the mother, and projects a new kind of meaning, separate from what she meant before, onto her. It's something romantic—not sexual, but it's erotic. If you're a little queer boy, mother doesn't *quite* cut the grade. In fact, she's nowhere on this issue. There's going to be someone more appropriate around, and if it's not father, it's someone else with a relatively mature penis. The father, however, usually happens to be the first likely object around that offers a serious vision of that inner deity. And from this flow all the implications.

Of course, a father can't be overtly sexual with his little queer kid because that would block off the child's development. But if the boy's yearning for the father is acknowledged in appropriately loving ways, that allows the inner relationship to develop over time. Gay boys have an inner queer father who when activated by romance teaches them in a homosexual sense and gives them all the incestuous love they're not going to get from the actual father.

Whether your father was good or bad to you around being queer is not an issue here. That's secondary. That's "vicissitudes," and we're all deeply wounded on that level. What's even more important is to talk about that inner love from its point of view, not from the ego's point of view, nor from a Western cultural point of view, but from the view of the archetype itself. Where it's coming from. That's the gay center. That's the cause of being queer. Not society. Not the mother and the father and their Oedipal games with you.

Here's the real question: How do we help gay men to mature this inner libidinal relationship with their inner queer father? What I'm saying concerns relationship with the inner world, with the inner father, the inner lover, the inner spirit. I cannot emphasize this enough. This is the real mystery of being gay.

When did you first begin to put a name on your own feelings of being different?

I'd had crushes on a number of boys from the time I was eleven and always felt very ashamed. I soon enough realized what was going on, but I didn't want to be this homosexual being I was seeing manifested through my budding sexuality. So one night, shortly after my bar mitzvah, I went to my mother and told her I had a problem I couldn't discuss and requested psychotherapy. She was nonplussed but took me to a child therapy center, and a nice woman behind the desk, a psychologist, was the first person I came out to. But I stopped going after three or four sessions when the therapy group they put me in folded. I decided that I could better deal with the dilemma on my own.

I inwardly knew I was queer all along. I was seeing things in a different way than the other children and adults around me. I probably first got the sense of that when I was four. I was taken to see Alexander the Great with Richard Burton and had my first conscious falling-in-love experience. He was so sexy with all those other Greek guys. I recall lying in my nursery school cot during nap the next day, staring at the ceiling, not sleepy but dreamily picturing the blond hero in his glorious armor, I at his side as beloved buddy and chief aide in adversity and triumph.

How do you nurture your gay soul today?

Some time ago I saw I had to be an avatar of the viewpoint I'm putting forth here, mainly because no one else was doing it. One of the main practices I try to do early each day is to sit with this inward deity, this consciousness or archetype we're talking about, and commune with it. We hang out together, so to speak. And, over time, we've gone through many different stages of development together. It's always a teaching relationship, but it's also an act of lovemaking. If I have big issues, he'll help me work on them in terms of how to act and be with things. I let him see through my eyes as much as possible, and vice versa, so together we experience what's happening in both worlds. That's how I live my life and why I live my life.

The "him" that you're describing is the archetype of gay love, or what?

I don't use any particular name for this character that I'm mentioning. He's both a "father" and a "male mother" and also their "other" son, my co-equal Twin brother/lover. He has many names, in many different tongues. It always turns out to be the same kind of thing, a "queer family" thing, and thereby you have a relationship with eternity that's not at all abstract. He's extremely queer and is purely gay-centered.

If you keep pursuing the questions you've been asking—What does it really mean to be gay? Is there something essential in gay love—you're always going to get to him. Because he's waiting inside at the center. That's what the Sufis say: He's waiting in your heart, and you're going to find him through love. But he's not the beautiful man/boy you once fell in love with, he's eternal. He's living moment by moment in your gay truth and experience.

Despite all you're saying, some people would say you're making an argument for exclusivity and superiority.

I would say that those critics are closet-queen homophobes. They are people caught in some kind of inner shame and guilt about their queerness, and that's where their criticisms are coming from. Their criticism is not at all about what they are criticizing but is rather projection of shadow. That's why in my opinion it's absolutely required that anyone who wants to become more hip as a gay person should enter therapy. Absolutely.

The primal battleground is in the inner world, not the outer. Efforts need to be focused on developing gay theory about the inner world of the homosexual libido and ways of initiation into it.

Is it really a matter of initiation, or rather just allowing what's inside to come out more fully?

If more of it comes fully out, one is plunged into a "dark night of the soul," and that's the fundamental initiation, where you have to confront all of your shadow, the inner demons and monsters, a descent, an encounter that's actually a journeying on an epic quest.

That can be an absolutely overwhelming, terrifying experience.

Of course, which is why people hide from coming out inside. That's been the whole need to establish a gay-centered depth psychology, a psychology of gay initiation. You have to establish a theoretical understanding as part of meeting this central developmental challenge, to guide and enable success. As inner understanding influences more and more queer individuals, they in turn will influence others. Working with psyche is always an individual quest and challenge.

But this is actually an archetypal way, the individuation path of an ancient gay heritage, as evolutionary change agents, as shamans and healers. Becoming gay has always been and always will be a spiritual process of inner initiation and unfolding, magically self-transformative, leading to queer treasures at a golden source.

Would some use of sexuality be an important part of this initiation process for gay men?

Psychotherapy and dream work are major ways to encounter and work with your shadow. Erotic body workshops, S/M and other rituals, tantric practices, and so on can also be useful ways of encountering one's psyche. If these mediums are used from a gay-centered place, with psychological mindfulness, they bring forth something that's not there otherwise. If not, they're going to be a big ripoff. But if they're truly gay centered, that means you're listening for the inner voice of that personified deity who brings you into relation with the beloved number one.

Developing a relationship with the inner Self is vitally important. To have that revolution go on in your own soul is much more profound than any revolution you can directly create around you in daily outer life. We'd make a lot more important progress with gay liberation in the outer world if more individual gays would wake up to this inner relationship.

All gay men have been divorced fundamentally from their gay souls, and yet the soul is the source of life. So we search for that cut off part of ourselves in bars and baths and images, in a series of partners. Most of us never get close to what we're looking for because we don't see it as an inner relationship and deal with it as such. Thus we only act out the shadows that swirl around that inner relationship. If we can but heal the old woundedness, then we go to the next step, which is the manifestation of gay spiritual wisdom that comes from inner knowing. As little queer kids, all we want is to wake up to that level of understanding.

If you had one thing to say to a young gay man just coming out, what would that be?

For true initiation in gay spirit, the way to reach the stars is by going within. All you're experiencing and thinking of as gayness and especially passionate love is the doorway to a world of spiritual truth, a kind of wisdom about self and the world, of what you are and what you can be. That's the inner world, the world of real magic. There's a level of reality in what you are beginning to experience that has the greatest human tradition connected with it. As much as possible, seek to understand that tradition and learn how to live in it by finding others of like mind in the past, present, and future. That's where the real inspiration in being gay resides: It's the most direct way of knowing God.

Through opening to your unconscious, you can meet and grow with the deeper, transpersonal forces that exist inside you, and maybe then they'll take you within the mysteries of gay love and transmutation. Not only are we recovering the most ancient of traditions but a new stage of gay liberation is upon us, and as we respond we will be birthing a necessary future, both for ourselves and the world.

BIBLIOGRAPHY

Baldwin, Guy. *Ties That Bind*. Los Angeles: Daedalus Publishing Company, 1993.

Boyd, Malcolm. *Take Off the Masks*. Rev. ed. San Francisco: HarperSanFrancisco, 1993.

——. *Are You Running with Me, Jesus?* Rev. ed. Boston: Beacon Press, 1990.

——. *Look Back in Joy: A Celebration of Gay Lovers*. Rev. ed. Boston: Alyson Publications, 1990.

——. *Gay Priest: An Inner Journey*. New York: St. Martin's Press, 1986.

Broughton, James. *Coming Unbuttoned: A Memoir*. San Francisco: City Lights Books, 1993.

——. *Making Light of It*. San Francisco: City Lights Books, 1992.

——. *The Androgyne Journal*. Seattle: Broken Moon Press, 1991.

——. *Special Deliveries: New and Selected Poems*. Seattle: Broken Moon Press, 1990.

Hall, Clyde [M. Owlfeather]. "Children of Grandmother Moon." In *Living the Spirit: A Gay American Indian Anthology,* edited by Will Roscoe. New York: St. Martin's Press, 1988.

Harvey, Andrew. *Hidden Journey: A Spiritual Awakening*. New York: Arkana/Penguin Books, 1992.

——. *The Web*. Boston: Houghton Mifflin Company, 1987.

——. *Burning Houses*. Boston: Houghton Mifflin Company, 1986.

——. *One Last Mirror*. Boston: Houghton Mifflin Company, 1985.

——. *A Journey in Ladakh*. Boston: Houghton Mifflin Company, 1983.

Hay, Harry. "A Separate People Whose Time Has Come." In *Gay Spirit: Myth and Meaning,* edited by Mark Thompson. New York: St. Martin's Press, 1987.

Hopcke, Robert H. *The Persona: Where Sacred Meets Profane*. Boston: Shambhala, 1995.

——. *Men's Dreams, Men's Healing*. Boston: Shambhala, 1990.

——. *Jung, Jungians, and Homosexuality*. Boston: Shambhala, 1989.

——. *A Guided Tour of the Collected Works of C. G. Jung*. Boston: Shambhala, 1989.

Isay, Richard A. *Being Homosexual: Gay Men and Their Development.* Rev. ed. North Vale, NJ: Jason Aronson, 1994.

Monette, Paul. *Last Watch of the Night.* New York: Harcourt Brace Jovanovich, 1994.

———. *Becoming a Man: Half a Life Story.* New York: Harcourt Brace Jovanovich, 1992.

———. *Borrowed Time: An AIDS Memoir.* New York: Harcourt Brace Jovanovich, 1988.

Ram Dass, and Mirabai Bush. *Compassion in Action: Setting Out on the Path of Service.* New York: Bell Tower/Crown, 1992.

———. *Journey of Awakening: A Meditator's Guidebook.* Rev. ed. New York: Bantam Books, 1990.

———, and Stephen Levine. *Grist for the Mill.* New York: Bantam Books, 1977.

———. *The Only Dance There Is.* New York: Anchor Books/Doubleday, 1979.

———. *Be Here Now.* Boulder, CO: Hanuman Foundation, 1971.

Ramer, Andrew. *Two Flutes Playing.* San Francisco, CA: Alamo Square Press, 1995.

Roscoe, Will. *Queer Spirits: A Gay Men's Myth Book.* Boston: Beacon Press, 1995.

———. *The Zuni Man-Woman.* Albuquerque: University of New Mexico Press, 1991.

Saslow, James M. *The Poetry of Michelangelo: An Annotated Translation.* New Haven, CT: Yale University Press, 1990.

———. *Ganymede in the Renaissance: Homosexuality in Art and Society.* New Haven, CT: Yale University Press, 1986.

Steinbrecher, Edwin C. *The Inner Guide Meditation: A Spiritual Technology for the 21st Century.* York Beach, ME: Samuel Weiser, Inc., 1988.

Walker, Mitch. *Men Loving Men: A Gay Sex Guide and Consciousness Book.* Rev. ed. San Francisco: Gay Sunshine Press, 1994.

———. *Visionary Love: A Spirit Book of Gay Mythology.* Berkeley, CA: Tree-roots Press, 1980.

Related Works of Interest

Berzon, Betty. *Setting Them Straight: A Guided Response to Antigay and Lesbian Bigotry.* New York: E. P. Dutton, forthcoming.

Conner, Randy P. *Blossom of Bone: Reclaiming the Connections Between Ho-*

Downing, Christine. *Myths and Mysteries of Same-Sex Love*. New York: Continuum, 1989.

Herdt, Gilbert, ed. *Third Sex, Third Gender: Beyond Sexual Dimorphism in Culture and History*. New York: Zone Books, 1994.

Hillman, James. *A Blue Fire*. New York: Harper & Row, 1989.

Hopcke, Robert H., K. L. Carrington, and S. Wirth, eds. *Same-Sex Love and the Path to Wholeness*. Boston: Shambhala, 1993.

Jackson, Graham. *The Secret Lore of Gardening: Patterns of Male Intimacy*. Toronto: Inner City Books, 1991.

———. *The Living Room Mysteries: Patterns of Male Intimacy,* Book 2. Toronto: Inner City Books, 1993.

Johnson, Robert A. *Inner Work*. San Francisco: Harper & Row, 1986.

Mains, Geoff. *Urban Aboriginals: A Celebration of Leathersexuality*. San Francisco: Gay Sunshine Press, 1984.

Monick, Eugene. *Phallos: Sacred Image of the Masculine*. Toronto: Inner City Books, 1987.

Moore, Robert, and Douglas Gillette. *King Warrior Magician Lover: Rediscovering the Archetypes of the Mature Masculine*. San Francisco: HarperSanFrancisco, 1990.

Moore, Thomas. *Care of the Soul*. New York: HarperCollins, 1992.

Ponce, Charles. *Working the Soul: Reflections on Jungian Psychology*. Berkeley, CA: North Atlantic Books, 1988.

Rinpoche, Sogyal. *The Tibetan Book of Living and Dying*. San Francisco: HarperSanFrancisco, 1992.

Singer, June. *Boundaries of the Soul: The Practice of Jung's Psychology*. New York: Anchor Books/Doubleday, 1972.

Stevens, Anthony. *Archetypes: A Natural History of the Self*. New York: Quill/William Morrow, 1983.

Thompson, Mark, ed. *Long Road to Freedom: The Advocate History of the Gay and Lesbian Movement*. New York: St. Martin's Press, 1994.

———, ed. *Leatherfolk: Radical Sex, People, Politics, and Practice*. Boston: Alyson Publications, 1991.

———, ed. *Gay Spirit: Myth and Meaning*. New York: St. Martin's Press, 1987.

Timmons, Stuart. *The Trouble with Harry Hay*. Boston: Alyson Publications, 1990.